The Comics of Joe Sacco

Critical Approaches to Comics Artists
David M. Ball, Series Editor

The Comics of Joe Sacco

Journalism in a Visual World

Edited by Daniel Worden

University Press of Mississippi   Jackson

www.upress.state.ms.us

The University Press of Mississippi is a member
of the Association of American University Presses.

Copyright © 2015 by University Press of Mississippi
All rights reserved
Manufactured in the United States of America

First printing 2015

∞

Library of Congress Cataloging-in-Publication Data

The comics of Joe Sacco : journalism in a visual world / edited by Daniel Worden.
    pages cm. — (Critical approaches to comics artists series)
  Includes bibliographical references and index.
    ISBN 978-1-4968-0221-7 (hardback) — ISBN 978-1-4968-0222-4 (ebook) 1. Sacco, Joe—Criticism and interpretation. I. Worden, Daniel, 1978– editor.
  PN6727.S14C66 2015
  741.5'092—dc23   2014047526

British Library Cataloging-in-Publication Data available

Contents

Acknowledgments vii

Introduction: Drawing Conflicts 3
   Daniel Worden

Section I. The Form of Comics Journalism

1. Time under Siege 21
   Jared Gardner

2. Inside and Outside the Frame: Joe Sacco's *Safe Area Goražde* 39
   Lan Dong

3. Drawing on the Facts: Comics Journalism and the Critique of Objectivity 54
   Isabel Macdonald

4. Views from Nowhere: Journalistic Detachment in *Palestine* 67
   Marc Singer

Section II. Space and Maps

5. Mapping Bosnia: Cartographic Representation in Joe Sacco's Graphic Narratives 85
   Edward C. Holland

6. A Thousand Plateaus: Mining Entropy in *Days of Destruction, Days of Revolt* 101
   Georgiana Banita

7. The Politics of Space in Joe Sacco's Representations of the Appalachian Coalfields 123
   Richard Todd Stafford

Section III: The Politics and Aesthetics of Joe Sacco's Comics

8. Little Things Mean a Lot: The Everyday Material of *Palestine* 141
   Ann D'Orazio

9. John's Story: Joe Sacco's Depiction of "Bare Life"   158
    Øyvind Vågnes

10. Sacco with Badiou: On the Political Ontology of Comics   168
    Alexander Dunst

11. Joe Sacco's Comics of Performance   184
    Rebecca Scherr

Section IV: Drawing History, Visualizing World Politics

12. Overtaken by Further Developments: The Form of History in *Footnotes in Gaza*   203
    Ben Owen

13. Graphic Representations of Language, Translation, and Culture in Joe Sacco's Comics Journalism   222
    Brigid Maher

14. What Washes Up onto the Shore: Contamination and Containment in "The Unwanted"   239
    Maureen Shay

15. Teaching World Politics with Joe Sacco: *Safe Area Goražde* in the Classroom   256
    Kevin C. Dunn

Appendix: Joe Sacco's Primary Works   273

Notes on Contributors   275

Index   277

Acknowledgments

First and foremost, Joe Sacco has made this book possible, by producing such astounding work and, more practically, by granting permission to reproduce images from that work. I hope that this book does something to confirm his already secure status as one of the most important figures not just in the history of comics, but in art, literature, and journalism, as well. This book would not have been possible had it not been for the support of "Critical Approaches to Comics Artists" series editor, David M. Ball. I thank him for his enthusiasm and advice from the conception to the production of this book. Many thanks, also, to Vijay Shah at the University Press of Mississippi. This book was a pleasure to edit because of the quality of each contributor's work, and to each of them I express my gratitude. A course offload from the University of New Mexico Department of English gave me the time to complete this project. I thank Jesse Alemán, Gary Harrison, Scarlett Higgins, Matthew R. Hofer, Melina Vizcaíno-Alemán, Kathleen Washburn, Kathryn Wichelns, and all of my colleagues at UNM for making me feel welcome and supported. Lastly, Catherine Zuromskis and Clementine give me a life that makes scholarship possible yet not solitary, and for that, among so many other things, I owe them everything.

The Comics of Joe Sacco

Introduction: Drawing Conflicts

Daniel Worden

> Make no mistake, everywhere you go, not just in Marvel Comics, there's parallel universes...
> —Joe Sacco, *Palestine*

Joe Sacco makes comics about conflicts—the Israel-Palestine conflict, the Bosnian War, the Iraq War, African immigration to Malta, the poverty faced by Native Americans on the Pine Ridge Reservation and coal miners in Appalachia, to name just a few. His comics neither romanticize suffering nor legitimate violence. To read Sacco's work is to enter into the messy complexity of history and everyday life, to feel oneself given up to historical necessity yet emboldened by the collective struggles that aspire to right wrongs and to resist military occupations, legal disenfranchisement, and economic inequality. A pioneer of comics journalism, Sacco has made it clear that comics have a representative force that can counter the amnesiac present tense of our media environment, and his work stands as a testament to cartooning's power to depict layers of experience, history, feeling, and action on a single page, in a single panel.

Sacco is best known for his groundbreaking work in comics journalism, including the contemporary masterpieces *Palestine, Safe Area Goražde, The Fixer,* and *Footnotes in Gaza*. His earlier work, much of which was originally published in alternative comics magazines and Sacco's own six-issue series with Fantagraphics, *Yahoo,* evidences the political concerns that underpin his comics journalism, yet the earlier work also bears clear traces of the influence of alternative and underground comics on his style. Often hilariously self-obsessed, grotesque, and parodic, Sacco's early works focus on subjects like the aggression of corporate culture in "Stanton K. Pragmatron, Part of a New Breed" and Sacco's own artistic pretensions and lack of dental insurance in "Cartoon Genius." Alternately, some of Sacco's early work is deeply historical and packed with information, such as the single-page illustrations in "When Good Bombs Happen to Bad People," about Britain's bombings in Germany during World War II and the United States's bombings in Libya in 1986, surrounded by quotations from military leaders and traditional print journalists.[1] Refined in works like *Palestine* and *Safe Area Goražde*, Sacco's juxtaposition of his own confessional, even narcissistic, concerns with larger historical structures—economic inequality, corporate labor, air war—resonates with other now-canonical comics like Art Spiegelman's *Maus*, a synthesis of caricature, testimony, history, and familial relations, and the work of R. Crumb, an influence on Sacco's cartooning style. As Sacco commented in an interview with Gary Groth, "I came out of that sort of autobiographical tradition that was very prevalent in the middle of the '80s, and is still prevalent to some degree. . . . But I'd also studied journalism."[2] Often remarking on the influence of Michael Herr's New Journalistic account of the Vietnam War, *Dispatches*, and the work of "gonzo journalist" Hunter S. Thompson on his own comics journalism, Sacco should be read not just as a figure in alternative comics, but also as a figure in journalism, and especially literary reportage or the New Journalism.[3] After all, the New Journalism emerged in the same historical moment as alternative comics—the 1960s and 1970s—and likewise strove to arrive at a politicized representation of events that speaks both to personal experience and impersonal social structures. Sacco's work is both comics and journalism, art and information, autobiography and history.

Life and Works

Joe Sacco's work ranges provocatively over some of the central military conflicts of the past twenty years, from the Bosnian War and the Israel-Palestine conflict to the insurgency in Chechnya and the Iraq War, and some of the major social issues of our time, including poverty, human rights activism, and dwindling support for investigative and print journalism. Along with these weighty subjects, Sacco's earlier work is about music and autobiographical themes much more familiar to the world of underground and alternative comics. Because of the scope of his work and his continued engagement with international crises, Sacco's career charts a compelling course not only from the world of comics publishing to the literary mainstream, but also from the autobiographical self to the world in all of its complexity and violence. Readers interested in Sacco's bibliography should consult the appendix to this book, which catalogs Sacco's major works.

Joe Sacco was born in 1960 on the island of Malta. His family immigrated to Melbourne, Australia, in 1961, and Sacco's childhood was spent in Australia until 1972, when his family moved to the United States.[4] In high school in a suburb of Portland, Oregon, Sacco worked on the school newspaper, contributing both news stories and editorial cartoons, and in 1978, Sacco entered the University of Oregon, where he majored in journalism. After graduating from college, Sacco would hold a number of jobs as a writer, including work writing a tour guide about Malta and a stint with the journal of the National Notary Association. In 1985, Sacco and Tom Richards founded the *Portland*

Permanent Press, a free magazine focused on Portland's comedy scene that also published comics, including work by Peter Bagge and an interview with Matt Groening. When the magazine folded in 1986, Sacco was offered a job at the *Comics Journal*, published by Fantagraphics Books. At Fantagraphics, Sacco would take over editorship of the comics series *Honk!*—which he would relaunch under the name *Centrifugal Bumble-Puppy*. An anthology series that consisted of primarily humor comics with occasional political satire, and only including a couple of comics by Sacco himself, *Centrifugal Bumble-Puppy* was canceled after eight issues. In 1988, though, Sacco would launch his own series with Fantagraphics, *Yahoo*, of which Sacco would publish six issues from 1988 to 1992. It is in *Yahoo* that Sacco began to develop and hone the political and social focus that would inform his longer works, especially in stories about the Gulf War ("How I Loved the War"), bombing campaigns ("When Good Bombs Happen to Bad People"), and his mother's experiences in Malta during World War II ("More Women, More Children, More Quickly"). Along with these stories, which led the way to his long-form comics journalism, Sacco also created a number of comics about music, including "In the Company of Long Hair," about Sacco's travels with the band The Miracle Workers. Along with many other comics artists, including Daniel Clowes, R. Crumb, Adrian Tomine, and Chris Ware, to name a few, Sacco has made comics about music and designed posters for bands; he even writes in *But I Like It*, a collection of his work about music, "I will write a book about the Rolling Stones when I get out of my saving-the-world phase."[5] Sacco's early work, originally published in the comics series *Yahoo* as well as in periodicals like *Centrifugal Bumble-Puppy*, *Prime Cuts*, and *Weirdo*, remains in print in the collected editions *Notes from a Defeatist* and *But I Like It*, making his entire career accessible to the scholar, student, and casual reader.

In 1991 and 1992, Sacco would visit Israel and Palestine, trips that would result in the nine-issue series *Palestine*, published from 1993 to 1995. *Palestine* was published serially, and the collected *Palestine* reflects the series' serial origin in its episodic structure. *Palestine* is a travelogue, and it follows Sacco as he meets and interviews both Palestinians and Israelis. In the 1990s, Sacco would also work as an artist for Harvey Pekar's *American Splendor* series, a cornerstone of alternative comics. *Palestine* received the American Book Award in 1996, signaling the critical acclaim that would greet his subsequent work. Sacco's next major work, *Safe Area Goražde*, was published as a single, long-form graphic narrative by Fantagraphics in 2000. Based on trips to Bosnia, and especially to the city of Goražde, that Sacco made during the Bosnian War, *Safe Area Goražde* has a more unified narrative than *Palestine*, though it is still divided into chapter-length episodes. Based on both firsthand interviews and research into the war and the region's history, *Safe Area Goražde* signals Sacco's shift away from the autobiographical focus of his early work, a focus that is still evident in *Palestine*, and to a concern with representing the complex histories that have led to contemporary conflicts. *Safe Area Goražde* received an Eisner Award in 2001, and Sacco would publish three shorter works drawn from his time in Bosnia, all of which would be eventually collected in *The Fixer and Other Stories*. Along with his work on Bosnia, Sacco would create a series of comics about labor struggles in the United States for Priscilla Murolo and A. B. Chitty's 2001 book *From the Folks Who Brought You the Weekend: A Short, Illustrated History of Labor in the United States*. After *Safe Area Goražde* and *The Fixer*, Sacco's next long-form project was *Footnotes in Gaza*, which received both an Eisner Award and the Ridenhour Book Prize in 2010. Building on the form that Sacco established with *Safe Area Goražde*, *Footnotes in Gaza* is a dense, rigorously researched graphic narrative about contemporary life in Gaza and its ties to the 1956 Rafah Massacre.

Following the success and critical acclaim of these works, Sacco received the PEN Literary Award in Graphic Literature for Outstanding Body of Work in 2012. Also in 2012, a volume titled simply *Journalism* appeared, collecting Sacco's comics journalism originally published in periodicals such as *Details*, the *Guardian*, *Harper's*, the *New York Times Magazine*, *Rolling Stone*, and *Time*. *Journalism* was followed by a collaborative book written by Chris Hedges and illustrated by Sacco, *Days of Destruction, Days of Revolt*, a book inspired by the Occupy Wall Street movement that moves from areas of poverty in the United States—the Pine Ridge Reservation, migrant labor camps in Florida, mining towns in Appalachia—to the Occupy encampment in Zuccotti Park. In 2013, Sacco's *The Great War*, a panorama of the first day of the Battle of the Somme, was published, signaling a potential shift in his work and its form. *The Great War* is a twenty-four-foot long silent panorama, packaged in a slipcase. With an accompanying book that gives some historical details about the battle scene as it unfolds, *The Great War* is more historical than Sacco's previous work, in which he nearly always appears as a character in the narrative, and more impersonal, lacking the first-person narrative voice that often positions the reader in relation to the violence represented on the page. Alternately, his newest work, published in late 2014, *BUMF*, volume 1: *I Buggered the Kaiser* continues the personal and political satire of his earliest comics. Sacco continues to develop as an artist and writer, and while his work already in print has unquestionably established him as one of the most significant comics artists of our time, his future work promises to do even more with the comics medium.

Underground Comics, the New Journalism, and Joe Sacco

The subtitle of this book, "Journalism in a Visual World," uses a phrase from an interview that Sacco gave to *Mother Jones* magazine. In the interview, Sacco is asked to describe the "advantage" of comics journalism, and he responds:

> It's a visual world and people respond to visuals. With comics you can put interesting and solid information in a format that's pretty palatable. For me, one advantage of comic journalism is that I can depict the past, which is hard to do if you're a photographer or filmmaker. History can make you realize that the present is just one layer of a story. What seems to be the immediate and vital story now will one day be another layer in this geology of bummers.[6]

Sacco's painstaking representations of contemporary conflicts and their long histories produce both knowledge and feeling. Through a work like *Footnotes in Gaza*, the reader both learns, through Sacco's painstaking research, about the 1956 Rafah massacre and its relevance to the contemporary struggles in Gaza, and feels the limitations, frustrations, and enthusiasms of the subjects produced in the wake of these events. Sacco's reaching through the personal to the historical places him in the tradition of the New Journalism, a style of literary reportage that is relevant now more than ever. As David Shields has argued in *Reality Hunger*, "the lure and blur of the real" is at the center of much contemporary art and literature.[7] Sacco's work places this contemporary artistic movement firmly in the traditions of underground comics and the New Journalism, two traditions that are deserving of more attention in our histories of twentieth-century art and literature.[8]

The New Journalism, especially as it was defined by Tom Wolfe in the 1970s, was premised on the investigation and elaboration of both the structural, or objective, and the personal, or subjective:

> [The New Journalists] were moving beyond the conventional limits of journalism, but not merely in terms of technique. The kind of reporting they were doing struck them as far more ambitious, too. It was more intense, more detailed, and certainly more time-consuming than anything that newspaper or magazine reporters, including investigative reporters, were accustomed to. They developed the habit of staying with the people they were writing about for days at a time, weeks in some cases. They had to gather all the material the conventional journalist was after—and then keep going. It

seemed all-important to *be there* when dramatic scenes took place, to get the dialogue, the gestures, the facial expressions, the details of the environment. The idea was to give the full objective description, plus something that readers had always had to go to novels and short stories for: namely, the subjective or emotional life of the characters.[9]

Sacco's comics journalism engages in this same synthesis, though Sacco's work builds less upon the tradition of the novel than the tradition of underground, confessional comics, combining the professional methods of the journalist and even the historian with the necessarily subjective, artistic filter of the comics artist.[10]

Working for Fantagraphics Books in the late 1980s, Sacco became a part of the alternative comics scene that had grown out of the underground comix movement of the 1960s and 1970s.[11] Published in *Weirdo* magazine, founded by R. Crumb, and close enough to Art Spiegelman that the famed creator of *Maus* would arrange a comics journalism assignment for Sacco with *Details* magazine, Sacco developed a style that is indebted to, but significantly different from, his predecessors.[12] While comics artists like R. Crumb, Justin Green, and Art Spiegelman would begin with and incessantly return to themselves—to their sexuality, their relationship with their families and spouses, their traumatized relation to past and present atrocities—Sacco would more persistently look outward rather than inward.[13] Even in his early editorial work, Sacco's degree of political engagement was evident. For example, in the first issue of *Centrifugal Bumble-Puppy*, published in September 1987, Sacco announces the "*Centrifugal Bumble-Puppy* Nicaragua Invasion Contest" to his readers:

> CONTEST! CONTEST!
> HELP YOUR PRESIDENT! UNDERMINE A CENTRAL AMERICAN NATION! WIN PRIZES!
> What you have to do:
> In 25 words or less, tell us why the United States is perfectly justified in invading Nicaragua!
> The top three entrants (as judged by your fearless editor) will have their statements sent to Ronald Reagan (that's right! Mr. Big himself!). That way he'll have some reasons ready for the American people when he finally does mount the invasion of Nicaragua!"[14]

This political satire differs in tone from Sacco's comics journalism, though his political consciousness is evident in all of his work. Even in his more autobiographical comics, such as "How I Loved the War," published in 1991, Sacco positions himself both in relation to media coverage of the Gulf War and Ali, a classmate of Sacco's in a German language course in Berlin (see Figure 0.1). Ali is a Palestinian "whose family fled Palestine in the 1948 fighting . . . whose house in Beirut was destroyed in the Lebanese Civil War . . . whose grandfather's brother was massacred at Shatila during Israel's 'Peace for Galilee' invasion."[15] The two panels at the top of Figure 0.1 move from Sacco's own emo-

Figure 0.1. Joe Sacco, "How I Loved the War," in *Notes from a Defeatist* (Seattle: Fantagraphics, 2003), 188.

tional state, his troubled long-distance relationship, and its ability to make the large-scale suffering of others insignificant; to the media, as Sacco flips on the television to get back in touch with others; and to the presence of, yet inability to experience, the suffering occasioned by the Gulf War and the conflicts that have preceded it. The large panel on the bottom half of the page contains a portrait of Ali, looking not at the viewer but up and off into the distance. Sacco has asked him what he thinks about the conclusion of the Gulf War. Ali registers both as being above us—above the mundane emotional difficulties of Sacco and others privileged with the burden of worrying predominantly about themselves—and also as being remote, removed from identification and sympathy. The page concludes with a statement of Ali's own difference from Sacco and, by extension, the reader—"You cannot imagine how I feel"—and Sacco's own reluctance to imagine how Ali feels: "I was afraid to even try."[16] This moment is an affirmation of the hazard negotiated by Sacco's comics journalism as well as the struggle that Sacco's work places himself and the reader within: by understanding the complex histories and lives of those we otherwise glimpse only through newscasts, we are forced not just to feel differently, but also to somehow act differently. At the same time, though, recognizing structures of violence also leads to the deflating realization that no matter how one feels or how one acts, structures remain. Our illusion of importance is pierced by the failure to identify, by the risk of realizing the histories that have led to our contemporary situation. Here and elsewhere in Sacco's work, the personal gives way on the page to the impersonal, and that process foregrounds both the insignificance of the individual and the necessity to think of individuals less as autonomous beings and more as the result of history, the outcome of structures of oppression.

This synthesis of the personal and the structural is the major accomplishment and the major challenge of Sacco's work. It is something of a truism today that contemporary subjects are unable to understand their place in the world. In one of his influential accounts of postmodernism, Fredric Jameson cites Michael Herr's New Journalistic account of the Vietnam War, *Dispatches*, as emblematic of the vertigo often thought to be intrinsic to life in late capitalism:

> This first terrible postmodernist war cannot be recounted in any of the traditional paradigms of the war novel or movie—indeed, that breakdown of all previous narrative paradigms is, along with the breakdown of any shared language through which a veteran might convey such experience, among the principal subjects of [*Dispatches*] and may be said to open up the place of a whole new reflexivity.[17]

This "new reflexivity," Jameson goes on to note, is facilitated by a "new and virtually unimaginable quantum leap in technological alienation," rendering the individual subject unable to find any stable vantage point, any objective or totalizing sense of her relation to the world.[18] This emblematically postmodern condition—namely, our inability to understand the violent world that we live in and how that violent world persists, indifferent to our own wishes—is one to which Sacco's "comics journalism" is uniquely suited to respond. And, to cite Jameson once more, if the challenge of representing war is constituted by the tension of "abstraction versus sense-datum," then Sacco's blending of his own experiences as reporter with witness testimony, historical research, and military mapping achieves a synthesis that posits a human collective that is interrupted or divided only by contingent differences, differences that are not real yet nonetheless provoke immense suffering.[19]

As Sacco remarks in his interview with Gary Groth, "With comics you can really reduce the scale to its earthly form."[20] This "earthly form" is rooted in Sacco's own critical lens, one that is present even in his earliest work in comics. Sacco's illustration style has expanded over the course of his career, beginning as a more cartoonish, caricature-based style in works like *Yahoo* and the opening chapters of *Palestine*, and eventually incorporating a crosshatched realism that balances more cartoonish elements, a synthesis visible in *Safe Area Goražde* and the silent, full-to-the-edge-of-the-page panorama of *The Great War*. Sacco's visual style captures realistic detail, yet also makes those details present through an inherently subjective, workmanlike series of pen strokes. In *The Fixer*, for example, Sacco draws a magisterial two-page spread of the dilapidated Holiday Inn in Sarajevo, and in the foreground, we see Sacco himself, drawn in the usual cartoonish style that he adopts to portray himself in his works.[21] His cartoonish presence in the strip serves less to differentiate him from his subjects than to draw attention to the mediated quality of the whole project—the fact that reality can never be represented in an objective or transparent way. In this image, Sarajevo itself is presented as a curious blend of the objective—the size of this image, the presence of the buildings on the page, the fine detailing of their cracks and ruination—and the subjective—Sacco is dwarfed by their presence, and the reader/viewer shares in his sense of awe and helplessness.

Sacco's realism is a clear stylistic choice, one that he has developed over the twenty years that his career has spanned to date. The great theorist of realism, Bakhtin, defines the novel quite loosely as "a diversity of social speech types ... and a diversity of individual voices, artistically arranged."[22] Sacco's work, with its emphasis on informants, fixers, and interview subjects, is mindful of voice as well, in a way that seems analogous to Bakhtin's realist novels. What seems unique to contemporary comics are the synthesis of a subjective frame in both the narration and the intimacy produced by the illustrations, a fidelity to the voice of others, and an interest in taking those two subjective modes of storytelling as evidence of larger social structures. Sacco is clearly invested in linking the subjective lens to power. His early work on air war and the Iraq War, for example, both collected in *Notes From a Defeatist*, juxtapose these two techniques. "When Good Bombs Happen to Bad People" is very abstract and historical, featuring drawings of military and political figures such as Ronald Reagan that resemble woodcuts. "How I Loved the War," on the other hand, focuses on Sacco's own anxiety during the Gulf War.

Sacco's later work synthesizes these two frames. For example, in *Safe Area Goražde*, Riki is a recurrent character. In Goražde on leave from the military, Riki serves as a tragicomic figure; he sings rock 'n' roll songs loudly, yet he is often melancholic because his life has been interrupted by the war. Riki is introduced in *Safe Area Goražde* as a humorous, enthusiastic exception to the somber reality Sacco experiences in Goražde. Sacco's writes, "In Goražde journalists were still exotics, guests from the outside—from *outside!* They welcomed us and all the promise our outsideness implied. . . . All that said, *nothing* had prepared me for Riki."[23] Riki is featured in a large panel, a halo of light around his head as he sings "Hotel California" and "Born in the USA" in large word balloons with accompanying musical bars. This moment of individuality is then followed by another shift to collective belonging as Riki greets Sacco by saying, "I would like to take this opportunity to thank the United States of America for what it has done for us" while shaking his hand.[24] This staged relation—of the individual and society, and of the individual as society—uses individual characters and subjects as both interesting in and of themselves, and as figures who represent larger categories such as the nation, the dispossessed, the veteran, the optimist. In moments like these, Sacco's work resonates as both an extension of the confessional tradition in underground and alternative comics and a major contribution to the tradition of immersive reporting consolidated by the New Journalism. Sacco's comics journalism makes the world legible and visible, in all of its complexity, and it does so by drawing lines from individual experiences to the larger structures that determine them.

Critical Approaches to the Comics of Joe Sacco

This book contains essays that further explore Joe Sacco's comics journalism, from a variety of disciplinary perspectives and with a variety of focal points, ranging from the history of journalism and the capacities of the comics medium, to the ways in which Sacco's comics journalism can be read alongside Giorgio Agamben's concept of "bare life" and Alain Badiou's political philosophy. Sacco's work has already found a place in some of the most important scholarship in comics studies. In two influential essays, Hillary Chute has read Sacco as emblematic of the comics medium's ability to represent history on the page as a kind of palimpsest.[25] Jeff Adams has convincingly placed Sacco in the category of "documentary graphic novels" that practice a critical social realism, and Amy Kiste Nyberg has defined the genre of comics journalism through Sacco's techniques.[26] Other influential readings of Sacco include Andrea A. Lunsford and Adam Rosenblatt's essays on Sacco's critical relationship to conventional journalism, as well as essays by Rose Brister and Belinda Walzer, Wendy Kozol, Brigid Maher, Rebecca Scherr, and Tristram Walker on Sacco's representations of conflict, violence, and human rights.[27] Along with interviews in magazines and newspapers, Sacco has taken part in a number of long interviews with Gary Groth in the *Comics Journal*, as well as with Hillary Chute in the *Believer* and Øyvind Vågnes in the *Journal of Graphic Novels and Comics*.[28] These interviews and the existing scholarship on Sacco give a sense of his importance to contemporary comics, art, literature, and journalism, not to mention global politics. The first book-length critical study of Sacco's work, *The Comics of Joe Sacco* seeks to build upon and consolidate this work. The book is divided into four sections, each of which explores a range of Sacco's texts and a range of those texts' themes, concerns, and formal elements.

The book's first section, "The Form of Comics Journalism," features essays that explore the meanings, history, and formal structures that constitute the unique blend of comics and reportage for which Sacco is best known. An overarching concern of the essays in the section is how Sacco both uses and critiques the standard of objectivity that has been prevalent in US journalism since the turn of the twentieth century. Placing comics journalism in relation to other media such as film, music, and magazines, Jared Gardner analyzes how Sacco manipulates time as both a thematic and a formal device that can pose alternatives to our Western notions of history and synchronicity. Looking at Sacco's *Safe Area Goražde*, Lan Dong analyzes Sacco's complicated negotiation of history and witness testimony, finding in Sacco's treatment of the Bosnian War a case study of how Sacco represents the stories of others in relation to his own presence as a reporter. In her reading of a four-page story originally published in the *New York Times Magazine*, Isabel Macdonald finds in Sacco a critique of the standard of objectivity, one that is shared by many journalists today and that Sacco is uniquely situated to visually articulate on the comics page. Concluding the first section, Marc Singer demonstrates how Sacco, often interpreted by scholars and critics as critical of the standard of objectivity, also employs the tactics of objective news reporting in his first long-form work, *Palestine*.

The second section, "Space and Maps," features essays that dwell on the many maps that feature prominently in Sacco's work, his use of aerial mapping and landscape images to visualize both the military and the slow violence of environmental degradation, and the strategies of detachment and involvement that his representations of space entail. Edward C. Holland's essay reads Sacco's maps and mappings of the Bosnian War as interventions in the traditional roles ascribed to cartography, bringing to bear the analytical tools of the discipline of geography to the study of comics. Georgiana Banita reads Sacco's contribution to his book with Chris Hedges, *Days of Destruction, Days of Revolt*, as partaking in the traditions of muckraking journalism and environmentalist documentary and photography, situating Sacco's landscapes of mountaintop-removal mining firmly in the tradition of environmental art and activism. Richard Todd Stafford also analyzes Sacco's representations of the Appalachian coalfields in *Days of Destruction, Days of Revolt*, finding in Sacco's landscapes and portraits a complex process of identification, spatialization, and ethical imbrication. Taken together, the essays in this section demonstrate how Sacco uses the inherently visual nature of the comics medium to produce new ways of seeing the world and others.

The third section, "The Politics and Aesthetics of Joe Sacco's Comics," contains essays that detail how Sacco's work makes demands on its readers, represents subjects in complex, historical registers, and foregrounds language and performance as necessary mediators of any journalistic text. These essays all share an interest in how Sacco's representations of history, subjects, and political difference enmesh the reader of his work in a revised relation to others and to everyday life. The usual becomes unusual; the norm becomes estranged. Using Bill Brown's thing theory and Jane Bennett's materialist theory, Ann D'Orazio analyzes how objects such as tea, tomatoes, trees, and the hijab function as nonhuman agents in Sacco's *Palestine*, endowing the text with a powerful depth and resonance. Øyvind Vågnes's essay is the first in the book to focus on Sacco's story "The Unwanted," and Vågnes demonstrates how one of Sacco's central devices—the portrait of an interview subject—functions as a means to represent the harms of "bare life" and to imagine an ethics of hospitality. While Vågnes draws on Giorgio Agamben, Judith Butler, and other theorists of human rights, Alexander Dunst draws on the philosophy of Alain Badiou to chart an important shift from Sacco's first long-form works of comics journalism—namely, *Palestine* and *Safe Area Goražde*—to the more recent *Footnotes in Gaza*. In *Footnotes in Gaza*, Dunst finds a shift away from ethics and toward a political aesthetic. Concluding this section, Rebecca Scherr draws on theories of performance and performativity to produce an account of both Sacco's performances on the page as an artist—the drawing of a line and how that line functions as a trace of the artist's presence—and his representations of himself as a "character" in his works. The essays in this section of the book develop multifaceted accounts of how Sacco's comics represent the world and address the reader through formal devices, representational strategies, and aesthetic principles.

The fourth and final section, "Drawing History, Visualizing World Politics," places Sacco's work in larger theoretical and practical contexts, by reading him in relation to the history of comics publishing, as well as an artist engaged with human rights crises, a journalist negotiating translation and linguistic difference, and a way to introduce students to world politics. Reading Sacco's *Footnotes in Gaza* as an entry in the tradition of book-length comics, a tradition about which comics artists, including Sacco, often express some ambivalence, Ben Owen argues that Sacco's representation of the 1956 Rafah Massacre produces an alternative sense of historical time in both its content and its form. Focusing on Sacco's *Palestine*, *Safe Area Goražde*, and *The Fixer*, Brigid Maher analyzes the role that translating and language play in Sacco's work. In his comics journalism, Sacco foregrounds translation as a process, producing a more nuanced relation of journalist to subject than one often finds in mainstream journalism. Returning to "The Unwanted," a work of reportage that is also one of Sacco's most autobiographical works in recent years, Maureen Shay argues that Sacco stages and then complicates the binary oppositions that structure the status and treatment of refugees to Malta. The final essay in this section considers the classroom, as Kevin C. Dunn elaborates how he has taught *Safe Area Goražde* in an introductory International Relations course. This essay should be of interest not just for its pedagogical argument, but also for its demonstration of how Sacco's work resonates beyond discourses more familiar to scholars in the humanities.

The four sections of *The Comics of Joe Sacco* overlap, of course, and the essays all share an investment in the exciting and intellectually challenging task of understanding Joe Sacco's comics. It is my hope that this book will both establish an interpretive and critical tradition for reading Sacco's comics, and also point to further research. While the essays in this collection range across Sacco's work, from *Palestine* and *Safe Area Goražde* to *Footnotes in Gaza* and the stories collected in *Journalism*, they are not exhaustive. Sacco's panorama of the Battle of the Somme, *The Great War*, was published in 2013, as this book was being written, and Sacco's newest work, *BUMF*, was not yet published when this book was completed. The critical approaches in this book are meant to inspire further approaches to the comics of Joe Sacco, comics that speak volumes about our contemporary world.

NOTES

1. These stories are all collected in Joe Sacco, *Notes from a Defeatist* (Seattle: Fantagraphics, 2003).

2. Gary Groth, "Joe Sacco, Frontline Journalist," in Joe Sacco, *Safe Area Goražde: The War in Eastern Bosnia, 1992–1995*, Special Edition (Seattle: Fantagraphics, 2011), 252. This interview was originally published in *Comics Journal* Special Edition (Winter 2002).

3. For example, in an interview for *Mother Jones* magazine, Sacco remarks that "the people whose work I've admired are people like George Orwell and others like Michael Herr and, of course, some of Hunter S. Thompson's work. I like good, straight reporting, too. Robert Crumb is an influence on how I draw, but not on the subject matter I take or my approach. One thing I do like about Crumb is that he's chronicled his age, his times, and I think that is what artists should do." See Dave Gilson, "The Art of War: An Interview with Joe Sacco," *Mother Jones*, July/August 2005, http://www.motherjones.com/media/2005/07/joe-sacco-interview-art-war.

4. I am indebted to Monica Marshall's biography of Joe Sacco for much of this information. See Monica Marshall, *Joe Sacco* (New York: Rosen, 2005).

5. Joe Sacco, *But I Like It* (Seattle: Fantagraphics, 2006), 107.

6. Gilson, "The Art of War."

7. David Shields, *Reality Hunger: A Manifesto* (New York: Knopf, 2010), 5.

8. For accounts of the New Journalism, see John C. Hartsock, *A History of American Literary Journalism: The Emergence of a Modern Narrative Form* (Amherst: University of Massachusetts Press, 2001); John Hollowell, *Fact and Fiction: The New Journalism and the Nonfiction Novel* (Chapel Hill: University of North Carolina Press, 1977); and Stacy Olster, "New Journalism and the Nonfiction Novel," in *The Cambridge Companion to American Fiction After 1945*, ed. John N. Duvall (New York: Cambridge University Press, 2012), 44–55. Accounts of underground and alternative comics include James Danky and Denis Kitchen, *Underground Classics: The Transformation of Comics into Comix* (New York: Abrams, 2009); Charles Hatfield, *Alternative Comics: An Emerging Literature* (Jackson: University Press of Mississippi, 2005); and Patrick Rosenkranz, *Rebel Visions: The Underground Comix Revolution, 1963–1975*, 2nd ed. (Seattle: Fantagraphics, 2008).

9. Tom Wolfe, "The New Journalism," in *The New Journalism*, eds. Tom Wolfe and E. W. Johnson (New York: Harper & Row, 1973), 20–21.

10. For a reading of Sacco and other comics artists in relation to the New Journalism, but one that ultimately posits a difference between comics journalism and literary nonfiction rather than the shared history that I am emphasizing here, see Rocco Versaci, *This Book Contains Graphic Language: Comics as Literature* (New York: Continuum, 2007), 109–38. For a reading of Sacco's *Safe Area Goražde* and Michael Herr's *Dispatches* that emphasizes the ethical mechanisms of each

text and the figure of the journalist, see Aryn Bartley, "The Hateful Self: Substitution and the Ethics of Representing War," *Modern Fiction Studies* 54.1 (Spring 2008): 50–71.

11. For a brief treatment of R. Crumb and underground comics' influence on Sacco, see Tristram Walker, "Graphic Wounds: The Comics Journalism of Joe Sacco," *Journeys* 11.1 (2010), 70–74.

12. Joe Sacco's short comic "Oliver Limpdingle's Search for Love" appeared in *Weirdo* 23 (Summer 1988). The story is collected in Sacco, *Notes from a Defeatist*, 20–21. Sacco's story "The War Crimes Trials," commissioned by Art Spiegelman, originally appeared in the September 1998 issue of *Details* and is collected in Joe Sacco, *Journalism* (New York: Metropolitan, 2012), 2–7.

13. For a thoughtful account of autobiographical comics and their emergence out of the underground comics tradition, see Jared Gardner, *Projections: Comics and the History of Twenty-First Century Storytelling* (Stanford: Stanford University Press, 2012), 107–48.

14. "Contest! Contest!" *Centrifugal Bumble-Puppy* 1 (September 1987), 29.

15. Joe Sacco, "How I Loved the War," *Notes from a Defeatist*, 188.

16. Ibid.

17. Fredric Jameson, "Postmodernism and Consumer Society," *The Cultural Turn: Selected Writings on the Postmodern* (New York: Verso, 1998), 16.

18. Ibid.

19. Fredric Jameson, *The Antinomies of Realism* (New York: Verso, 2013), 256.

20. Groth, "Joe Sacco, Frontline Journalist," 247.

21. Joe Sacco, *The Fixer and Other Stories* (Montreal: Drawn and Quarterly, 2009), 12–13.

22. Mikhail Bakhtin, "Discourse in the Novel," in *The Dialogic Imagination: Four Essays*, ed. Michael Holquist, trans. Caryl Emerson and Michael Holquist (Austin: University of Texas Press, 1981), 262.

23. Joe Sacco, *Safe Area Goražde: The War in Eastern Bosnia, 1992–1995* (Seattle: Fantagraphics, 2000), 24.

24. Ibid., 25.

25. Hillary Chute, "Comics as Literature?: Reading Graphic Narrative," *PMLA* 123.2 (March 2008): 452–65; and "Comics Form and Narrating Lives," *Profession* (2011): 107–17.

26. Jeff Adams, *Documentary Graphic Novels and Social Realism* (New York: Peter Lang, 2008), 121–60; and Amy Kiste Nyberg, "Comics Journalism," in *Critical Approaches to Comics: Theories and Methods*, eds. Matthew J. Smith and Randy Duncan (New York: Routledge, 2012), 116–28.

27. Andrea A. Lunsford and Adam Rosenblatt, "'Down a Road and into an Awful Silence': Graphic Listening in Joe Sacco's Comics Journalism," in *Silence and Listening as Rhetorical Arts*, eds. Cheryl Glenn and Krista Ratcliffe (Carbondale: Southern Illinois University Press, 2011), 130–46; Adam Rosenblatt and Andrea A. Lunsford, "Critique, Caricature, and Compulsion in Joe Sacco's Comics Journalism," in *The Rise of the American Comics Artist: Creators and Contexts*, eds. Paul Williams and James Lyons (Jackson: University Press of Mississippi, 2010), 68–87; Rose Brister and Belinda Walzer, "*Kairos* and Comics: Reading Human Rights Intercontextually in Joe Sacco's Graphic Narratives," *College Literature* 40.3 (Summer 2013): 138–55; Wendy Kozol, "Com-

plicities of Witnessing in Joe Sacco's *Palestine*," in *Theoretical Perspectives on Human Rights and Literature*, eds. Elizabeth Swanson Goldberg and Alexandra Schultheis Moore (New York: Routledge, 2012), 165–79; Brigid Maher, "Drawing Blood: Translation, Mediation, and Conflict in Joe Sacco's Comics Journalism," in *Words, Images, and Performances in Translation*, eds. Brigid Maher and Rita Wilson (New York: Continuum, 2012), 119–38; Rebecca Scherr, "Shaking Hands with Other People's Pain: Joe Sacco's *Palestine*," *Mosaic* 46.1 (2013): 19–36; Tristram Walker, "Graphic Wounds: The Comics Journalism of Joe Sacco," *Journeys* 11.1 (Summer 2010): 69–88.

28. Groth, "Joe Sacco, Frontline Journalist"; Gary Groth, "Joe Sacco on *Footnotes in Gaza*," *Comics Journal* 301 (2011): 376–426; Hillary Chute, "Joe Sacco (Comics Journalist)," *Believer*, June 2011, http://www.believermag.com/issues/201106; Øyvind Vågnes, "Inside the Story: A Conversation with Joe Sacco," *Journal of Graphic Novels and Comics* 1.2 (December 2010): 193–216.

Section I
The Form of Comics Journalism

1. Time under Siege

Jared Gardner

As a storytelling medium, comics are burdened by inefficiencies and obstacles. While scholars devoted to nourishing the emerging field of comics studies are often temperamentally disinclined to discuss these facts, cartoonists themselves are quite articulate on the subject. And for the cartoonist perhaps no issue looms larger than that of time.

Chris Ware, for example, has more than once commented on how profoundly "uneconomical" comics are "work-to-reading-time-wise."[1] In an interview in 2001, he even attempted to calculate the ratio: "about an hour and a half of work per second of reading time." In 2001, experiencing mainstream exposure for the first time following the publication of *Jimmy Corrigan*, Ware found himself feeling like Washington Irving's Rip van Winkle: "Lately, I can't shake the feeling that I've been living a dream for the last 10 years or so; I can't account for most of my 20s, and I have to continually remind myself that certain people are dead now and many of my friends have children."[2]

Ware's experience is a familiar one. In 2008, the cartoonist Alec Longstreth vowed not to shave until he finished his graphic novel, *Basewood*, eventually releasing a time-lapse video documenting the growth of his hair and beard over the course of the next three years, four months, and two days while he worked daily on his comic, eventually producing 125 pages and 14.5 inches of beard.[3] The video is an effective commentary on the vast amount of time required to produce an ambitious comic, but it also eloquently describes the profound dislocations in space-time the creation of these works can produce for its creators—dislocations that amplify an already highly charged relationship between cartoonist and reader. Comics, after all, are a form that require an active readership ready and willing to engage in a collaborative act of meaning-making, filling in the gaps between panels, setting still images into imaginative motion, and navigating two often competing semantic systems—word and image. Ideally, the cartoonist might fantasize a reader ready and willing to put in the cognitive labor that would correspond to the creative labor of its creation, as Ware, for example, diagrams in painstaking detail in the prefatory pages to *Jimmy Corrigan*.[4] But in the end, all cartoonists are deeply aware that they are and will remain on the short end of the temporal economies of comics creation and reading.

Of course, temporal gaps and disjunctions are fundamental to comics in other ways as well. By the time Einstein first theorized that time was not absolute, as Newtonian physics had insisted, but was in fact relative to space, comics were already busily navigating this newly discovered space-time. The consequences for physics and philosophy of Einstein's 1905 theory of Special Relativity would take generations to fully sink in, but comics had already begun mapping an approach to time that was not rigidly bound by our conventional *experience* of time as "tensed"—that is, defined by a real present which moves inexorably and steadily away from a lost past and towards an imagined future. As cartoonists and readers discovered early in the form's development, to read comics is necessarily to see past, present, and future at once, and to experience time not (only) as serial but also as simultaneous. Indeed, arguably the most significant consequence of Einstein's theories for the philosophy and science of time is that it demonstrates time as itself a dimension that functions akin to the spatial dimensions we *do* experience every day. Comics have spent the better part of their history not only illuminating Einstein's theory of Special Relativity, but also pointing readers towards ways of navigating a previously unimaginable *tenseless* model of time.[5]

More than a century later, however, faith in time as something universally shared by all shows little sign of being shaken. In fact, despite repeated proofs of Einstein's theory in the intervening decades, our practices in relationship to time have become, in many respects, *more* committed to a notion of absolute time. We synchronize our growing networks, economies, and broadcast schedules across continents with ever greater precision, contributing to the illusion—so vital to our twenty-first-century global economy—that time moves the same in one part of the world as it does in another.

In what follows, I want to argue that one of the most powerful and potentially transformative contributions of Joe Sacco's work as a comics journalist has been its dedication to exploring the *politics* of time and the very different ways in which it moves and is experienced in different places and by different peoples. If part of being a cartoonist is, as Ware suggests, to be Rip van Winkle, Sacco dedicates his comic art not so much to the achronicity of the artist but to the rendering of the temporal experiences of those who find themselves outside of "absolute" time.

Time in Goražde

The hybrid category we deploy to describe Sacco's work—comics journalism—is, of course, something of an oxymoron, especially in the twenty-first century, when news cycles are increasingly measured in hours and when global new media provides instant access to images, tweets, and other bytes from around the world at the touch of a screen. Sacco began serializing his first major work of comics journalism, *Palestine*, as journalism was going through its most profound changes since the birth of the penny press in the 1830s. As the new twenty-four-hour cable news station, pioneered by Ted Turner's CNN in the 1980s, merged with the rise of the World Wide Web in the 1990s, time constraints, which had always been one of the journalist's most pressing challenges, were compounded exponentially. Satellite television and the Internet, two networks that depend on the shared fiction of synchronized time, have combined to make the world feel "smaller," collapsing distances and creating the demand for "real-time" access to news and information. While political leaders, like Tony Blair in 2007, worry that the pace of journalism in the twenty-first century is such that both facts and opinions "harden within minutes," such laments have done little to change the pace of journalism or the expectations of its audiences.[6]

Of course, even as satellites and servers spread out across the globe creating the illusion for producers and consumers of an interconnected "small world"—an imagined global "here" that shares the same clocktime: a fantastical "now"—much of the world finds itself most definitely not included in that dominant "here and now." It is this dark side of the digital divide, and the stories of daily life that unfold in that other world, that have been the subject of Sacco's comics journalism over the course of the last two decades, the same decades in which the "digital divide" and its impacts first became visible. Needless to say, what divides his subjects—their stories, their daily rhythms, their visions of the past and the future—from his imagined readers involves far more than Internet access. But for a cartoonist employing his time-intensive craft to convey stories from conflict zones in an age of tweets, blogs, and twenty-four-hour breaking news, this "digital divide" perhaps best represents what separates *him* from his journalistic peers.

Of course, many other changes were underway as Sacco began his career as a comics journalist, including increasing concentration of media ownership, the collapse of print economies (especially impacting newspaper and independent journalism), and the concomitant rise of social media (providing each networked individual with a printing press on which to record their every mood and appetite). On the other side of the world, other trends beg for attention.[7] Perhaps most notable for Sacco's journalism, we see the dramatic shift in the number of civilian casualties in conflict zones around the world. A century ago, 85–90 percent of casualties in war were military. By the late 1990s, approximately 80 percent of all casualties in military conflicts were civilian.[8] What does "here and now" look and feel like for the inhabitants of these conflict and sacrifice zones? This has been a driving preoccupation of Sacco's journalism: to tell the story of those who by the standards of modernity have no story to tell, precisely because they have no future towards which to move.

The German social theorist Niklas Luhman has argued that the modern, Western conception of the future emerges only with the rise of bourgeois society in the seventeenth century, linked with the rise of market capitalism and its (newfound) need for a future in which to invest.[9] Much of modernity as we know it in the West can be linked to this new conception of the future and its most powerful product: the "series of things" (*series rerum*) as a model for temporal progress. Everything from the inventions of the modern nation-state, race (and racism), and global capitalism depends fundamentally on the belief in progress that remains at its core linked to Enlightenment stadialism—a vision of individuals and societies evolving from savagery to civilization, from a benighted Past to an imagined Future. Print technology has from very early in its history been dedicated to promoting and protecting this vision, and the forms that have risen within the new economies of print—including journalism, the novel, biography—all have at their core this fundamental story. It is a story as old as (our modern conception of) time itself: the story of our inevitable and inexorable movement from a lost Past towards an imagined Future, a story which reinforces and naturalizes our experience of time and faith in an inheritance which awaits, just around the corner.

Yet, for many individuals in the world, time does not move in this way. Often it does not move at all. In *Safe Area Goražde*, Sacco describes in detail a relationship to time for the inhabitants of the besieged city that is completely out of sync with the "outside world." "There'd been nothing new for years, no new films, no new fashion," Sacco writes.[10] One young man, Haris, describes his longing to see the Quentin Tarantino film *Pulp Fiction* he had learned of from a magazine left by British peacekeepers. For him, the film represents the "new," change in opposition to the timelessness of a city under siege. *Pulp Fiction* is a particularly interesting cultural text for the young Bosnian to focus on. Most notably, the film can be identified as an important precursor in a cycle that would grow in visibility at the start of the new century, films that deliberately break with traditional narrative chronology and invite, even require, repeated viewings in order to navigate the story and the many "clues" scattered across the fragmented narrative. For Tarantino, the technology that allowed for these repeated viewings was the VCR.[11] By 2000, when *Goražde* was published, the new technology of the DVD afforded unprecedented abilities for the viewer to time-travel across a cinematic text, past, present, and future. Beginning with *Memento* and *Mulholland Dr.*, a wave of films would follow from the template established by *Pulp Fiction* in exploring a Hollywood cinema liberated from the linear timeline.

Longing for *Pulp Fiction*, therefore, is more than simply a longing for something "new"—it is a longing for temporal movement, for the freedom to move between a past, present, and future. It is a longing for the kind of mobility that Sacco, for example, possesses, able to hop on a UN convoy back to "civilization" and its conventional time whenever he flashes his credentials. "They *had* to love me in Goražde," Sacco writes, "I *was* movement."[12] Further, Sacco could leave knowing that on his return he would always find "my pals, their familiars, and everyone else still surrounded in the enclave just where I'd left them."[13]

On one such return Sacco meets his friend, Riki, one of *Goražde*'s most colorful characters. Riki characteristically breaks into song—always an American pop tune from another era, in this case, the Eagles's 1977 hit "Hotel California": "You can check out any time you like, but you can never leave." Like the allusion to *Pulp Fiction*, Riki's choice shows an understanding of American popular culture as representing something specifically related to time—and particularly a relation to time that the residents of Goražde find themselves longing for. Unlike Sacco, the residents of the besieged city "can never leave," and even nearby Sarajevo "may as well have been a million miles away." "We're afraid we're losing time," says one young woman, while Edin, Sacco's friend and guide, has remained stalled for four years "stranded in Goražde, 15 minutes from his degree" at the university.[14] Fifty miles from Sarajevo, less than 500 miles from Vienna, the inhabitants of Goražde are close enough geographically and historically to dominant time to feel the "loss" of time as measured by the world just beyond their grasp. During the time Sacco was in Goražde, the future of the city and of the former Yugoslavia in general was in limbo, as diplomats met in Dayton to work on a comprehensive peace agreement to bring an end to the war that had raged for more than three years. The residents of Goražde were well aware of the fact that their status represented an obstacle to a resolution to the war with which Western media and their audiences had grown weary ("I wish Goražde would go away," Sacco quotes one American journalist as saying).[15] At the time of Sacco's extended stay in the city, the inhabitants hang between two fates, only one of which would reconnect them to the capital, to the West, to education, to time.

For the residents who awaited the decisions being hammered out in Ohio, it was all about time—or, more specifically, about *Time*. Roughly halfway through the volume, Riki again performs for his friends, this time not an American pop song but an article from an issue of *Time* magazine he had memorized when he was in the trenches in 1994. "Paula Jones, who was 24 then, sued President Clinton for $700,000 for allegedly violating her civil rights by making unwelcomed sexual advances toward her in a Little Rock hotel," Riki recites earnestly, while Sacco looks on in slack-jawed amazement.[16] Even more starkly than the allusions to "Hotel California" and *Pulp Fiction*, that the magazine in question is "*Time*" underscores a larger concern with what it means for those living in conflict and sacrifice zones to be outside of dominant *Time*: not written about in its pages, not perceived as being of interest to the readers of this magazine, once itself a cornerstone of Time Warner, the world's largest media conglomerate and the epitome of Big Media. From the beginning of the war to its end, *Time* magazine covered the fate of those in Goražde sporadically at best, and in the May 16, 1994, issue which Riki had memorized in the Bosnian trench, there is not a single mention of the Bosnian War then entering its third year.[17]

It is, of course, impossible not to miss the tragic irony of Riki's reading and rereading this "news" magazine from the trenches of a war that is forgotten even as it is waged, and on the wrong side of the religious lines quickly emerging as surrogate for Cold War divisions and borders. And yet, for better or worse, this was the *Time* to which these besieged citizens longed to be reunited, if only because alternatives were few and far between. Sacco attempts to provide one such alternative, however small and however inadequate: an approach to journalism and time entirely different than that represented by *Time* and its compatriots. The dominant approaches are described in *Safe Area Goražde*: "Journalists blew in with the U.N. convoy in the morning... did some man-in-the-street and/or a quickie stand-up on the second bridge, and blew out with the U.N. convoy in the afternoon."[18] After all, "they needed their journalism *now*, for the top of the hour," and, as Sacco describes, familiarly threw candy into the streets to prompt a mad scramble of kids in order to spark a ready-made "scene."

Of course, Sacco's journalism is not the stuff of an hour, or even a year. "Hotel California," *Pulp Fiction*, and even the issue of *Time* that Riki reads over and over are all "old news" by the time of Sacco's stay in Goražde in the fall of 1995. *Pulp Fiction*, which represented all that was "new" for Haris, is already last year's phenomenon, replaced in the autumn of 1995 by new time-bending indie hits like *The Usual Suspects* and *12 Monkeys*. And *Time* magazine was on to newer and more urgent topics as well. But by the time Sacco finishes the pages on which these events are recorded, still more time has passed. For example, the page on which Haris in 1995 bemoans his lack of access to the 1994 film *Pulp Fiction* was completed in November 1998. The page in which Riki recites the 1994 issue of *Time* was completed in February 1999.

That we know the dates on which Sacco finished particular pages is in itself an unusual feature of this work: his system of dating by month and year each of the pages he produces, a practice few other long-form cartoonists employ. When asked about the practice in an interview with Hillary Chute, Sacco said:

It's sort of a weird, anal thing, but I want to know that I'm producing. It's sort of a spur to produce, and it reminds me sometimes that I left a certain page for a while. For example, there's a page early on that was penciled for a long time, but I didn't have an Egyptian uniform. I finally found a book for that. It took a year. I didn't actually date the page until I was finished with that panel.[19]

On the one hand an attempt to "demystify" the process for his readers—"letting people know your pace and your rate"—Sacco's dating system also serves to remind us how very "old" his "news" always is. Not unlike the inhabitants of Goražde, Sacco's journalism is always "late," the processes of travel, interviews, photographs and recordings, transcriptions, and, of course, the meticulously crosshatched drawings with often highly detailed architectural and environmental backgrounds staggering and fracturing the "news cycle" in manifold ways. Like the inhabitants of Goražde, Sacco's "news" is always caught in the past. In 2000, the year of the publication of *Safe Area*, Goražde was not mentioned once in either the *New York Times* or *Time* magazine, save in reviews of Sacco's book itself.[20]

And that is part of the mandate of Sacco's comics journalism. Its slow, handmade, stutter-step production and dissemination necessarily brings old news back into focus. Long after the Dayton accords effectively ended the war, Sacco was still telling stories about its people and its aftermath. For example, in *The Fixer: A Story from Sarajevo*, Sacco seeks out the "fixer" who was his guide through the city back in the late days of the war in 1995, a mysterious man named Neven—half-swashbuckler, half-con man—who finds himself now adrift. An ethnic Serb who had fought for the Bosnians in the war before becoming a fixer for the journalists in Sarajevo covering the war from its cosmopolitan capital, Neven at war's end finds himself completely dislocated from even his own memories. Holding a photograph of his old comrades, he muses, "The worst thing is now I can't remember the names of most of those guys. . . . I can't remember the names of my friends who were killed."[21] The city is moving on, as Sacco notes at the book's beginning. In Sarajevo,

> the shops are open . . . the trams are running . . . the cafes are housing the idle and spewing a relentless Eurobeat. . . . And with every few steps one relentless Eurobeat drowns out another; but all the relentless Eurobeats cannot drown out the silence, which is the most relentless thing of all.[22]

Whereas in 1995, with Sarajevo under siege, Sacco found numerous individu-

Figure 1.1. Detail of Joe Sacco, *The Fixer*, in *The Fixer and Other Stories* (Montreal: Drawn & Quarterly, 2009), 4.

als willing to share their stories and revisit traumatic memories; in 2001, the relentless Eurobeat carries everyone on a "procession" away from his table and his desire for conversations about the past. "I can hardly get this city to tell me about my broader subject, much less whisper any of its terrible secrets."[23] Only the hope of finding Neven, whom no one has seen in years, keeps Sacco rooted at the café table, hoping against hope that he is not, as he fears, "wasting my time again."[24] The book's first prologue, set in 2001, gives way to a second prologue set in 1995 when Sacco and Neven first meet; here Neven sits waiting for a journalist, any journalist to come by and give him work, to redeem the long wait (see Figures 1.1 and 1.2). "Put yourself in Neven's shoes," the narrator tells us, which is precisely what Sacco in the first prologue has done, as *he* is now the one sitting waiting for Neven to give him a reason for being at the café.

One of the remarkable features of comics is its ability to allow us to occupy two temporalities at once. This is precisely the effect of this two-page spread that ends the first prologue and begins the second, as the reader's eye moves and marks both the parallels and differences between Sarajevo in 2001 and the same city in 1995. The crowds, the beat, the commerce, and the idle chat-

Time under Siege   29

Figure 1.2. Detail of Joe Sacco, *The Fixer*, in *The Fixer and Other Stories* (Montreal: Drawn & Quarterly, 2009), 5.

ter on the left, the ominous silence, and the eerie solitude of a hotel lobby on the right. For Neven in 1995, the war was winding down and with it any sense of vocation. No longer a soldier, now even his stack of business cards from journalists represents only memories of the fading "crowded months and 150 dm days."[25] All the "real" journalists now "have followed the flies to somewhere else"; Bosnia is no longer where the "action" is to be found. Which is, of course, where our comics journalist walks in, the last journalist to arrive, the last one to "report" from the war, the only one to return in 2001 in search of new stories about a past which now no one wishes to recall. Except for Neven, if he could only remember.

Sacco is conscious of his own desires, as arguably the world's slowest journalist, to freeze his subjects in place—as he says of Riki at the end of *Safe Area Goražde*, "I hoped he'd be there when I got back . . . just where I left him . . . with Creedence or the Eagles on his lips . . . and still sure his world was about to be put right. I hoped he could go . . . but I wanted to hold him there."[26] In one respect, which Sacco explicitly acknowledges, his desire to hold his subjects in place and in time is potentially just the obverse of the conventional journalists' need to make his subjects *move* (by, for example, throwing candy to a crowd of children), to move the story towards a resolution in time for the evening news. But in a world driven by the demand for the news—for the new—the cartoon journalist's ability to speak for those who are unmoored from this networked time at the very least serves to remind us that time as measured by CNN or *Time* is not absolute or universal.

Beyond the Eurobeat

As Sacco puts it in *Palestine*, "make no mistake, everywhere you go, not just in Marvel Comics, there's parallel universes."[27] For the residents of Goražde, time had been fractured by the war, the wound fresh and raw, and ultimately repairable. For many of the survivors, time would be resynchronized back to the Eurobeat with the war's end. But alongside Bosnia, Sacco has spent a lot of time covering conflicts and occupations in places where generations have been born and died, denied the belief in a future, and where the attempt to recover history, as Sacco does in *Footnotes in Gaza*, is like writing on sand. I want to conclude by returning to Sacco's first trip to Palestine—and his first extended work of comics journalism in a conflict zone—where he first discovered these "parallel universes" where time operated very differently and began learning how to tell time by their clocks.

Palestine is a very different conflict zone than Goražde. Early in *Safe Area Goražde*, Edin takes Sacco on a tour of the city in search of traces of the history of violence that has ravaged his city—"the car of one of his best friends, killed on the first day of the attack on Goražde," "marks in the road where a Serb tank had stopped and turned."[28] In Gaza, however, all traces of the houses leveled by Israeli bulldozers are lost beneath "the ground where they have been swallowed."[29] For Palestinians, as Sacco describes it in *Footnotes in Gaza*, time operates in ways that those who live outside of the occupied territories can never truly comprehend. Here, "events are continuous,"[30] but recorded only as yet another "footnote" in a larger history which "can do without its footnotes"—footnotes that "trip up the greater narrative," to be ultimately sloughed off in new editions, presenting ever tighter narrative versions of the "truth" and, of course, room for newer "footnotes" ("Here, where the ink never dries").[31]

Traditional history—the attempt to recover the past—fails when it comes to Palestine, calling for alternate methods of historiography.[32] But journalism—the attempt to record the present—fails no less spectacularly, and that failure first brought Sacco to Gaza in late 1991. As Edward Said puts it in his introduction to the collected *Palestine*, what we call journalism is in fact overwhelmingly "controlled and diffused by a handful of men sitting in places like London and New York," men representing media conglomerates with little interest—political or financial—in the perspectives of the Palestinians.[33] In an interview in the *Comics Journal* in 1995, Sacco described his painful discovery in 1989 of "how the media had manipulated my perception of Palestinians."[34] But the solution was not as simple as going to Gaza and getting "the other side." It involved entering a space under siege where events moved in ways traditional journalism had no methods to record or recover.

For example, early in the series, traveling from Cairo to Palestine, Sacco passes tanks burned out and discarded in the sands—"since when? '73? '67? '56?"[35] As he will record in painstaking detail in *Footnotes in Gaza* more than a decade later, the attempts to pin time down according to the conventional timelines of history fail in a landscape littered with the detritus of endlessly repeated cycles of violence and revenge. So it is that, even before arriving in Palestine, Sacco's sense of time is totally askew: "It's a long way to Palestine and slow going," he writes, against the image of one of the twisted tanks, "But I've been speeding, man. I've been speeding. I'm already there."[36]

This dislocation from time and space—such that he can be simultaneously progressing slowly *and* "speeding," "a long way" away *and* "already there"—causes Sacco to abandon pretenses to journalistic objectivity and style at the border. In its place, he first turns to a ready-made toolset drawn from the New Journalism, adopting a present-tense subjectivity and proclaiming himself now, "three weeks later," "good at this"—"this" being his ability to get Palestinians talking.[37] "I'm a charmer . . . a real innocent."[38] The security of his new method is interrupted, however, by a memory of a Berlin conversation from 1985 about the execution of the American Jew Leon Klinghoffer by the Palestinian Liberation Front, a memory seared in his consciousness by the "human interest" the media brought to Klinghoffer's death. Meanwhile, Sacco now realizes of the Palestinian lives lost in the intervening years, "even when it's made the evening news I never caught a name or recall a face."[39] Faced with the seeming unnarratability of a people whose story has been systematically untold for generations, Sacco's first impulse is to make the story about *himself*—to be the "human interest." But his memory of his earlier response to the execution of Klinghoffer—a tirade on the streets of Berlin fueled by lust, jealousy, and ego—reminds him of the fallibility of his present-tense self as the filter for the story he needs to tell.

Instead, he soon discovers, it will be his first (seemingly broken and paradoxical) articulation of time in the Sinai desert—slowly/speeding, distant/present—that will serve as the method by which he will immerse himself in a time that stands still even as events move so fast that the "ink never dries." What emerges in this, Sacco's first extended work of comics journalism, is a method of alternating between the slowness of seemingly empty, timeless moments and the chaotic "speeding" of events tumbling one on top of another. Both defy the techniques of journalism and the privileging of a story with a beginning, middle, and end. But both prove open, in ways that perhaps Sacco did not anticipate when he began the project, to the unique affordances of comics. For example, in Chapter 5, at the center of the collected volume, Sacco describes a day in Ramallah which begins with a splash page depicting what could be any Saturday in the occupied city: Israeli soldiers move through the streets pirouetting anxiously every which way (what Sacco calls "the West Bank 'Swan Lake'").[40] But then, just when our protagonist is once again ready to give up hopes that "Ramallah will deliver" "some bangbang" for his "comics magnum opus," the protestors appear and the splash page is replaced by an increasingly chaotic jumble of panels and narration boxes—first three panels, then four, then sixteen panels tumbling against a thickly crosshatched background.[41] "Jesus, that was quick," a breathless narrator notes as the protesting youth come racing past him at the bottom of the page.

This alternation between two radically different experiences of time—the splash page, representing the repetition of what the narrator experiences as countless Saturdays spent waiting on the streets of Ramallah for the "story," and the jumble of panels, representing the "speeding" of events tumbling faster than they can be processed—will evolve over the course of the next two decades as Sacco's crucial tool for describing the "parallel universes" his experiences in Palestine have opened up to him. It is a toolset that is, in a sense, bestowed on him by listening to the story of Ghassan, the subject of "Moderate Pressure," which immediately precedes "Ramallah." Ghassan recounts his recent experiences in Israeli detention. The story begins with a full half-page panel devoted to representing Ghassan's experience of waking up in his home one night to discover the place crawling with Israeli soldiers and policemen. Below, two panels represent Ghassan being informed that he is being arrested on suspicion of belonging to a terrorist organization. In the pages that follow, the passage of time during his confinement and interrogation is represented by increasingly small boxes, the pages divided up first into six, then nine, twelve, sixteen, twenty panels. Here, the panels describe not only the increasingly claustrophobic spaces in which Ghassan is confined, but also the fracturing of his sense of time after days and weeks in solitary confinement, hooded, sleep-deprived, cut off entirely from the outside world. Recalling the events, Ghassan tries to count the hours—"They changed my position every four or five hours"—and the days—"After four days without sleep, I began to have hallucinations."[42] But all he can know with certainty is what his hallucinations showed him at the time: "My daughter is dead," "my brother is dead," "my father is dead."[43]

The status of these visions as "hallucinations" is, of course, clear to Ghassan by the time he recounts his experiences to Sacco. But in his cell they were not hallucinations but realities: "My daughter *is* dead." When finally Ghassan is released after nineteen days, the story ends as it began with a full half-page panel—this time representing not Ghassan's home but the East Jerusalem street traffic that swallows up his story, his experience in its procession of traffic, shoppers, and lovers all following the "Eurobeat" of dominant time. Despite being now returned to his middle-class living room, with his daughter asleep in his arms, Ghassan cannot recover that beat, knowing that at any moment of any night a dozen soldiers might appear in his kitchen to haul him or any member of his family away—for weeks, forever.

As we saw in *Goražde*, to be in the rhythms of conventional time requires having a future. It also assumes the rhythms of daily life, the security of home, the safety of sleep, a clock that needs punching in the morning. None of these are available to those who are born, live, and die under occupation. When home, job, or even sleep are insecure, the present cannot be—as we experience it conventionally—a place from which one can move, inexorably, forward in time. The present is instead only a point of perpetual, timeless uncertainty. Ghassan's is therefore a story uniquely his own, but also one shared by countless other Palestinians detained for weeks, months, indefinitely. Sacco's rendering of Ghassan's story is a metaphor for the parallel experience of time of a people living under occupation. Yet neither the slowing down of the splash page nor the speeding up of the smaller panels can by themselves adequately describe how time is experienced in these conditions. And, of course, as a journalist, an outsider, Sacco could not presume to know the experience of being born, coming of age, and growing old in such a world, however many interviews he records or reference photos he takes. There are only his own experiences—his boredom, his fear, his sense of time shifting suddenly from capacious sameness to frenetic movement. Sacco's experiences in Ramallah bear no similarity to those of Ghassan. But in telling Ghassan's story, Sacco discovers a vocabulary that teaches him to tell time as it is experienced in this parallel world: not as a flow of neatly ordered events all marching in time to the Eurobeat, but as an expanding and contracting frame in which everything, and nothing, happens in each and every moment.

This "everything and nothing" defines what has become arguably Sacco's most distinctive visual feature, especially in his comics journalism devoted to Palestine: the panorama. He uses it to striking effect in Chapter 6 of *Palestine* to represent across two densely illustrated pages what he calls "Refugeeland"—

Figure 1.3. Joe Sacco, *Palestine* (Seattle: Fantagraphics, 2001), 211.

a Palestinian refugee camp in the Gaza strip that is not precisely identified in terms of time or space. In the image spread out before us, we see a couple of dozen figures move through cratered streets awash with mud, trash, sewage. Looking down on the scene from a bird's-eye view, we cannot identify any individual figure below, but we see details in the larger environment that Sacco's street-eye subjective view could not provide: the cinderblocks holding down tarps on corrugated tin roofs, the horse-drawn carts, the goats working their way into overflowing dumpsters. Only the vehicles—a van, a handful of cars—assure us that we are in fact in the late twentieth century. And these vehicles look as liable to be washed away or devoured by the mud as any of the anonymous individuals walking across its surface.

A short time later, in an installment aptly named "Rewind," Sacco describes vividly the experience of being in one of those cars, as his guide Sameh drives him through torrential rains down the impossible streets of Jabalia, "a Disneyland of refuse and squalor," running into one dead end after another.[44] The purpose of this trip turns out to be to share with Sameh's friends an illegal video—a compilation of violence, burials, military exercises, marches. As they watch the video the first time, Sacco obsesses over the passage of time as the 8 o'clock curfew approaches—the everyday violence, physical and rhetorical, of life in Palestine. So caught up in the video are his colleagues, that they do not notice the passage of clock time, whereas Sacco cannot see anything else (see Figure 1.3). The next day, forced to watch the video once again, he is finally able to relax. "That's the good thing about video, you can rewind it, watch it over, eliminate all surprises. . . . Step outside, however, in present time, and all bets are off."[45]

Here, the compulsive re-watching of the video of past violence and conflict is comparatively safe to the uncertainty of the present—or better put, the video represents a fixed version of the "present" now safe for watching and rewinding, whereas the present itself only carries the certainty of new violence. And unlike that recorded on the videocassette, the new violence might involve you on the screen, memorialized for countless re-watchings to come. Or more likely, and more terrifying, not recorded at all. The violence of the recorded past is a comforting antidote to the uncertainty of everyday life "in present time," where "all bets are off"—because wagers, like economies more broadly, require at least the possibility of a future that might turn out different, better than the past being rewound, time and time again, or the present, poised, waiting to spring, just outside the door.

For Haris, in *Safe Area Goražde*, the desire to watch *Pulp Fiction* was about the desire to be reconnected not only to the "new" of the "now"—but also a now that promised movement. When films like *Pulp Fiction* broke with conventional linear time, they created a puzzle that, through the VCR or DVD, could be restored to its "proper" narrative timeline. For the residents of Jabalia, however, the VCR does not provide access to the "new," but instead to a safely prerecorded rewind-able version of an eternal, recurring now. For Sacco, the comics form—uniquely flexible in terms of its representation of space-time—opens up opportunities for representing experiences of time outside the dominant "proper" time of global capitalism and its networks so that different kinds of history and journalism might take shape to record its stories. He uses comics' visualization of time as space to show his readers *both* the flow of "universal" time and time's stutter-stop motion in worlds under siege. It's a small world only if we imagine, as Sacco refuses to allow us to do, that we are all experiencing the "flow" of time—past, present, and future—in sync and in the same way. Time has a politics, and only by denaturalizing the universal claims of networked time can those of us measuring our days by its relentless "Eurobeat" begin to recognize the common humanity of those living in parallel worlds under siege.

NOTES

1. "Live Webchat: Chris Ware," *The Guardian*. August 15, 2013, http://www.theguardian.com/books/booksblog/2013/aug/15/live-webchat-chris-ware-graphic-novelist.

2. Keith Phipps, "Chris Ware," *AV Club*, December 31, 2003, http://www.avclub.com/article/chris-ware-13849.

3. Alec Longstreth, "The *Basewood* Beard," December 10, 2011, https://www.youtube.com/watch?v=___4kLh5zhs.

4. Chris Ware, *Jimmy Corrigan: The Smartest Kid on Earth* (New York: Pantheon, 2000).

5. I discuss this at length in a forthcoming essay in *Time: A Vocabulary of the Present*, eds. Joel Burges and Amy J. Elias (forthcoming).

6. Quoted in John Keane, *Democracy and Media Decadence* (Cambridge: Cambridge University Press, 2013), 174.

7. As Sacco and his collaborator Chris Hedges remind us in *Days of Destruction, Days of Revolt*, such "sacrifice zones" are just as liable to be right down the road, however invisible, as on the other side of the world. See Chris Hedges and Joe Sacco, *Days of Destruction, Days of Revolt* (New York: Nation, 2012).

8. Mary Kaldor, *New & Old Wars. Organized Violence in a Global Era*, 2nd ed. (Stanford: Stanford University Press, 2007), 107.

9. Niklas Luhmann, "The Future Cannot Begin: Temporal Structures in Modern Society," *Social Research* 43 (Spring 1976): 130–52.

10. Joe Sacco, *Safe Area Goražde: The War in Eastern Bosnia, 1992–1995* (Seattle: Fantagraphics, 2000), 73.

11. Tarantino's "film school," the source of his encyclopedic range of allusions and references, was the California video store he worked at until 1990.

12. Sacco, *Safe Area Goražde*, 64.

13. Ibid.

14. Ibid., 98.

15. Ibid., 4.

16. Ibid., 99.

17. In this week's installment of the magazine's column "Winners and Losers," Robert Bennett is lauded for securing as his client not only Clinton but the embattled Congressman Dan Rostenkowski, while the new Denver International Airport is named the week's "big loser" for its delays in baggage handling.

18. Sacco, *Safe Area Goražde*, 130.

19. "Joe Sacco," in Hillary L. Chute, *Outside the Box: Interviews with Contemporary Cartoonists* (Chicago: University of Chicago Press, 2014), 148.

20. A survey of LexisNexis suggests only one English-language news story on Goražde in 2000, from the London *Financial Times* on December 18, 2000.

21. Joe Sacco, *The Fixer*, in *The Fixer and Other Stories* (Montreal: Drawn & Quarterly, 2009), 100.

22. Ibid., 2.

23. Ibid., 4.

24. Ibid., 5.

25. Ibid.

26. Sacco, *Safe Area Goražde*, 221.

27. As Mary Layoun puts it, "one of the most powerful of the structural relations traced in *Palestine* is its turn on the comics' convention of parallel universes. . . . If comics are the deliberate sequential juxtaposition of panels of words and images that tell a story, the convention of parallel universes in comics is a visual culmination of the genre's possibilities." Mary Layoun, "Telling Stories in *Palestine*: Comix Understanding and Narratives of Palestine-Israel," in *Palestine, Israel, and the Politics of Popular Culture*, eds. Rebecca L. Stein and Ted Swedenburg (Durham: Duke University Press, 2005), 317.

28. Sacco, *Safe Area Goražde*, 16.

29. Joe Sacco, *Footnotes in Gaza* (New York: Metropolitan, 2009), 181.

30. Ibid., 252.

31. Ibid., 9, 12.

32. See Ben Owen's essay in this volume.

33. Edward Said, "Homage to Sacco," in Joe Sacco, *Palestine* (Seattle: Fantagraphics, 2001), iii.

34. Thom Powers, "Joe Sacco," *Comics Journal* 176 (1995): 102.

35. Sacco, *Palestine*, 3.

36. Ibid.

37. Ibid., 4.

38. Ibid., 5.
39. Ibid., 8.
40. Ibid., 118.
41. Ibid., 118, 125.
42. Ibid., 108, 109.
43. Ibid., 109.
44. Ibid., 208.
45. Ibid., 213.

2. Inside and Outside the Frame: Joe Sacco's *Safe Area Goražde*

Lan Dong

Widely recognized for his comics journalism, Joe Sacco has written extensively about his travel experiences in such war-torn regions as the Gaza strip and Eastern Bosnia. In this essay, I examine how Sacco's *Safe Area Goražde: The War in Eastern Bosnia, 1992–1995* produces a sense of subjective truth as well as objective fact about the Bosnian War through the use of a hybrid genre that combines life writing and journalism in a graphic narrative. In *Safe Area Goražde*, Sacco explores the ethnic cleansing that occurred during the Eastern Bosnian conflicts through the particular lens of Goražde, a Muslim-dominated enclave; this settlement, located on the Drina riverbank, is a United Nations-designated "safe area" that is surrounded by Serb-controlled regions and that had been constantly under attack since the beginning of the war in 1992. Based on and reflecting his multiple trips to Goražde from late 1995 to January 1996, the graphic narrative is divided into dozens of chapters. These short episodes, ranging from two to fifteen pages, focus on many facets of the struggle: they portray various local residents along with refugees from other areas, document their memories of the war, depict the lasting impact of multiple military offensives, provide a historical context of the conflicts in the region and the international communities' responses to them, and address the political uncertainties within the settlement.

When Sacco first arrived in Goražde with a United Nations convoy in 1995, the town and its 57,000 residents had been cut off from the rest of the world for over three years. The four-page opening chapter, entitled "Go Away," begins and ends with splash pages (in which the illustration runs to the edge of the page) that help introduce the setting of the book, both in terms of the geographical location of the story and its historical and political context, namely the ongoing peace talks in Dayton, Ohio that would directly affect the future of the town and its people. As Will Eisner has pointed out, a splash page is like "a launching pad" for a graphic narrative because it establishes "a frame of reference."[1] The chapter "Go Away" begins with a full-page splash. The lack of a panel border calls the reader's attention to what is beyond the frame of the page as well as to what is on the page. The effect of visual images literally being

Figure 2.1. Splash opening page introducing the landscape near Goražde. Joe Sacco. *Safe Area Goražde: The War in Eastern Bosnia, 1992–1995* (Seattle: Fantagraphics, 2000), 1.

cut off at the edge of the physical page also indicates the limits of what can be captured in words and visuals within the pages of the book (see Figure 2.1).

In discussing comics as literature, Hillary Chute proposes that "Sacco spatializes the elliptical prose style of avant-garde writers such as Louis-Ferdinand

Céline, fragmenting boxes of text and floating them over his images. Spatializing the verbal narrative to dramatize or disrupt the visual narrative threads ellipses into the grammar of a medium already characterized by the elliptical structure of the frame-gutter-frame sequence."[2] The narration on the opening page is framed in three captions that are positioned triangularly, dividing the image (without panels) into three parts. In the middle is a team of United Nations vehicles on a narrow road that is partially destroyed, "nearing Goražde."[3] The damaged road and debris on the roadside correspond with the landscape on both sides of the road: trees with bare branches; visibly inhabitable and inhabited buildings and other constructions with missing roofs, windows, doors, walls, and holes of varied sizes; and an abandoned, obviously non-operational skeleton of a car. Whereas these visual elements allude to the town's history and reality, the text on the bottom of the page focuses on its uncertain future: "In the fall of 1995, the future of Goražde and its 57,000 inhabitants was by no means clear."[4] Further away are hills with scattered houses, identified as "no-man's-land."[5] There are no people in sight on this page, as if the convoy were driving into an empty town. The "non-frame" of this splash page "speaks to unlimited space" and "has the effect of encompassing unseen but acknowledged background."[6] The unseen subjects acknowledged by the narrative, Goražde's 57,000 inhabitants, are arranged deliberately on another splash page that concludes this short chapter.

Presented from the author's perspective—from inside one of the United Nations vehicles—Sacco portrays the local residents standing on both sides of the damaged road, looking outward and expectantly, while armed military guards manage the lines of people and keep order. The crowd, made up of men, women, and children of differing ages, seems endless, suggesting a pointed irony to the narration in the only caption on the page: "'I wish Goražde would go away,' I heard one American correspondent say . . ."[7] The people in Goražde are waiting not only eagerly for the United Nations procession but also anxiously for the result of the peace talks that would decide their fate and the future of their town. This splash page without the caption makes up the cover image of the 2008 edition of *Safe Area Goražde*. As such, Sacco leads the reader into Goražde and introduces the residents who, instead of going away, are right there visually in front of the reader's eyes.

As the above examples demonstrate, Sacco plays multiple roles simultaneously in *Safe Area Goražde*: author, artist, narrator, and journalist. Instead of trying to present a view of the military conflicts and Bosnians' suffering and dislocation from a conventional journalistic perspective, Sacco is a first-person narrator who befriends local residents and participates in social gatherings; at the same time, he is also a journalist who interviews people, observes their lives, and functions as a conduit to introduce to the reader multiple testimonies about the war. Thus, his graphic narrative both informs and challenges its readers, prompting them to navigate various subjective truths and objective facts in order to comprehend the complex history and reality of Goražde. This essay focuses on three aspects of *Safe Area Goražde*. First of all, it examines how Sacco frames the multiple first-person narratives and differing points of view provided by himself, the local residents, and the refugees stranded in Goražde in order to convey the episodic nature of survivors' testimonies and to connect the past with the present. Secondly, it addresses how the book reveals Sacco's "anti-official and anti-corporate attitude," to borrow Rocco Versaci's words, towards not only Western journalists who often report superficial and at times erroneous facts but also the failure of the UN, NATO, and the Clinton administration to intervene and prevent massacres in the region.[8] Thirdly, it looks at how Sacco's work visualizes multiple narrators and narratives, contextualizes personal stories with historical references, and represents Goražde through the author's simplistic, cartoonish self-portrait juxtaposed with his detailed, realistic visual representation of the local people and landscape.

A Journalist Inside and Outside the Frame

The comics medium is integral to Sacco's critical assessment of the situation in Goražde, together with its traumatic history and uncertain future. *Safe Area Goražde* visualizes war and its effects through survivors' testimonies. Aided by his guide and translator, Edin, Sacco interviews a number of Goražde residents as well as refugees from Visegrad and Foca where ethnic cleansing took place in 1992. Generally speaking, these testimonies are the longer chapters in the book. Hillary Chute has argued that "comics can express life stories, especially traumatic ones, powerfully because it makes literal the presence of the past by disrupting spatial and temporal conventions to overlay or palimpsest past and present."[9] Besides the presentation within the panel that "makes literal the presence of the past," actions and meanings also can be articulated in the white space between panels, commonly known as the gutter. In *Safe Area Goražde*, pages in the chapters of survivors' stories are framed in black borders; thus, the usual gutter as white space becomes black space, calling the reader's attention to the disruption of space and time and ultimately to this dark chapter of Eastern Bosnian history. Whereas the images for the most part depict historical atrocities, the text conveys the intertwining of the past and present. As Andrea A. Lunsford and Adam Rosenblatt have pointed out:

> Knowing that his dependence on mediators, as well as the complexity of the situations he is faced with, makes it impossible to tell even a single absolute

or positivistic "truth" about war or occupation, Sacco is content to try for the truth as he apprehends it. That truth, significantly, turns out to hinge on a series of human relationships involving everything from friendship to codependence and commerce. More often than not, the relationships Sacco builds in search of his "story" wind up *becoming* the story. (emphasis in original)[10]

Sacco's work covers not only the survivors' experiences and memories of war but also the process of his investigating the events: on the one hand, his interviews explicate "large, impersonal political machinations" in which political power shifts are entangled with ethnic and national pride; on the other hand, they burrow into "the individual lives of those affected" whose testimonies preserve the history of numerous mass murders and military assaults.[11] During such a process, Sacco, as a journalist and character, is visually present at times within the panels or pages, yet at other times he is outside the frame.

Taking advantage of the comics medium, Sacco presents varied actions, emotions, and narrative voices on the same page to provide different perspectives. His presence on some pages is a direct reminder of the journalist's mediating role in documenting and reporting particular events or topics. In an interview with Ernesto Priego in 2002, Sacco states:

> I don't really believe in objective journalism. To me all journalism is subjective; even that journalism that pretends to be objective, because writers come from a view point; they come from a culture. I don't think they can be objective about things or places they don't know much about. So I think it's important to depict myself for that reason. I want the reader to know that this is me and these are the things seen through my eyes.[12]

Sacco considers himself "a filter," and through the inclusion of his visual presence, he makes the reader aware of his role and perspective. Accordingly, his visual absence on other pages foregrounds the survivors' narratives, through which the reader is able to witness the traumatic past with all its visceral details.

In the chapter entitled "15 Minutes," Sacco juxtaposes his interview subject and her narrative with his personal experience and observations. In so doing, he depicts how the war and its aftermath have interrupted and continue to affect the Goraždan children's education. This page's top panel, without a border, portrays the skeleton of a school building whose visual details echo Sacco's narrative that "this secondary school, one of three in Goražde, had been gutted."[13] The low angle from which the remains of the school building are projected onto the page amplifies the bare, "gutted" structure. The two bottom panels on the left side focus on the dire need for qualified teachers and adequate classrooms. A schoolgirl's words, presented in word balloons, are supplemented by additional facts in captions about truncated class time and the shortage of instructors. One assumes the girl is talking to Sacco during one of his interviews, although he is not visually present in these panels. The bottom panel on the right—a bleed panel—transitions to another scene. This illustration depicts three children following Sacco and asking him for pencils, highlighting the lack of school essentials and disrupting the spatial and temporal continuity of the narrative. Together, the bottom panels—two of them framed and the other unframed—juxtapose his role as a journalist who conducts interviews outside the frame with his presence as a character who interacts with local residents inside the frame. In these four panels, Sacco's juxtaposition of subjective truths (his observation as well as the schoolgirl's words filtered by him) with objective facts (what's left of the school building and shortened school hours) powerfully reveals the inadequacy of the school facilities, the understaffed and overcrowded classes, and the lack of basic supplies, all of which pose challenges to educating children in Goražde during and after the war.

Besides appearing literally in the images as a character and participant in daily life as well as at social events in Goražde, Sacco's visual absence—usually paired with a textual presence—also facilitates the narrative in the book. One such example is Sacco's repeated portraits of Rasim. A refugee from Visegrad, Rasim is a self-identified "eyewitness" to the massacre in spring 1992, "when Serbs brought Muslims to the bridge on the Drina and pushed them into the river and shot them."[14] The chapter entitled "Around Goražde, Part I" begins with a shoulder portrait of Rasim, looking directly at the reader. This image reappears several times throughout the chapter, while Sacco visualizes Rasim's recollection of violence, deaths, injuries, and displacements during the war. Each time, Rasim's portrait is accompanied by his first-person narration framed in word balloons. In his analysis of the power of Sacco's depiction of "graphic wounds," Tristram Walker argues that Sacco's work requires readers to "mentally construct the reality of trauma. The 'white screen' of the spectacles and the gutter may allow for our own interpretation and imagination but ultimately we are guided in deciding the degree of brutality between frames by the images and written narration provided by Sacco."[15] For instance, in one moment of Rasim's narrative, Sacco depicts the brutal slaughter within the panels as well as through the scene-to-scene transitions, juxtaposing the witness and victim with the "graphic wounds." Rasim's role as a survivor is reinforced by his recurring portrait and statement: "I was an eyewitness."[16] His matter-of-fact words and passive facial expression in the last panel pose a sharp contrast to the graphic images of chaotic displacement and mass murder illustrated in the other panels on this page: massive blood spilled on and dripping over the bridge, highlighted by the usage of black shading, a dark river with bodies floating in it, and Serb soldiers in uniforms covered in blood dragging men, women, and children to the edge of the bridge for execution. Will Eisner considers the two kinds of frames in sequential art—the page border and the panel border—as "controlling devices."[17] He further contends: "The use of the panel border as a structural element within the setting... serves to involve the reader and encompasses far more than a simple container-panel. The sheer novelty of the interplay between the contained space and the 'non-space' (the gutter) between the panels also conveys a sense of heightened significance within the narrative structure."[18] Scott McCloud later conceptualizes the importance and creative possibility of the gutter between panels in a chapter entitled "Blood in the Gutter."[19] On this particular page, the black (instead of the usual white) space between panels is the same shade as the victims' blood. The comics page itself is structured by the violence Rasim witnessed.

Although Sacco is visually absent (since he was not a firsthand observer of the massacre that is visualized in most of the panels in this chapter), questions framed in word balloons and directed toward Rasim—"Were people resisting? / Were they screaming? / Were they tied? / But did they still kill women and children?"—remind the reader of his presence outside the frame.[20] As a journalist conducting an interview, Sacco prompts Rasim in order to probe for additional details or to verify specifics. Sacco's questions interrupt the spatial and temporal coherence of Rasim's narrative and connect the past with the present. Furthermore, Sacco puts Rasim's first-person narrative recounting his traumatic experience in quotation marks throughout the chapter, calling the reader's attention to Sacco's role as a mediator who recites the words of his interview subject. In retelling Rasim's story in words and images, Sacco's framing devices remind the reader that memory is "a doubly mediated representation by both the informant and the narrator."[21] In this episode, the Chetniks' massacre of Muslims in Visegrad is doubly mediated through Rasim the informant, as well as through Sacco the narrator. Walker argues that "although explicit violent imagery could be considered exploitative and voyeuristic, Sacco uses it to restore a sense of humanity to those dehumanized by the pace of globalized media."[22] Using his trademark comics journalistic approach, Sacco thereby rehumanizes the local residents and refugees in Goražde who have been "dehumanized and violated by their experiences in war."[23]

Media, Politics, and the "Real Truth"

Along with interviews and survivors' testimonies, *Safe Area Goražde* also includes background information about Bosnia's history, ethnic tensions, and conflicts, as well as the involvement (or lack thereof) of the United States, the

UN, and NATO in the region. In discussing comics journalism as a new genre inspired by the New Journalism, Rocco Versaci contends:

> Comics journalists have taken full advantage of the graphic language of the medium to reanimate the most salient feature of New Journalism: the foregrounding of the individual perspective as an organizing consciousness. In addition, comics journalists achieve layers of meaning inaccessible to prose journalism alone because of comics' graphic language that blends words and images. What is more, like the New Journalists, comics journalists embrace a pointed anti-"official" and anticorporate attitude. However, unlike the absorption of New Journalism into the mainstream and the resulting dilution of its radical message, comics journalism retains, paradoxically, a powerful marginal status that will make it difficult for these works to ever be fully "co-opted."[24]

A journalist by vocation and a comics artist in practice, Sacco foregrounds his own perspective as "an organizing consciousness" in *Safe Area Goražde*. With this approach, he directs the reader's attention to the problematic media coverage of the Eastern Bosnian war and the peace negotiation process. Shortly after his arrival, he alludes to his "anti-'official' and anticorporate attitude," by positioning himself against Western journalists rushing to Goražde by critiquing the short-lived and superficial representation of Goražde.

As Susan Sontag has stated pointedly, "Unlike the genocide of the Armenians during World War I and of the Jews and the Gypsies in the late 1930s and early 1940s, the genocide of the Bosniak people has taken place in the glare of worldwide press and TV coverage."[25] The problem is not whether Eastern Bosnia in general and Goražde in particular has a presence in news coverage; rather, it is how they have been covered. Sacco's criticism "isn't leveled merely at the moral grey zone created during the Bosnian war: he is more interested in the framework of representations themselves that mediate, authorize, commemorate and circulate trauma in different ways."[26] The page reproduced as figure 2.2 juxtaposes a Western news crew in the foreground with local residents in the background. In the image, while two reporters report on-site, several cameramen shoot footage and two journalists interview a child on the street; meanwhile the local people appear as a mass at the margin of the scene. The visual presence of these locals is interrupted by an inset panel (a panel contained within a larger panel) and by several captions. The focal point of the image appears to be on the Western journalists in Goražde rather than on Goražde's residents. The panel as a whole is visually disjointed by Sacco's satirical remarks presented in fragmented captions: "Goražde! / which had just

Figure 2.2. Splash page introducing the residents of Goražde. Joe Sacco. *Safe Area Goražde: The War in Eastern Bosnia, 1992–1995* (Seattle: Fantagraphics, 2000), 4.

wrested the spotlight from that media darling Sarajevo! / Goražde! / which was getting CNNed! NPRed! BBCed! / But its proverbial 15 minutes were ticking away! / Pretty soon no one was gonna remember Goražde! / Gora-wuh? / Hunh?"[27] The multiple frames on this page—captions, word balloons, varied panel borders, and the page itself—not only function as a narrative device but also provide structural support.[28] The deliberate fragmentation implies Sacco's criticism of the lack of consistent and in-depth news coverage regarding Goražde. "Journalistic economy—finding the best representative images and quotes in the least amount of time—here erases all that is not apparent to the eye and all that cannot be encapsulated in a brief sound-byte [sic]."[29] In contrast, Sacco's work, as presented in *Safe Area Goražde*, positions the people of Goražde centrally. Instead of jotting down a few quotes and flashing the camera for some images before taking off in a hurry, he stays, listens, and observes. The inset panel featuring Sacco and his colleagues visually positions him among Western journalists yet simultaneously separates him from them.

In examining the tension between the ethical and the political in war journalism, Aryn Bartley asks: "What are the ethical implications for journalists whose task is to represent war? Can war representation ever assume an ethical responsibility before its subject matter? What is the relation between an ethics and a politics of representation?"[30] *Safe Area Goražde* asks the reader to contemplate both the ethics and the politics of representing experiences of the conflicts in Eastern Bosnia. Distinct from the traditional journalistic approach, Sacco takes advantage of comics' blending of words and images to embody local residents as individuals and their personal stories as elements of history. He explains why he comes to Goražde when addressing the question raised by students in Edin's trigonometry class. Sacco presents his answer in a double-page spread, in which he breaks his first-person narrative into fragments framed in captions across the page: "Why? / Because you are still here / not raped and scattered / not entangled in the limbs of thousands of others at the bottom of a pit / Because Goražde had lived, and— / How?"[31] The image, without frames and bleeding to the edge of the pages, underscores the contrast between the Goraždans "still here" and the traumatic history and reality of the town. On the one hand, the local people portrayed on this page seem busy carrying on their day-to-day life, adults and children alike: chopping wood, hanging laundry, pushing a wheelbarrow, and playing soccer. On the other hand, the buildings and roads bear the obvious marks that result from multiple bombing, shelling, and other military assaults. The glimpse of the town's life presented on this page echoes the irony in the book's title "safe area," a UN designation that has hardly materialized. Being cut off from the outside world and surrounded by armed Serb forces, Goražde is, after all, anything but "safe." As a comics artist as much as a journalist, Sacco's works "blend actual reportage with his ruminations on the media industry. . . . [His] emphasis on the transcultural coverage of these traumas, with his comic avatar as the international journalist relaying information on the Bosnian war, emphasizes how trauma must be understood in relation to international circuits of mediation and commodification."[32] For him, the "real truth" encompasses how Goražde and its residents have lived, are still here, and will move forward, a narrative of survival to which Western media usually fails to devote time.

The Act of Seeing: Visualizing Personal and Public History

Safe Area Goražde negotiates and synthesizes journalistic, documentary, and graphic narrative forms through visualizing multiple narrators and narratives. Sacco foregrounds personal stories, through which he makes complex histories of Eastern Bosnia present and calls the reader's attention to international relations. He frames the residents and refugees' personal narratives with narratives of how he comes to know them. Thus, throughout the book, he draws and narrates not only his interviewees' memories, but also the process of meeting and interviewing people around the town, as well as his own experiences and observations. In this sense, *Safe Area Goražde* becomes a graphic representation of the ways in which one comes to learn about other people's histories and in which one connects the past with the present. Here, the visual elements of comics come into play. In her editor's column for *PMLA* in 2004, Marianne Hirsch writes:

> With words always already functioning as images and images asking to be read as much as seen, comics are binocular texts par excellence. Asking us to read back and forth between images and words, comics reveal the visuality and thus the materiality of words and the discursivity and narrativity of images. . . . Comics highlight both the individual frames and the space between them, calling attention to the compulsion to transcend the frame in the act of seeing.[33]

Taking advantage of the visuality and materiality of words and the discursivity and narrativity of images, *Safe Area Goražde* bears witness to Sacco's own interpretation and perception of the complex history of Eastern Bosnia. As Jared Gardener has stated, Sacco's work does not offer answers nor attempt to present a definitive history of events; rather, "its words and pictures reflect brutal and critical honesty towards all the players in this ongoing tragedy, including himself."[34] Sacco changes the size of panels, creates panels without borders, and draws images that bleed across the borders into other panels to signal narrative shifts and to show the various ways in which the journalist and his interview subjects interact with each other. Such methods connect the present with the past as well as the personal with the public; in this process, these approaches highlight not only what is being seen within and between the panel borders but also the "act of seeing" itself.[35]

Within the pages of *Safe Area Goražde*, the reader comes in contact with many historical and cultural references that supplement and contextualize the testimonies that Sacco collects along with the life he experiences in Goražde. There are images of historical maps; political leaders, including Josip Broz (commonly known as Tito), Serbia's president Slobodan Milosevic, President Clinton, and Lieutenant General Rose (the UN's top military commander in Bosnia); and cultural icons of the time period, including basketball player Clyde Drexler and Quentin Tarantino's film *Pulp Fiction*. Sacco blends these images and representations of public history with his interviewees' personal stories. Such a combination creates a strong connection between the public and the personal.

During his multiple trips, Sacco becomes friends with his translator and guide, Edin. Interwoven with numerous interviews and conversations translated by this character, Sacco also documents Edin, a person born and raised in Goražde whose story would otherwise not have been covered in Western news media; he then layers these narratives with the historical context of the region. Their many conversations at various places and times reveal the traumatic experience of Edin and his family. Sacco's framing of these episodes within historical references thus establishes a close connection between personal story and public history. Edin was a college student studying mechanical engineering in Sarajevo before the war. He completed all the coursework and requirements except for an oral defense. Now that he is stranded in Goražde, the distance between him and his degree is indefinite. As Sacco puts it, Edin has been "15 minutes from his degree for the past three and a half years" (98). Such a methodology prompts the reader "to consider the idea that truth is never completely objective and that the facts alone do not necessarily reveal a given event in the most meaningful way."[36] The chapter entitled "Brotherhood and Unity" is one example in which Sacco juxtaposes Edin's personal story with the public history of Yugoslavia after World War II. Taking advantage of comics' ability to register temporality spatially,[37] Sacco visualizes the following statement of Edin: "I spent a very nice childhood."[38] Condensed into four panels that portray him as a child, an adolescent, and a young man spending time with Serb, Croat, and Muslim friends, Edin's personal experiences help to highlight ethnic diversity before the Bosnian War began in 1992. Sacco contextualizes Edin's personal narrative with maps and a portrait of the Communist resistance leader Tito. The maps introduce the geographical location and demographics of Goražde, while the narration emphasizes the ethnic diversity in Bosnia. The side-by-side arrangement of Edin's portrait and childhood with images of Tito and the six Yugoslav republics allows for the convergence of personal story with public history.

The medium of comics also affords Sacco the freedom to step out of the narrative of the Goraždans and the refugees' personal histories in order to share with the reader his own reactions to and interpretation of the stories. As a character, Joe experiences life in Goražde moment-by-moment; as the author and artist, Sacco pieces the narrative together in retrospect, based on his notes, sketches, and photographs taken in the field.[39] Alla Gadassik and Sarah Henstra argue that "Sacco's driving question isn't just how to tell the silenced stories but how to approach the subject most ethically, given the conflicting interests. . . . Rather than asking readers to accept the truth of his account, he constructs a narrative that encourages us actively to interpret and reflect on what we're reading."[40] For instance, throughout the book Joe consciously highlights the mobility and access afforded by his privileged role as an American journalist, which poses a sharp contract to people living in isolated Goražde.

As Sacco puts it, "They *had* to love me in Goražde / They *had* to want me. / I *was* movement" (emphasis in original).[41] While his privilege affords Sacco more opportunities to befriend Goraždans (by transporting unavailable and desired goods—such as Levi's jeans—and passing gifts and messages back and forth between families and relatives separated geographically), his privilege is also emblematic of the uneven and even unjust relationship between Sacco and his subjects.

In the chapter entitled "America Man," Sacco recounts an incident during his first trip to Goražde. While going out with Edin and his colleague Whit, Sacco meets a man identified as F, who has been stranded and separated from his wife for years. Confronting Sacco, F declares, "America man thinks Bosnia man primitive," and he demands to know, "Journalist / Why you come?"[42] Juxtaposing F's angry, looming face with Sacco himself withdrawing into a corner, Sacco visualizes F's rage and resentment over the failure of international intervention alongside his own feelings of helplessness and defenselessness. F's wide-opened eyes, gritted teeth, and raised fist—all presented in exaggerated fashion—complement his words: "I become angry; very angry."[43] In contrast, Sacco is cornered on the page. Unable to defend himself, he admits: "I wanted out, out of there / I wanted to put a hundred thousand miles between me and Bosnia / between me and these horrible, disgusting people and their fucking wars and pathetic prospects . . ."[44] At that moment, Sacco is forced to face his positionality as a privileged American journalist who has the freedom to visit and leave. His self-criticism is embedded in his involvement with and detachment from the local people and their affairs. Even though Sacco and F both wear glasses, F's eyes are featured prominently in the panels while Sacco's eyes are not visible behind the blankness of his glasses, thus calling the reader's attention to the act of seeing. His self-reflexivity as "a reporter/narrator includes scrutinizing the extent to which his understanding relies on, and is limited by, his role as a Westerner visiting the region."[45] Moreover, this simplistic cartoonish self-portrait poses a sharp contrast to the detailed, realistic visual representation of the local people and landscape, thus further portraying his status as an outsider.

In conclusion, as Edward Said has pointed out, what ultimately makes Sacco an unusual "portrayer of life" is his complex representation of "history's victims"; Sacco's *Safe Area Goražde* "has the power to detain us, to keep us from impatiently wandering off in order to follow a catch-phrase or a lamentably predictable narrative or triumph and fulfillment."[46] Through the juxtaposition of personal stories with journalistic reporting and public history, Sacco's transcriptions and visualizations of survivors' testimonies provide a rich, in-depth documentation of the history of the town of Goražde and the experiences of its residents. Through recording the result as well as the process of his acts of journalism, Sacco uncovers and emphasizes the subjective experiences as well as the objective facts of the Bosnia War, thereby presenting a nuanced and inherently "graphic" picture of the region and its history.

NOTES

1. Will Eisner, *Comics and Sequential Art: Principles and Practices from the Legendary Cartoonist* (New York and London: Norton, 2008), 64.

2. Hillary Chute, "Comics as Literature?: Reading Graphic Narrative," *PMLA* 123.2 (2008), 460.

3. Joe Sacco, *Safe Area Goražde: The War in Eastern Bosnia, 1992–1995* (Seattle: Fantagraphics, 2000), 1.

4. Ibid.

5. Ibid.

6. Eisner, *Comics and Sequential Art*, 44.

7. Sacco, *Safe Area Goražde*, 4.

8. Rocco Versaci, *This Book Contains Graphic Language: Comics as Literature* (New York and London: Continuum, 2007), 111.

9. Hillary Chute, "Comics Form and Narrating Lives," *Profession* (2011), 109.

10. Andrea A. Lunsford, and Adam Roseblatt, "'Down a Road and into an Awful Silence': Graphic Listening in Joe Sacco's Comics Journalism," in *Silence and Listening as Rhetorical Arts*, eds. Cheryl Glenn and Krista Ratcliffe (Carbondale: Southern Illinois University Press, 2011), 132.

11. Gary Groth, "Joe Sacco on *Footnotes in Gaza*," *Comics Journal* 301 (2011), 380.

12. Ernesto Priego, "'I'm a Filter': Joe Sacco," *Comics Grid*, August 2, 2011, http://www.comicsgrid.com/2011/08/sacco-interview/.

13. Sacco, *Safe Area Goražde*, 97.

14. Ibid., 109.

15. Tristram Walker, "Graphic Wounds: The Comics Journalism of Joe Sacco," *Journeys: The International Journal of Travel and Travel Writing* 11.1 (Summer 2010), 76.

16. Sacco, *Safe Area Goražde*, 110.

17. Eisner, *Comics and Sequential Art*, 41.

18. Ibid.

19. Scott McCloud, *Understanding Comics: The Invisible Art* (New York: HarperPerennial, 1993), 60–93.

20. Sacco, *Safe Area Goražde*, 111.

21. Wendy Kozol, "Complicities of Transnational Witnessing in Joe Sacco's Palestine," in *Theoretical Perspectives on Human Rights and Literature*, eds. Elizabeth Swanson Goldberg and Alexandra Schultheis Moore (New York: Routledge, 2012), 165.

22. Walker, "Graphic Wounds," 69.

23. Aryn Bartley, "The Hateful Self: Substitution and the Ethics of Representing War," *Modern Fiction Studies* 54.1 (2008), 51.

24. Versaci, *This Book Contains Graphic Language*, 111.

25. Susan Sontag, "A Lament for Bosnia," *Nation*, December 25, 1995, 819.

26. Terri Tomsky, "From Sarajevo to 9/11: Travelling Memory and the Trauma Economy," *Parallax* 17.4 (2011), 50.

27. Sacco, *Safe Area Goražde*, 6.

28. Ibid., 130.

29. Bartley, "The Hateful Self," 54.

30. Ibid., 51.

31. Sacco, *Safe Area Goražde*, 14–15.

32. Tomsky, "From Sarajevo to 9/11," 50.

33. Marianne Hirsch, "Editor's Column: Collateral Damage," *PMLA* 119.5 (October 2004), 1213.

34. Jared Gardner, "Comic Journalism, Comics Activism," *Public Books*, August 28, 2012, http://publicbooks.org/multigenre/comics-journalism-comics-activism.

35. Hirsch, "Editor's Column," 1213.

36. Versaci, *This Book Contains Graphic Language*, 110.

37. Chute, "Comics as Literature," 452.

38. Sacco, *Safe Area Goražde*, 18.

39. Alla Gadassik, and Sarah Henstra, "Comics (as) Journalism: Teaching Joe Sacco's *Palestine* to Media Students," in *Teaching Comics and Graphic Narratives: Essays on Theory, Strategy and Practice*, ed. Lan Dong (Jefferson, NC: McFarland, 2012), 248.

40. Ibid., 246.

41. Sacco, *Safe Area Goražde*, 65.

42. Ibid., 191.

43. Ibid., 192.

44. Ibid.

45. Gadassik and Henstra, "Comics (as) Journalism," 249.

46. Edward Said, "Homage to Joe Sacco," in Joe Sacco, *Palestine* (Seattle: Fantagraphics, 2001), v.

3. Drawing on the Facts: Comics Journalism and the Critique of Objectivity

Isabel Macdonald

This chapter discusses the significance of Joe Sacco's comics journalism in the light of the shortcomings of the traditional model of "objective reporting." The chapter begins by looking at how Sacco approaches these shortcomings in the preface to his book *Journalism*, in which he elaborates on the theory and methods that guide his work.[1] This first part of the chapter examines Sacco's arguments about the benefits of comics journalism in the context of a broader shift amongst journalists away from the traditional conception of objectivity, and particularly the requirements for journalists to espouse a neutral tone and rely on authoritative sources. The second part of the chapter explores how he puts this approach into practice. I will argue that by drawing himself into his journalism, Sacco simultaneously draws attention to the complex practices and dynamics of reporting that have long been eclipsed by journalists' standard claims that they just "report on the facts." Drawing on a close reading of his comic "The Underground War in Gaza," I will show that this approach addresses the limits of "objective reporting" on multiple levels.[2]

Joe Sacco and the Critique of Objectivity

In the preface to his book *Journalism*, Sacco contrasts his comics journalism to the model of reporting in which he was trained at the University of Oregon, which emphasized "objectivity." In the context of journalism, the concept of objectivity refers to the strict rules around "factuality," "detachment," and balance, first institutionalized in the North American press in the early twentieth century.[3] This "doctrine of objectivity," as Stephen A. Ward calls it, mandates that journalists be neutral and detached. The only allowable opinion is that attributed to an authoritative source or one who "can speak for a group or institution."[4] Journalists, on the other hand, are to refrain from inserting their own interpretations, values, or opinions into news reporting. "Objective reporters" are also expected to balance their stories by seeking out both sides of any controversial issues.

In his preface to *Journalism*, Sacco frames the form of comics journalism as a counterpoint to this traditional concept of objectivity, which he critically refers to as "American journalism's Holy of Holies," and he argues that his own approach has advantages over the model of objective reporting.⁵ For instance, he argues that reporting in an implicitly subjective form allows him to better acknowledge the role of his social position and values. Like growing numbers of journalists, Sacco is critical of the assumption that a journalist can ever be neutral. In his preface, Sacco remarks that requiring that journalists approach a story with no preconceived ideas is a fine idea, but "the problem is I don't think most journalists approach a story that has any importance in that way. I certainly can't."⁶

Sacco's bold move to draw himself into his journalism addresses one of the major weaknesses that have been observed in journalism's traditional theoretical framework. In light of growing awareness of how knowledge is influenced by the values and culture of those producing it, the notion that journalists can be neutral, objective observers is increasingly recognized as a myth.⁷ More specifically, Sacco's move to acknowledge his position as a foreign reporter is significant in light of the particular shortcomings "objective reporting" presents in the field of international reporting.⁸ In outlining the theory behind comics journalism, Sacco implicitly addresses the shortcomings of the traditional journalism model. In contrast to purportedly "objective reporters," Sacco explains, he "embraces the implications of subjective reporting."⁹ Drawing himself as a character in his work, he explains, he gives himself "journalistic permission to show [his] interactions with those [he] meet[s]. Much can be learned from these personal exchanges, which most mainstream newspaper reporters, alas, excise from their articles."¹⁰

In drawing himself into his stories, Sacco also brings attention to his own process of reporting. This addresses another weakness of the traditional journalism model, which has been faulted not only for its failure to acknowledge the reporter's social position, but also for masking the process of reporting. As Ward has argued, historically, the concept of objectivity in journalism was heavily influenced by the idea of scientific objectivity that prevailed in popular culture at the turn of the twentieth century, when the norm of objectivity was first codified in journalism ethics codes and textbooks. The North American newspaper editors who were early proponents of journalistic objectivity drew uncritically on a then-popular view of scientific objectivity, which was understood to entail a "passive, careful observation of facts."¹¹ Inspired by this now-widely disputed view, proponents of journalistic objectivity stipulated that "the objective reporter should not taint data with subjective interpretation."¹² Early journalism textbooks instructed aspiring journalists to "keep yourself out of the story" and report solely "on facts" and "the truth or reality of the event," as one journalism textbook put it.¹³ Editors would go on to defend "reports as objective—allegedly the factual statements of a passive observer." As Ward argues, the theory of journalistic objectivity thus early on became wedded to "an epistemologically indefensible position and an inaccurate representation of the reporting process." Those who invented objectivity in journalism "ignored the obvious activity of reporting and news editing."[14]

In contrast to this erasure of the journalist's reporting process in the traditional model of objective reporting, Sacco's approach foregrounds his process of reporting. As he explains in his preface to *Journalism*, "By admitting that I am present at the scene, I mean to signal to the reader that journalism is a process with seams and imperfections practiced by a human being—it is not a cold science carried out behind Plexiglas by a robot."[15] By consciously drawing himself into his journalism, along with the "seams and imperfections" of his reporting process, Sacco's approach thus posits an alternative to traditional reporters' characteristic erasure of their own role in what they report.

While the drawn, interpretive, and subjective form of comics does appear to contrast with journalism's quest for objective truth, Sacco nonetheless argues that "facts (a truck carrying prisoners came down the road) and subjectivity (how the scene is drawn) are not mutually exclusive."[16] Like other journalists who have in recent years written critically about the model of objective reporting, Sacco continues to uphold the importance of standard journalistic methods for witnessing, verifying, and reporting facts. In his preface, he references some of these methods, including his reporting notes taken in the field, recorded interviews, and extensive background research. As such, comics journalism is no less able than any form of reporting to meet "the journalist's standard obligations—to report accurately, to get quotes right, to verify claims."[17]

In his preface, Sacco also notes the ways in which his methodology differs from that of the traditional journalism model. For instance, he consciously breaks from traditional mandates that "objective reporters" seek out authoritative sources and report two sides of any given story. As he explains in distinguishing his approach from the mainstream concept of balanced journalism, "The powerful should be quoted, yes, but to measure their pronouncements against the truth, not to obscure it."[18] Unlike the dominant model of reporting, the sources in his comics journalism are overwhelmingly ordinary people consistently neglected by objective journalism. As Sacco's preface makes clear, this alternative pattern of sourcing is a conscious decision. Yet the unusual form of comics journalism also plays a role. For Sacco observes that reporting in comics, a medium that lacks the cultural status of more standard forms of journalism, complicates his access to elite sources.

Sacco's critical approach to powerful sources addresses some of the concerns sociologists have long raised about the dominant Anglo-American model of objective reporting.[19] Three studies have found that the stipulation that reporters must rely on authoritative sources tends to disproportionately privilege the perspectives of powerful institutions and officials. Comics journalism's more critical approach to authority figures, and its alternative focus on the perspectives of ordinary people, directly addresses this important shortcoming of the traditional reporting model.

Sacco's bold break from the model of "objective reporting" dovetails with broader efforts to reconceptualize journalism's traditional theoretical framework. While much of English-language newspaper reporting in North America continues to abide by some variant of the objectivity doctrine, requiring that reporters write "balanced" reports, using a neutral tone, there have been moves in professional journalism to replace the concept of objectivity with other professional ideals.[20] In 1996, the Society for Professional Journalists, who had up until that point enshrined objectivity as the central tenet of their influential Code of Ethics, dropped the term, and replaced it with the words truth, accuracy, and "comprehensiveness."[21] Objectivity is tellingly not amongst the ten fundamental "elements" or principles of journalism identified by journalists Bill Kovach and Tom Rosenstiel, in the latest edition of the influential book, *The Elements of Journalism: What Newspeople Should Know and The Public Should Expect.*

With the rise of new media platforms such as blogs and social media, which privilege more subjective forms of writing and multimedia presentation, some journalists have recently argued that the idea of journalistic objectivity is so untenable that it should be abandoned altogether, as what one prominent new media journalist famously declared a "false God."[22] Others defend objectivity as an ideal, but advocate major revisions to the codes and rules by which it has historically been institutionalized in North American news reporting.[23] Even journalists and educators who argue that objectivity is still a useful ideal for journalists are critical of traditional stipulations for "objective reporters" to abide by "the supposedly neutral style of newswriting."[24] Such mandates are seen to be increasingly out of step with current practices in journalism. Moreover, in recent years, there has been growing recognition of the benefits of interpretation and analysis in journalism.

In *The Elements of Journalism*, Kovach and Rosenstiel advocate abandoning the term "objectivity" altogether, arguing that journalism should be understood as a "discipline of verification."[25] Thus, regardless of whether or not journalists adhere to a neutral style of writing, what is most important is the quality of the journalist's reporting methods. As an approach grounded in standard reporting methods, Sacco's approach strongly resonates with such efforts to reformulate journalism's theoretical framework. The authors of *The Elements of Journalism* propose that, instead of the contested notion of objectivity, journalists should understand their work in terms of a broader set of principles, including that "journalism's first obligation is to the truth."[26] Yet as these two influential journalists acknowledge, truth is a highly complex concept that might best be understood in journalism "as a goal—at best elusive."[27] Too often, they say, journalists have neglected this larger goal, and resorted instead to mere facticity, a much narrower approach of merely recording facts. Yet in the absence of critical reflection on the broader implications of these facts, such an approach can constitute "a kind of distortion all its own" (as in the case of stories that pointlessly emphasize the race of suspects, and thus play to racial stereotypes).[28]

In addition to warning of the dangers of an approach of narrow facticity in journalism, Kovach and Rosenstiel argue that journalists should embrace a greater "spirit of transparency" in their work. The authors of *The Elements of Journalism* explain that journalists should be more open about their methods and techniques of reporting, as well as about the limits of their knowledge. Yet as Kovach and Rosenstiel acknowledge, this more transparent form of reporting "runs contrary to what most journalists do."[29] Indeed, journalists' own standard language for discussing journalism works powerfully against such a self-reflective turn in journalism. When journalists talk publicly about what they do, they have been observed to often fall back on clichéd metaphors, such as that of journalism being a mirror of reality or a window on the world. Or, they use stock phrases about reporting "just the facts." When journalists talk about truth, Kovach and Rosenstiel observe, they often elide the complexity of this concept, describing truth as if it were "something that rises up by itself, like bread dough."[30]

Such language, implying that the journalist's role is passive and neutral, is particularly prevalent when it comes to discussions of traditional visual journalistic forms like photography, which have typically been valued in journalism for their purported capacity to "reflect what 'is there,'" show "things 'as they are,'" and "capture life on its own terms."[31] As Sacco observes in his preface, the visual medium of comics, in contrast, is read quite differently, because drawings are typically understood to be "by their very nature subjective." "Drawings are interpretive even when they are slavish renditions of photographs, which are generally perceived to capture a real moment literally," he argues.[32] The form of comics thus has the potential, he implies, for a very different kind of journalism. By drawing attention to mediation, comics journalism implicitly challenges journalists' standard claims that they just report facts. Moreover, by emphasizing the "seams and imperfections" of the reporting process, Sacco's approach has particular relevance for casting light on the complex dynamics and practices of journalism that have long been eclipsed by both objective reporting, and by journalists' standard language for talking about their work. In the following section, I will explore how Sacco puts his approach into practice in "The Underground War in Gaza."

The Practice of Comics Journalism: The Case of "The Underground War in Gaza"

Sacco's "The Underground War in Gaza" was first published in the *New York Times Magazine* in 2003, and there, Sacco faced the kinds of space constraints common in more standard forms of journalism. As he explains in his notes contextualizing the piece, his editors at the magazine gave him only four pages. This would seem to make it a more appropriate point of comparison to mainstream journalism than the book-length works of comics journalism that have received more attention in scholarship on Sacco. Moreover, in his book *Journalism*, Sacco identifies "The Underground War in Gaza" as a successful example of comics journalism, despite the piece's short length.

In this brief work of comics journalism, Sacco reports on an Israeli military campaign to eliminate tunnels on the border of the Gaza Strip and Egypt. The piece documents the Israeli army's concerns that Palestinian militants were using the tunnels to smuggle weapons into Gaza Strip, and examines the human effects of the military campaign to eliminate these tunnels. At the time of Sacco's research, this campaign had demolished hundreds of Palestinian homes in the Palestinian border town of Rafah. In "The Underground War in Gaza," Sacco draws on standard reporting techniques, including interviews both with Palestinians directly effected by the campaign, and with Israeli army officials, as well as his own eyewitness observations from his reporting trip in Gaza. Citing reports from Palestinian officials, as well as the United Nations Relief and Works Agency, his comic also relies on official documents of the kind it is standard for journalists to use in their background research.

As Amy Kiste Nyberg has observed, Sacco's comics reportage often bears striking parallels with the presentation strategies of television reportage, another visual form of journalism that also breaks from the traditional doctrine of objectivity.[33] Like television reporting, Sacco's work relies heavily on images of the journalist reporting in the field, a presentation format that implicitly appeals to the assumption that reporters have a privileged access to reality because of their status as on-the-ground witnesses. Accordingly, "The Underground War" contains numerous panels visually depicting Sacco at different moments in his reporting process.

Despite its short length, the comic communicates extensive factual informa-

Figure 3.1. Joe Sacco, "The Underground War in Gaza," in *Journalism* (New York: Metropolitan, 2012), 23.

tion about the Israeli army's campaign to destroy tunnels into Gaza, including details about the Israeli military protocols for demolishing homes, and various official estimates of how many Palestinian homes they had destroyed. Through a drawn map included on the first page, Sacco also provides the reader with details about Rafah's geographic location. This short, yet informative, piece thus supports Sacco's argument that the interpretive, subjective form of comics is compatible with the journalist's obligation to accurately present facts.

Yet "The Underground War" presents a far more complex picture of the facts than his preface to *Journalism*. For this short comic implies that even the most basic facts of the military campaign Sacco is reporting on are far from straightforward. For instance, Sacco reveals that even such a simple question as how many houses the Israeli military campaign destroyed is frustratingly difficult to answer. While an Israeli army spokesman estimates the figure to be 300–400, the Rafah governorate puts the number at 860, while the United Nations Relief and Works Agency (Unrwa) says 580 houses were destroyed. However, he notes that Unrwa "counts even a multi-unit structure as a single house."[34] While presenting the basic facts about these home demolitions, his comic subtly explores the ways that facts are shaped by different bureaucratic institutions, each of which has its own interests and particular recording mechanisms. By highlighting these confusingly conflicting accounts, "The Underground War" suggests that reporting is much more complex and uncertain than is implied in journalists' standard language for talking about their work. Contrary to standard notions about recording objective facts, the work of reporting is here shown to also entail a confusing process of navigating competing truth claims by different bureaucratic institutions.

"The Underground War" also offers a much more ambivalent view of the reporter's role as witness than does Sacco's preface to *Journalism*. While scenes of Sacco's work reporting in the field help legitimate his reporting by implicitly appealing to assumptions about the credibility of eyewitness reporting, Sacco's drawings of himself also address the limits of what he witnesses. For instance, in one of the first panels in which the comics journalist appears, he is standing side by side with an Israeli army official "behind a 25-foot-high metal wall, which his forces are building as cover from Palestinian sniping," as Sacco explains in his narration (see Figure 3.1).[35] The comics journalist is dressed in an Israeli military uniform—replete with flak jacket and camouflage hard hat.

In a short text in *Journalism* addressing the context of his reporting in "The Underground War," Sacco explains, "representing the *New York Times Magazine* opened doors for me at the Israeli Foreign Press Office, and Israeli spokespersons asked if I would like to spend a day and night with Israel Defense Forces soldiers manning their positions along the Egyptian border."[36] In the comic, he does not explain this in so many words. However, characteristic of Sacco's approach of showing the process of his reporting, the piece offers revealing visual reflections on the embedded conditions of his reporting. For instance, in the scene where the reporter is first clearly depicted, standing at the army official's side, Sacco's (and the reader's) field of vision is entirely blocked off by the twenty-five-foot metal wall built by the Israeli military (see Figure 3.1). Thus, despite Sacco's reliance on the strategies used in more conventional visual forms of reporting for legitimating the "reality" of what the reporter witnesses in the field, "The Underground War" also draws attention to the limits of what Sacco witnesses while embedded with the army.

The implicitly subjective, interpretive comics medium adds a further layer of meaning to Sacco's drawn depictions of himself, dressed in Israeli military garb, interacting with army officials. For by their very form, comics call attention to their own constructed nature. Sacco's drawn depictions of his own process of reporting on this military campaign for the *New York Times Magazine* thus calls critical attention to how the reality of this Israeli campaign is being constructed both by, and for, an American comics journalist embedded with the Israeli army.

"The Underground War" offers a good example of Sacco's conscious efforts to deal more critically with powerful sources than is typical in "objective reporting." While he does interview "authoritative" sources of the kind privileged in the traditional journalism model, his comic also draws on interviews with other, less powerful, sources. Meanwhile, his comics reportage helps the reader to critically evaluate the claims of powerful sources. To do so, he relies on some strategies that are quite common in any form of journalism that seeks to hold the powerful to account. The facts presented to Sacco by the officials are counterposed with conflicting evidence, from both official documents, and from Sacco's interviews with other parties with stakes in the issue, namely some of the Palestinians he met during his reporting in Rafah, where the campaign was being waged. The account of one of these Palestinians, whose home was destroyed by the Israeli army, directly contradicted some of the Israeli military officials' claims. While the army officials told Sacco that they only destroyed homes being used for smuggling or to harbor gunmen, this Palestinian man said his home had been neither. Similarly, Sacco cites reports suggesting the number of houses demolished was far higher than the number estimated by the army spokesman he interviewed. In other words, the comic exemplifies what Kovach and Rosenstiel argue to be the very essence of journalism, the verification of facts.

As Sacco notes, he quotes powerful sources in order "to measure their pronouncements against the truth."[37] Indeed, although Sacco extensively cites the words and perspectives of army officials in the "The Underground War," the comic does not provide an uncritical platform for these powerful sources' statements. Yet the strategies Sacco uses to evaluate the version of events presented to him by army spokesmen are far more complex than what is generally implied when a journalist invokes a quantifiable idea of the truth. In addition to examining what his powerful interviewees tell him about their military campaign in terms whether what they say is true or false, the piece also works on a whole other level to call into question the official version of events. Moving beyond a reductive approach of facticity, "The Underground War" also works to address the broader implications of these facts, and of Sacco's reporting, by touching upon the human effects of this military campaign.

Drawing attention to the language used by the Israeli military and its spokesmen, this piece also works to critically interrogate the bureaucratic frameworks by which the reality of this campaign is constructed. Making use of comics' textual elements, Sacco's comic foregrounds the terminology mobilized by the Israeli military in promoting their campaign to the press, and by implication, to the public. For instance, Sacco writes, "the IDF claims 'terrorists' sometimes slip through the tunnels."[38] The quotation marks around the term "terrorists" demarcates it from the language of Sacco's narration, which refers instead to "Palestinian militants."

Sacco's comic also highlights the language and rationales military officials use in explaining their contentious demolitions of Palestinian homes. In one scene, for instance, an army official nicknamed "Colonel Pinky" tells the embedded journalist, "We have a legal right to destroy a home when the home is used for terror operations." Further details of the military's rationale for the home demolitions are provided in Sacco's narration: "Houses are destroyed, he says, if they serve as 'piers' for tunnels . . . or if Palestinian militants use them to launch rifle, grenade or anti-tank attacks on his men."[39] The page concludes with a panel in which Pinky's battalion commander elaborates on the details of the policies and procedures for demolishing Palestinian homes. He explains, "We don't just randomly destroy homes." Further, Sacco's narration adds, "To demolish a home, he says he must submit a request that goes all the way up to the 'legal adviser of the entire army' (According to the I.D.F., though, this procedure only applies to houses it considers 'inhabited')."[40] Such scenes work to address the limitations of standard "objective reporting," which has been faulted for adopting the same bureaucratic terms, language, and frameworks of knowledge as journalists' powerful bureaucratic sources. While Sacco devotes considerable space to the army spokesmen's explanations of the official protocols, legality, and the procedures for demolishing Palestinian homes, the effect is not to naturalize this bureaucratic version of reality, but rather to critically explore it. There is also a visual layer to these explorations of his sources' bureaucratic perspectives. For instance, Sacco depicts details of the banal institutional setting of his interview with the battalion commander, who, in Sacco's drawing, speaks from behind his desk, while smoking a cigarette.

Drawing on comics' noted strengths in communicating dialogue, the third page of "The Underground War" introduces a view of this campaign that is starkly different from that painted by the highly abstracted, legalistic language of the military officials. This page opens with a panel in which Sacco asks the battalion commander "about the destruction of one particular home. It belonged to someone I know—let's call him T.—and it was demolished not four days before, along with a few other dwellings." The narration paraphrases part of the colonel's response: "Colonel Avi knows the houses. He says gunmen used them as cover to shoot at a bulldozer." This army official is quoted saying that it was an "empty home, a vacant home that no family is living in." "You call this a home, we call this a military position," he tells Sacco.[41]

The adjacent panel draws on Sacco's interview with "T." to offer an alternate view of this "military position." Reflecting the strengths that have been noted in the comics medium for communicating environmental details and affective content, this panel depicts a Palestinian man standing, shoulders hunched, a forlorn expression on his face, amidst a pile of rubble that had previously been his home. Sacco explains that the Israeli claims that they only destroy "empty homes" "may be technically accurate, but Palestinians say that it turns the truth on its head. For example, T.'s home was 'empty'—but only, he says, because he and his family were chased out by constant Israeli gunfire."[42] In one of the final scenes of "The Underground War," T. is standing in front of a desolate background of rubble, speaking to Sacco. "T. doesn't seem bitter yet about the destruction of the house that he says he 'spent all my life dreaming about,'" Sacco's narration begins. "In fact, after agonizing for weeks as the bulldozers drew nearer, he seems almost relieved now that the deed is done," Sacco continues, in a caption beside a drawing of T., whose face is marked with worry lines. In the final panel of this scene, the Palestinian man is quoted, "Yes, I used to have hope, but now it's finished."[43] By juxtaposing the explanations of the official Israeli protocols with the account of this directly affected Palestinian, this piece exposes the limits of the bureaucratic framework and language by which the army officials present the situation to Sacco.

"The Underground War" also explores the related, yet subtly distinct, question of how the campaign is articulated by various individuals involved in the campaign. The opening scenes of "The Underground War" communicate how the "success" of this campaign is measured in the eyes of a "man nicknamed Colonel Pinky," who is in charge of the military campaign to destroy the tunnels in Rafah (see figure 3.1).[44] Sacco explains that "Colonel Pinky judges his success by the price of a bullet in Rafah. The fewer the tunnels, the higher the price. He says a bullet now costs up to 21 shekels (about $4.50), the highest it's ever been."[45] An ironic twist to the words of the Israeli colonel who professes to measure success by the price of bullets is introduced on the concluding page of "The Underground War in Gaza." In this scene, a man with a gun in his arms tells Sacco that the armed movement to which he belongs has begun manufacturing their own bullets in Gaza. Sacco's drawing of this undeterred armed man hints at the intractable, cyclical dimensions of the conflict between Israel and Palestine.

This chapter began by looking at the theory and methods of comics journalism explained by Sacco in his book *Journalism*. Resonating with broader, recent efforts to reformulate journalism's traditional theoretical framework, Sacco's approach consciously breaks from the traditional concept of objectivity. While he upholds the importance of standard journalistic methods for reporting facts, he also embraces an implicitly interpretive, subjective form of reporting that allows him to be more critical of powerful sources, and more open and transparent about his own reporting process. In "The Underground War in Gaza," Sacco puts this approach into practice. Sacco's comics journalism works on multiple levels to address the limitations of the traditional Anglo-American journalism model, and one of its particular strengths is how it casts light on the complex practices of reporting that have long been elided by purportedly objective journalism.

NOTES

1. Joe Sacco, "A Manifesto, Anyone?" in *Journalism* (New York: Metropolitan, 2012), xi–xiv.

2. Joe Sacco, *Journalism* (New York: Metropolitan, 2012), 26. "The Underground War in Gaza" was first published in *New York Times Magazine*, July 6, 2003, and collected in *Journalism*, 22–25.

3. Stephen J. A. Ward, *The Invention of Journalism Ethics: The Path to Objectivity and Beyond* (Montreal: McGill-Queen's University Press, 2004), 214.

4. Ibid., 20.

5. Sacco, "A Manifesto, Anyone?" xiii.

6. Ibid., xiii.

7. See David T. Z. Mindich, *Just the Facts: How 'Objectivity' Came to Define American Journalism* (New York: New York University Press, 1998), 4

8. See Mark Pedelty, *War Stories: The Culture of Foreign Correspondents* (New York: Routledge, 1995).

9. Sacco, "A Manifesto, Anyone?" xiii.

10. Ibid.

11. Ward, *The Invention of Journalism Ethics*, 198.

12. Ibid.

13. Charles G. Ross, *The Writing of News*, cited in Ward, *The Invention of Journalism Ethics*, 214.

14. Ward, *The Invention of Journalism Ethics*, 198.

15. Sacco, "A Manifesto, Anyone?" xiii.

16. Ibid.

17. Ibid., xii.

18. Ibid., xiv.

19. See Gaye Tuchman, *Making News: A Study in the Construction of Reality* (New York: Free Press, 1978); Richard Ericson, Patricia Baranek, and Janet Chan, *Negotiating Control: A Study of News Source* (Toronto: University of Toronto Press, 1989); and Mark Fishman, *Manufacturing the News* (Austin: University of Texas Press, 1980).

20. Mindich, *Just the Facts*, 9.

21. Ibid., 5–6.

22. Jon Katz, "No News is Good News," *HotWired*, October 9, 1996, Web.

23. Ward takes this latter approach, arguing that "opinion surveys show that a substantial portion of the public continues to expect reporters to provide fair, objective information," and that it would thus be inadvisable for journalists to abandon the contested concept altogether. While distancing himself from the doctrine's traditional mandate of neutrality, he emphasizes the ongoing importance of objective methods in journalism. Ward, *The Invention of Journalism Ethics*, 14.

24. Bill Kovach and Tom Rosenstiel, *The Elements of Journalism: What Newspeople Should Know and The Public Should Expect* (New York: Three Rivers Press, 2007), 83.

25. Ibid., 6.

26. Ibid., 36. In 1996, the Society for Professional Journalists, who had up until that point enshrined objectivity as the central tenet of their influential Code of Ethics, dropped the term, and replaced it with the words truth, accuracy, and comprehensiveness.

27. Ibid., 45.

28. Ibid., 42.

29. Ibid., 95.

30. Ibid., 41.

31. Barbie Zelizer, *About to Die: How News Images Move the Public* (Oxford: Oxford University Press, 2010), 3.

32. Sacco, "A Manifesto, Anyone?" xi.

33. See Amy Kyste Nyberg, "Comics Journalism," in *Critical Approaches to Comics: Theories and Methods*, eds. Matthew J. Smith and Randy Duncan (New York: Routledge, 2012), 116–28.

34. Sacco, "The Underground War," 23.

35. Ibid.

36. Sacco, *Journalism*, 26.

37. Sacco, "A Manifesto, Anyone?" xiv.

38. Sacco, "The Underground War," 23.

39. Ibid.

40. Ibid.

41. Ibid., 24.

42. Ibid.

43. Ibid., 25.

44. Ibid., 23.

45. Ibid.

4. Views from Nowhere: Journalistic Detachment in *Palestine*

Marc Singer

Joe Sacco has won accolades not only for his vivid and compelling works of comics journalism, but also for his criticism of how he and other journalists represent and exploit violent conflicts. In comics such as *Palestine, Safe Area Goražde*, and *Footnotes in Gaza*, Sacco insistently foregrounds his own position as a reporter, an outsider, a tourist, and an artist whose work depends on appropriating stories of other people's misery, dispelling any claims to journalistic detachment or impartiality. This apparent deviation from the practices of contemporary American-style journalism has earned attention and praise from other journalists, critics, and scholars, who typically celebrate Sacco for challenging journalism's presumption of objectivity. While they have devoted considerable attention to Sacco's representation of his own subjectivity, few scholars have examined how Sacco also aligns his work with the practices of objective journalism. This alignment is especially pronounced in *Palestine*, his first book-length work of comics journalism.

In the winter of 1991 and 1992, in the waning days of the first intifada, Sacco spent two months in the Palestinian territories. As he would tell Peter Aspden in 2003, "It is almost preposterous to think that a western reporter could be objective in a situation like that."[1] This lack of objectivity extended to his representation of the lives of the Palestinians he met: he told Aspden "that is why it is important to write in the first person. It would be very difficult to get that feeling across if you were pretending you were not even there, as traditional US journalism does."[2] Despite Sacco's disparagement of journalistic pretenses to objectivity, *Palestine* also replicates many of those same practices. Some of the testimonies he records, particularly (though not exclusively) stories of intra-Palestinian violence, prompt Sacco to fall back on the neutralistic detachment and professional objectivity of American journalism, presenting secondhand accounts and conflicting views without expressing his own opinions. This practice allows reporters to maintain the appearance of impartiality that press critic Jay Rosen, adapting a term from philosopher Thomas Nagel, calls "the view from nowhere."[3] Contrary to its reputation as the most overtly subjective and self-critical of Sacco's major works of journalism, *Palestine* periodically resorts to this mode of viewless objectivity, selectively suspending Sacco's willingness to comment on the stories he hears. Critical accounts of Sacco's defiance of journalistic objectivity should consider both the many meanings of that contested term and the degree to which Sacco's journalism has always been grounded in some of the same traditions that he opposes.

Objectivity and Experience

Objective journalism flourished after World War I in response to anxieties over the subjectivization of knowledge, particularly as it was revealed by the rise of both wartime propaganda and public relations.[4] As promoted by journalist Walter Lippmann and editor Charles Merz, "objectivity" described the pursuit of a scientific method of verification and transparency that could authenticate and validate journalistic work. This method, however, was immediately subject to contestation and transformation. Michael Schudson speculates that most reporters in Lippmann's day used the term in a very different sense: "their concept of 'objectivity' was simply the application of a new label to the naive empiricism which reporters of the 1890s had called 'realism,'" namely the belief that simply reporting the facts will produce a story free of any ideology or worldview.[5] By the 1930s, objectivity had become "an articulate professional value in journalism," though it was a value applied more often to the journalists themselves.[6] As the concept has migrated from a method of verification to a standard of impartiality—a standard that many journalists and press critics believe is impossible to uphold—objectivity has increasingly become conflated with what Rosen terms the view from nowhere.

Rosen describes the view from nowhere as

> a bid for trust that advertises the viewlessness of the news producer. Frequently it places the journalist between polarized extremes, and calls that neither-nor position "impartial." Second, it's a means of defense against a style of criticism that is fully anticipated: charges of bias originating in partisan politics and the two-party system. Third: it's an attempt to secure a kind of universal legitimacy that is implicitly denied to those who stake out positions or betray a point of view. American journalists have almost a lust for the View from Nowhere because they think it has more authority than any other possible stance.[7]

Rosen is careful to distinguish this viewlessness from other definitions of objectivity, such as "trying to ground truth claims in verifiable facts" or "the struggle to get beyond the limited perspective that our experience and upbringing afford us," which he wholeheartedly supports.[8] The view from nowhere is Rosen's attempt to label the position of impartiality adopted by many contemporary journalists and isolate it from the methods and standards of verification that also go by the name of objectivity.

When critics laud Sacco for breaking away from journalistic objectivity, then, they typically mean that he does not pretend to write from a neutral, uninvolved, or viewless position. Adam Rosenblatt and Andrea A. Lunsford state that "Sacco's work is closer to traditional journalistic practices" than that of any other comics creator, but they nevertheless maintain that he "uses comics not just to create a new kind of journalism, but also to question the orthodoxies of more traditional reporting. . . . In stressing his subjective position, Sacco distinguishes himself from the traditional journalistic aims of distance and objectivity."[9] Kristian Williams suggests this challenge is endemic to the field of comics journalism, whose "inherent subjectivity contrasts sharply with the newsroom's dispassionate prose"; he cites Sacco as an exemplary comics journalist who interrogates his own experience rather than adhere to journalistic conventions of balance or impartiality.[10] Rocco Versaci locates Sacco and other comics journalists in the tradition of the New Journalists who "questioned the very possibility of objective truth."[11] However, no critic carries this contrast between subjectivity and objectivity to greater extremes than Benjamin Woo, who suggests that Sacco's representation of subjective experience disqualifies his work from consideration as journalism.

Woo proposes a number of reasons why Sacco's work is not journalistic, but most of them boil down to Sacco's refusal of the formulas, conventions, and publication channels that mark journalism in its most traditional forms:

> I do not consider *Palestine* a work of journalism. For one thing, it was produced without the support of a news agency and released by a publisher of alternative and pornographic comic books. For another, Sacco has effectively abandoned the traditional indices of newsworthiness: comics are labor-intensive and slow to produce; chapters are organized thematically rather than chronologically; he meets no "notable" people; and there is, sadly, nothing novel about injustice and grinding deprivation.[12]

Many of these objections seem both petty and exclusionary. Fantagraphics Books does indeed publish pornographic comics, particularly under its Eros Comix imprint, but *Palestine* was not an Eros book and the publisher's other titles have little bearing on whether it constitutes a work of journalism or not; Woo might as well argue that no article published in *Playboy* can be journalism either. Equally rigorous applications of Woo's other criteria would rule out any stories by independent journalists, stories not written for the daily news cycle, stories not organized chronologically, or stories about average citizens. Most problematically, Woo's last objection would seem to disqualify any story about injustice or deprivation as he apparently deems these subjects insufficiently newsworthy.

Woo's major argument for reclassifying *Palestine* proves equally arbitrary, based on a definition of journalism that is highly favorable to the kind of reporting Sacco's work challenges. Citing Walter Benjamin, Woo draws a sharp distinction between "the relaying of information and the communication of experience," associating Sacco with the latter and journalism exclusively with the former.[13] In his view, *Palestine* is a work of storytelling and the documentary tradition, not reporting. But Woo admits that his definition is built on ideal types, not empirical descriptions of existing examples.[14] His rigid partition of information and experience leaves no room for narrative journalism, also known as literary journalism or New Journalism, which blends journalistic and novelistic techniques to tell a story "that fundamentally engages the subjectivities of author and reader."[15] Those techniques include "immersion reporting, complicated structures, character development, symbolism, voice, a focus on ordinary people" and "a consciousness on the page through which the objects in view are filtered," as well as journalistic standards of accuracy.[16] The form erases Woo's distinction between the documentary and reporting—indeed, it is sometimes identified with the phrase "documentary reportage."[17] Many scholars place Sacco in this tradition, recognizing that journalism already has an institutional space for his type of reporting.[18]

Michael Schudson observes that journalism has always pursued ideals of storytelling alongside ideals of information: information journalism's claims to moral or professional superiority over narrative journalism are products of their struggle for market position and at least in part "a cover for class conflict" between their historical constituencies, but the informative model is "not necessarily more accurate" than the narrative one.[19] Other scholars of journalism similarly complicate Woo's assumption that information and experience can be neatly separated. G. Stuart Adam defines journalism as "the product of reporting—the gathering and presentation of slices and bits of human experience and thought," while Amy Kiste Nyberg states that "journalists distill experience into story" and notes that their techniques are as suited to conveying experiences as they are to relating facts.[20] If journalism is the distillation of experience into story as Nyberg and Adam suggest, then Sacco's work qualifies on the most important count. Woo says he only wants "to clarify the regime of authenticity that pertains to so-called comics journalism," but in defining the field so narrowly, he effectively reinforces the regime of authenticity claimed by so-called objective journalism.[21] His statement that "Information, like journalism, is a form of representation that strives to transmit the real as objectively and transparently as possible" presumes the very assumptions that Sacco's work questions.[22] Contrary to his own acknowledgment of the "ideological labor" that supports traditional journalism's claims to objectivity, Woo's idealized conception of journalism explicitly endorses those ideologically freighted claims.[23] It should be no surprise, then, that Sacco's reportage will not fit within the narrow confines of Woo's definition.

This disjunction is doubly ironic since Sacco's comics journalism is far more traditional than his critics, his defenders, or most of his interlocutors acknowledge. In a rare departure from the prevailing critical discourse, Nyberg describes how "15 Minutes," one of the stories in *Safe Area Goražde*, relies on the conventional narrative structures and reporting devices of print and broadcast journalism.[24] For Nyberg, comics journalists adopt the practices of traditional journalism just as much as they adapt them; those practices include "the ways in which comics journalists absent themselves in response to the journalistic norms of objectivity and distance."[25] While *Palestine* is more typically recognized for its subjective attention to Sacco's experience and the experiences of Palestinians, it, too, is invested in these journalistic conventions. For all that Sacco foregrounds his own presence in *Palestine*, he selectively absents himself and his opinions to achieve, however fleetingly, the putative objectivity and distance of traditional journalism.

Viewless in Gaza

Certainly, Sacco has been critical of such pretenses towards impartiality, whether in journalistic, diplomatic, or political contexts. He mocks this viewpoint early in *Palestine* when he watches a dual demonstration unfold: the Israeli activist group Peace Now protests settlements in occupied East Jerusalem while counter-protestors call the Peace Now group traitors to Israel. Sacco writes, with hyperbole shading into transparent irony, "here's *both* sides of the settler issue for consideration!"—the joke being that this common journalistic formulation, which reduces complex issues to two and only two highly polarized sides, completely excludes the Palestinian residents whose lives and homes are most affected by the settlements.[26] A few chapters later, Sacco presents another, equally false posture of objectivity when an Israeli soldier tells a Palestinian whose home has been attacked by settlers, "Look, on your side there are some extremists, and on our side there are some extremists."[27] Sacco has no patience for such claims of equivalence, particularly when, as his Palestinian informant observes, the two sides are not treated equally under the laws the Israeli soldier represents and enforces. Nevertheless, when Sacco is reluctant to question, criticize, or judge his subjects he can fall back on his own posture of journalistic detachment—not claims of balance or equivalence, but a simple muting of his own views. Sacco is particularly silent in Chapter Six, which addresses the subject of Palestinian violence against Israelis and against other Palestinians who are suspected of collaborating with Israelis.

In the story titled "Rooms," an American teacher named Larry, who serves as Sacco's guide in the Gaza Strip, takes him to meet some friends in the home of a Palestinian named Ibrahim, who celebrates Palestinian attacks on Israelis.[28] At the very beginning of *Palestine*, Sacco mentions how similar incidents, particularly the murders of the Munich Olympians and American tourist Leon Klinghoffer, colored his own perceptions of the Palestinian cause prior to his trip to Palestine.[29] When the men in "Rooms" ask Sacco how Americans view Palestinians, however, he offers no opinion on these attacks. Instead, he shifts subjects and says "the killing of collaborators hasn't gone over too well," as if that were the violence that had generated the most opposition in America.[30] Undeterred, Sacco's informants defend the torture, disappearance, and execution of suspected collaborators. Sacco notes that from 1990 to 1991, intra-Palestinian violence killed two and a half times as many Palestinians in Gaza as Israeli security forces did in the same period, but otherwise does not question his informants' defense of these killings. This silence does not connote endorsement on Sacco's part, merely a willingness to allow his informants to indict themselves in their own words. As he told Mark Nevins, "I think I tried to present things as accurately as possible ... If Palestinians said things that made themselves look bad, those were also included. I didn't try to hide anything."[31] Neither does he try to challenge them, even in the narration he composes after the fact. Other men in Ibrahim's room criticize the tactics of violence and terrorism, but Sacco doesn't weigh in. This is the posture of objectivity—hiding nothing, questioning nothing, and repeating the testimony of others, often without comment—that defines Rosen's view from nowhere.

If Sacco's textual narration refuses to adopt any but the mildest disapproval of this violence, his visual framing of these stories is even more ambiguous. Sacco routinely illustrates the stories he hears from his informants, investing them with the same visual presence he gives to events he witnesses firsthand.[32] The stories of Palestinian violence in "Rooms," however, are presented at a double remove. Sacco illustrates them in a series of isolated images—two of Palestinian attacks on Israelis, one of Palestinians beating an alleged collaborator, and one of Palestinians listening to a collaborator's confession on a cassette tape—while the accompanying narration and the surrounding panels depict the conversation in Ibrahim's room (see Figure 4.1). Whereas stories of Israeli abuses like the harrowing imprisonment of "Moderate Pressure" or the

Figure 4.1. Joe Sacco, *Palestine* (Seattle: Fantagraphics, 2001), 155.

tragic succession of deaths and burials in "Pilgrimage" receive multi-page dramatizations, sometimes including dialogue and always showing a continuous sequence of actions and consequences, these stories of Palestinian violence are reduced to discrete moments and filtered through the comments of other Palestinians. They also display two telling absences: Sacco does not draw any of the Israeli victims except as distant silhouettes, and he does not portray himself taking part in the conversation. Panels depict the other men addressing him, showing him their work permits, and asking him for a light, images that are clearly drawn from Sacco's point of view, but it's a disembodied one—a view from nowhere. "Moderate Pressure" and "Pilgrimage" leave no doubts as to Sacco's opinion of the Israelis' abuses, but any similar judgments are left implicit in "Rooms." The viewlessness distances Sacco from his subjects and releases him from any obligation to comment on matters that trouble his own sympathies.

The next story, "Law," follows directly from "Rooms" and continues the focus on intra-Palestinian violence.[33] This time, the art offers an even more graphic demonstration of Sacco's equivocations. In this story, Sacco speaks with a Palestinian lawyer who is defending a family that has committed an honor killing of their fifteen-year-old daughter, strangling her because she committed adultery with a collaborator. Sacco dramatizes this murder in the grotesque caricature that was typical of his work at the time (see Figure 4.2). On the facing page, Sacco asks the lawyer about his other cases and receives a litany of tortures and abuses inflicted by the Israeli security forces on his clients. The uppermost panel illustrates one of them, showing an Israeli man pressing a teenage boy's face onto a hot plate (see Figure 4.3). The body language and the panel composition are virtually identical to the illustration of the honor killing on the preceding page, establishing a direct and immediate parallel between the two acts. But if the compositions invite a comparison between these two crimes with young Palestinian victims, the framing does not give them equal weight. The boy's torture by the Israelis dominates the layout, floating over the lawyer and bleeding out to the edges of the page, while the girl's murder by her own family is bound by a much smaller panel and relegated to an interior corner. This juxtaposition illustrates Sacco's vacillation on his own journalistic position. Parallels are unavoidable when adjacent compositions are so similar, but judgments are not parceled out equally when one image is so much more prominent than the other. Despite the striking composition, these pages in some ways represent the worst practices of both objective and subjective journalism—Sacco draws precisely the sort of equivalency he derided earlier, but then weights it to minimize the murder in comparison to the torture.

These juxtaposed images become a way of presenting and withholding comment, much like traditional journalists' practice of letting their sources answer each other. At the end of Chapter Six, Sacco discusses the day's testimonies with his guide, Larry. It is Larry, not Sacco, who voices his discomfort with the stories they have heard in Gaza: "You know that family honor killing that lawyer was handling? That really shook me up. What did you think?" Instead of recording his answer, Sacco skips ahead in the next panel to present more of Larry's objections: "The idea of armed struggle bothers me. I think the taking of someone's life under any circumstances is wrong. Killing someone is negating that person."[34] Rather than voice his own opinion, Sacco allows his sources to debate each other, a practice that Rosen and other press critics have termed "he said, she said journalism."[35] In this style of journalism, reporters quote clashing truth claims but do not assess them, assigning equal value to claims of varying accuracy or merit. This is slightly different from Sacco's position in "Rooms" and "Law," where the disagreements revolve around matters of opinion and moral judgment rather than fact, but he still allows Larry to take up the burden of challenging his other sources. Economics reporter Peter Goodman, who left the *New York Times* for the *Huffington Post* because he wanted "a chance to write with a point of view," described this practice as "almost a process of laundering my own views, through the tried-and-true technique of dinging someone at some think tank to say what you want to tell the reader."[36] Sacco's own views remain unspoken, with Larry serving at best as a proxy for Sacco, or at the very least as a late and barely audible counterpoint to the views of the lawyer and the other Palestinian sources.

Sacco has particular difficulty writing about the hijab, the veil or headscarf worn by many Muslim women, although he opens the story "Hijab" with a chastening anecdote that suggests he sometimes has good reasons for withholding his own views.[37] Sacco is quite free with his opinions on the first page, confessing, "I blank out most all the women who wear [the hijab], they're just shapes to me, ciphers, like pigeons moving along the sidewalk" until he is jolted out of this dismissive attitude by an unexpected conversation with a woman in hijab who speaks "perfect English! The King's!"—a suggestively patriarchal reference as the monarch of England, then as now, is a queen.[38] Sacco depicts himself as a poor authority on gender roles in Palestinian society, a Western man who initially accepts Orientalist narratives of silent, subjugated, and undifferentiated Muslim women.[39] In fact, he briefly floats the idea that "the hijab was more my problem than hers" before he reports that "the hijab *is* a focal point of some debate here" and proceeds to present that debate through the words and experiences of a number of women.[40] After his initial self-exposure, however, Sacco keeps his thoughts to himself. Even his self-criticisms are filtered through his informants' views, or rather, his imagining of their views:

Figure 4.2. Joe Sacco, *Palestine* (Seattle: Fantagraphics, 2001), 160.

Views from Nowhere: Journalistic Detachment in *Palestine* 77

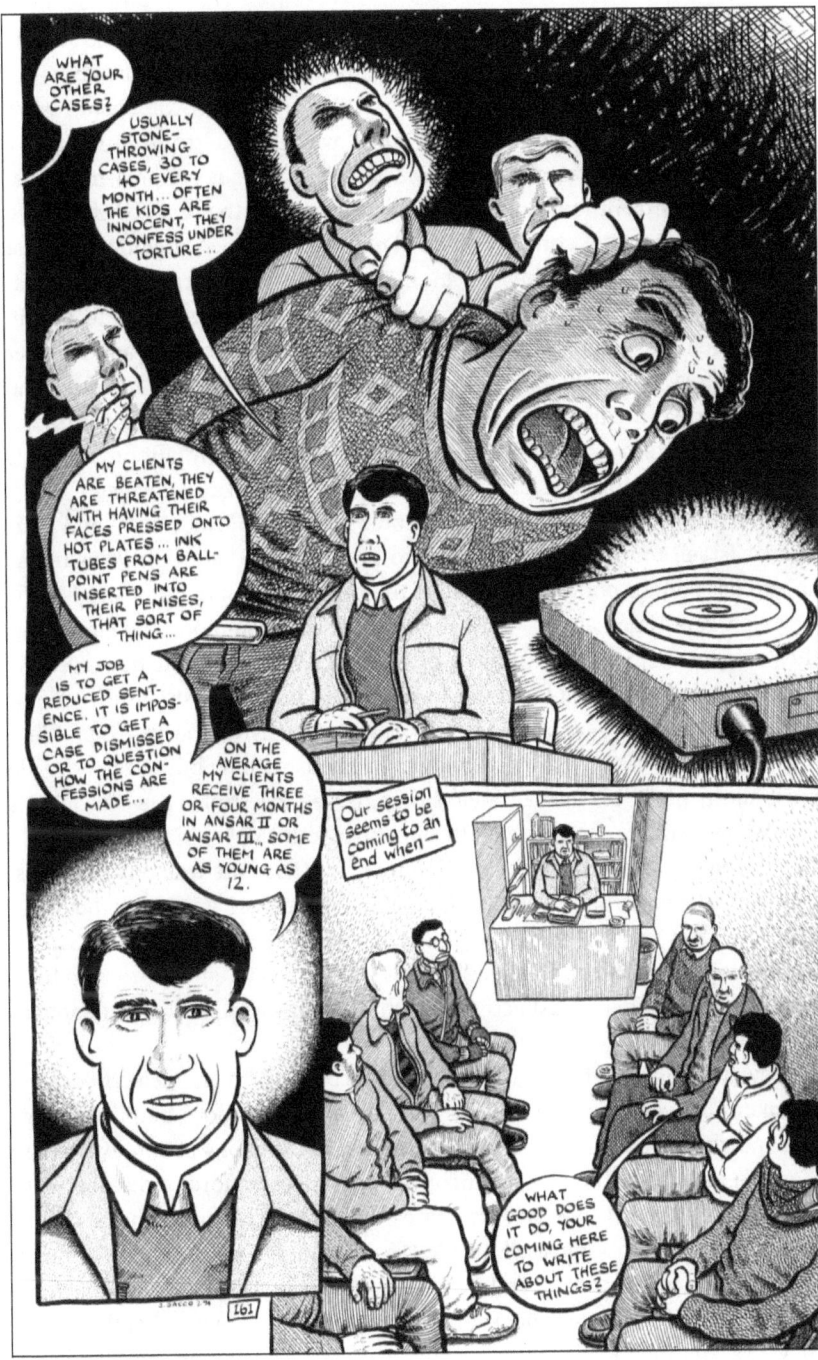

Figure 4.3. Joe Sacco, *Palestine* (Seattle: Fantagraphics, 2001), 161.

"One of the women seems put off by my questioning, like who am I to strut in with my Western, patronizing air?"[41] Sacco is understandably reluctant, after his first encounter, to project or impose his opinions on the women, but while he "does not trump the women with a voice-over that asserts an authoritative perspective," he still uses traditional journalistic techniques to present opposing viewpoints.[42] Although the women say they wear the hijab by their own choice and not at the compulsion of Hamas (the Islamist organization that controls the Gaza Strip), they all reveal that some other form of social pressure—from family, school, or religious faith—has motivated them to don it. One of them has begun applying such pressure to her friends, and another relates a story of how she witnessed some young men stoning a doctor who wasn't wearing the hijab.[43] Once again, Sacco allows his sources to contradict themselves instead of challenging their statements directly, although in this case he presents himself as poorly qualified to issue such a challenge.

He is not always so reticent. In Chapter Nine, he allows Naomi and Paula, two Israeli tourists from Tel Aviv, to present their views on Palestine as an explicit counterpoint to the rest of the book's presentation of the Israelis "through Palestinian eyes."[44] But Sacco interjects his opinions and challenges their arguments in a way he rarely if ever does with his Palestinian sources. As Sacco notes after Naomi asks him to see "our side of the story, too"—an appeal to conventions of journalistic balance and objectivity—he has no problem hearing the Israeli side of the conflict; he's "heard nothing but the Israeli side most all my life."[45] He instead invites them to see Palestinian life through his eyes when he offers to walk them through the Arab Market in Jerusalem's Old City. Ironically, the request backfires: rather than allay the women's concerns, their fear spreads to Sacco, who ends up viewing the market through their eyes after all.[46] This reversal notwithstanding, the episode revolves around Sacco's wholesale abandonment of objectivity, his willingness to empathize with both Israeli and Palestinian perspectives, and his invitation to Naomi and Paula to do the same.

However, this rejection of objectivity turns out to be highly selective. Sacco alternates between his own subjective viewpoint and a more traditional view from nowhere that absolves him from voicing his opinions in contexts where they would prove professionally inconvenient. He can afford to disagree with Naomi and Paula because they are less essential to his reporting; he has heard their side of the story most all his life. The Palestinian point of view is much harder for Sacco to access, and he cannot afford to alienate his sources. He effaces himself at the moments that most disturb his own liberal humanist views—moments when Palestinians express their support for attacks on civilians or collaborators, for anti-Semitic threats or conspiracy theories, for pressuring women to wear the hijab, for defending a family that murders their fifteen-year-old daughter. Sacco normally displays an admirable willingness to reveal and criticize his own viewpoint as a Western journalist in Palestine, but he conceals his opinions when they would most contest the views of the people he writes about.

Sacco's more recent work has moved away from this recourse to mute objectivity and he-said she-said journalism—although other critical accounts once again differ from this assessment, largely because of a countervailing shift in Sacco's art. Rosenblatt and Lunsford note that his drawing style has changed from "the highly caricatured, always askew style he used in *Palestine* and other works" to a "near-obsessive hunger for visual detail," particularly in his renderings of landscapes and locations; they conclude that Sacco "seems less aggressive in his focus on his own subjectivity and more in tune with the traditional journalistic search for realism and objectivity."[47] While Sacco is much less likely to make himself the subject of his later works, his journalism has continued to emphasize not only his own subjectivity but also the subjectivity of his sources. In *The Fixer*, Sacco repeatedly asks readers to "put themselves in the shoes" of the people he meets, particularly Neven, the eponymous fixer and potential fabulist who guides Sacco through Sarajevo.[48] This refrain invites empathy, not impartiality, even as Sacco attempts to cut through the rumors and tall tales to get at the truth of what happened in the Bosnian war. He assumes an even more subjective posture at the end of *Footnotes in Gaza*, where he presents the final three pages from the first-person perspective of one of the Palestinians who was beaten and killed in a 1956 massacre.[49] By placing the reader in the viewpoint of his subjects, Sacco renders his meticulously researched findings with visceral immediacy while obliterating any claims to journalistic detachment. He frames these pages, in fact, as a rebuke of his own pretenses to an objective command of the facts, of his arrogant belief that he "knew more about that day" than the men who survived it.[50] Rejecting his earlier complicity in the conventions of objectivity, this graphic display suggests that good journalism—dedicated to an honest representation of experience rather than the pursuit of an arbitrary impartiality—is always grounded in a view from somewhere.

NOTES

1. Peter Aspden, "'Tugged by the forgotten places,'" *Financial Times*, June 27, 2003, 15.

2. Ibid.

3. Jay Rosen, "The View from Nowhere: Questions and Answers," *PressThink*, November 11, 2010, http://pressthink.org/2010/11/the-view-from-nowhere-questions-and-answers/; see also Thomas Nagel, *The View from Nowhere* (New York: Oxford University Press, 1986).

4. Michael Schudson, *Discovering the News: A Social History of American Newspapers* (New York: Basic, 1978), 121–44.

5. Ibid., 155.

6. Ibid., 155–57; see also Bill Kovach and Tom Rosenstiel, *The Elements of Journalism* (New York: Crown, 2001), 74.

7. Rosen, "The View from Nowhere."

8. Ibid.

9. Adam Rosenblatt and Andrea A. Lunsford, "Critique, Caricature, and Compulsion in Joe Sacco's Comics Journalism," in *The Rise of the American Comics Artist: Creators and Contexts*, eds. Paul Williams and James Lyons (Jackson: University Press of Mississippi, 2010), 69.

10. Kristian Williams, "The Case for Comics Journalism: Artist-Reporters Leap Tall Conventions in a Single Bound," *Columbia Journalism Review* (March–April 2005), 52, 55.

11. Rocco Versaci, *This Book Contains Graphic Language: Comics as Literature* (New York: Continuum, 2007), 114.

12. Benjamin Woo, "Reconsidering Comics Journalism: Information and Experience in Joe Sacco's *Palestine*," in *The Rise and Reason of Comics and Graphic Literature: Critical Essays on the Form*, eds. Joyce Goggin and Dan Hassler-Forest (Jefferson, NC: McFarland, 2010), 173.

13. Ibid., 172.

14. Ibid., 171–72.

15. John C. Hartsock, *A History of American Literary Journalism: The Emergence of a Modern Narrative Form* (Amherst: University of Massachusetts Press, 2000), 40.

16. Norman Sims, *True Stories: A Century of Literary Journalism* (Evanston: Northwestern University Press, 2007), 6–7.

17. Ibid., 10.

18. Ibid., 285–86; Versaci, *This Book Contains Graphic Language*, 130–31; Rosenblatt and Lunsford, "Critique, Caricature, and Compulsion," 71.

19. Schudson, *Discovering the News*, 89–90, 118–19.

20. G. Stuart Adam, "Notes Towards a Definition of Journalism," in *Journalism: The Democratic Craft*, eds. G. Stuart Adam and Roy Peter Clark (New York: Oxford University Press, 2006), 347; Amy Kiste Nyberg, "Comics Journalism," in *Critical Approaches to Comics: Theories and Methods*, eds. Matthew J. Smith and Randy Duncan (New York: Routledge, 2012), 118–19.

21. Woo, "Reconsidering Comics Journalism," 173.

22. Ibid., 172.

23. Ibid., 170.

24. Nyberg, "Comics Journalism," 120–24.

25. Ibid., 119.

26. Joe Sacco, *Palestine* (Seattle: Fantagraphics, 2001), 18, his emphasis. Two pages later, Palestinians assert their "side" of the story by picking up discarded Peace Now signs and conducting an impromptu "mini-demonstration": "They march a few dozen yards . . . chanting their heads off

... raising more decibels in two minutes than I've heard all afternoon ... I mean, they're screaming like their lives depended on it!" (20).

27. Ibid., 67.

28. Ibid., 150–58.

29. Ibid., 6–8.

30. Ibid., 155–56.

31. Mark David Nevins, "'Drawing from Life': An Interview with Joe Sacco," *International Journal of Comic Art* 4.2 (Fall 2002), 34.

32. Woo, "Reconsidering Comics Journalism," 174.

33. Sacco, *Palestine*, 159–63.

34. Ibid., 177.

35. Jay Rosen, "He Said, She Said Journalism: Lame Formula in the Land of the Active User," *PressThink*, April 12, 2009, http://archive.pressthink.org/2009/04/12/hesaid_shesaid.html.

36. Howard Kurtz, "Huffington snags N.Y. Times star," *Media Notes*, September 21, 2010, http://voices.washingtonpost.com/howard-kurtz/2010/09/huffington_snags_ny_times_star.html.

37. Sacco, *Palestine*, 137–40.

38. Ibid., 137.

39. Wendy Kozol, "Complicities of Witnessing in Joe Sacco's *Palestine*," in *Transmedial Perspectives on Human Rights and Literature*, eds. Elizabeth Swanson Goldberg and Alexandra Schultheis Moore (New York: Routledge, 2012), 167, 172–73.

40. Sacco, *Palestine*, 137, his emphasis.

41. Ibid., 139.

42. Kozol, "Complicities of Witnessing," 173.

43. Sacco, *Palestine*, 139–40.

44. Ibid., 256.

45. Ibid.

46. Williams, "The Case for Comics Journalism," 54–55.

47. Rosenblatt and Lunsford, "Critique, Caricature, and Compulsion," 83.

48. Joe Sacco, *The Fixer* (Montreal: Drawn & Quarterly, 2003), collected in Joe Sacco, *The Fixer and Other Stories* (Montreal: Drawn & Quarterly, 2009).

49. Joe Sacco, *Footnotes in Gaza* (New York: Metropolitan Books, 2009), 386–88.

50. Ibid., 385.

Section II
Space and Maps

5. Mapping Bosnia: Cartographic Representation in Joe Sacco's Graphic Narratives

Edward C. Holland

In the fall of 1995, Joe Sacco traveled to Bosnia. The country's three-year-long civil war was at last coming to an end. Working counter to the narratives and depictions found in mainstream portrayals of the conflict and its leading actors, Sacco crafted a series of nonfiction graphic narratives about his experiences in the country. The topics were varied: the experience of the war in Goražde, a Muslim town in the country's southeast surrounded for much of the war by Serbian forces and paramilitaries; the story of Šoba, a hard-living soldier in the Bosnian army who moonlights as a rock star; and a meditation on the International Criminal Tribunal for the Former Yugoslavia, which in its early existence failed to capture those most responsible for the crimes committed during the conflict.[1] Sacco tells these stories with his characteristic blend of journalism and artistry in the comics medium. Sacco's virtuosity lies in his authorization of feeling: "This is hard stuff. It's brutal stuff. Some of it's downright evil. So why should you be reading it? You should read about it because you care about it."[2] The characters, stories, and techniques of narration all work to cultivate an emotional response in Sacco's readership.

Building on this argument, in this essay I consider the use of maps and mappings as narrative technique in the work of Joe Sacco. The geography of Sacco's work—specifically, the variety of cartographic representations that appear in "Christmas with Karadzic" and *Safe Area Goražde*, two of Sacco's comics on the 1992–95 war in Bosnia—relies both on traditional cartography, through the representation of places, boundaries, and territories from a Cartesian viewpoint, and a grounded perspective that inserts the reader into the action and attempts to replicate the experience of war through the visual negotiation of the conflict landscape. This essay is in conversation with existing work in the disciplines of geography and comics studies that consider the use of representation and narrative in the comics medium to challenge mainstream interpretations of political conflict. I also integrate recent work on the retheorization of maps, and suggest that comics and maps perform a similar function through their varied and processual representations of space. The result in Sacco's work is the use of maps and mappings to communicate and critique predominant narratives and interpretations of the war in Bosnia.

In making this argument, I open by discussing the ways in which these comics communicate the story to the reader and make possible a varied set of readings and interpretations of a range of topics, from geopolitical events to everyday experiences. Specific narrative techniques—including the insertion of the historical interlude and the depiction of banality—facilitate such critical readings.³ I further synthesize this existing work with the emergent critique of cartography present in the discipline of geography. The interpretation of maps has shifted away from the fixed ontology of maps-as-objects towards an increased engagement with the practice of mapping.⁴ While Sacco's work includes maps-as-text—with their traditional demarcation of borders and territories and a bird's-eye view of space—there is also an emergent depiction of space from a grounded perspective. The process of mapping is made possible by the comics medium and Sacco's nuanced and varied representation of space.

Graphic Narrative and the Representation of Space

Graphic narrative as a medium is itself subject to many possible readings and meanings. Scott McCloud's *Understanding Comics* considers the form, the basic elements, and the process of creating comics.⁵ Essential to the comics medium is the juxtaposition of images as presented in sequence; the viewer, in turn, interprets these images.⁶ In the discipline of geography, Jason Dittmer has built on McCloud's work to interrogate the process through which the reader—as a nomadic subject—engages with the comic book medium.⁷ Comic books offer the possibility for unique readings in both time and space in comparison to media such as literature and film: "The practice of reading comic books ... enables a variety of image-sequences to be produced from the same images by the reader."⁸ The spatial layout of the comic, with its panels and gutters—both of which are, potentially, communicative sites where the narrative progresses and creative sites where the reader interprets the direction of the story—makes possible these emergent readings. McCloud refers to this as "the *visible* and the *invisible*," an interplay that is unique to comics; in turn, "no other artform gives so much to its audience while asking so much *from* them as well."⁹

Other work in geography has focused more on the content of graphic narrative and the varied narrative techniques employed by comics creators in communicating their stories. This literature builds on the concept of critical geopolitics, which interrogates the "convenient fiction" of mainstream interpretations of geopolitical events and actions.¹⁰ These interpretations privilege the state and geography as defined through the delineation of the state as a form of spatial-political organization, which, in turn, results in the production of discourse.[11] Gearóid Ó Tuathail suggests that geopolitical discourse can be classed into three categories: formal geopolitics, the geopolitical visions and high-level study of world politics by "intellectuals of statecraft"; practical geopolitics, or the narratives through which statesmen and political leaders communicate on the subject of geopolitics to the general public (the annual State of the Union address is an oft-cited example); and popular geopolitics, the lowbrow formats (including movies, newspapers, and comic books) found in popular culture that inform and structure simplified understandings of global politics.[12] Comic books, as a medium, generally invoke popular narratives while appealing to young men through genres varying from heroism to war to horror. In the critical geopolitics literature, comic books have primarily been theorized as a mechanism for reproducing popular interpretations of geopolitical events: the binaries of good and evil during World War II, the Cold War, and the post-September 11 War on Terror. Particularly notable in such work on comics is the role of nationalist superheroes—primarily Captain America, but also Captain Canuck, Captain Britain, and Union Jack—who serve as signifiers of the nation-state for their audiences.[13]

Counter to this existing work, I have previously argued that Sacco constructs his comics to challenge mainstream interpretations of geopolitical events.[14] Sacco's graphic narratives eschew the oversimplifying binaries of mainstream comic books; while the format and structure are consistent, the content and narrative process depart from the tropes commonly found in the comics medium. For example, in his short piece "Chechen War, Chechen Women," about life for those displaced in Russia's North Caucasus as a result of the second war in Chechnya, Sacco relies on three narrative techniques—the historical interlude, the singular panel, and the depiction of the banal—to communicate the situation's complexity and the need for alternate and nuanced readings.[15] The narrative incorporates a brief history of the deportation of the Chechens to Central Asia during World War II to underscore the consequences of displacement as previously experienced by the ethnic group. Similarly, Sacco's use of the singular panel effectively depicts the September 1999 terrorist attacks in three Russian cities that served as the impetus for the broadening of a second campaign in the region in October of that year. The lives of those displaced by the conflict take on a routineness and tedium that reflects the realities of war without any hint of glory—this is depicted through the banal experiences of refugees living in camps in neighboring Ingushetia. And Sacco's positionality as a journalist—the incorporation of "on-the-ground elements of witness and reportage" into his work—leads to the implicit questioning of who should serve as the subject in the depiction of conflict.[16]

In this essay, I want to build on this existing scholarship in two ways. First,

I am interested in the role of the map as a narrative technique; like the techniques introduced above, Sacco's use of maps simultaneously reproduces their traditional function and form while also allowing for a more critical interpretation of the experience and consequences of conflict. With respect to the first point, and like other elements of narration, the maps included in Sacco's work are intended to inform the reader and condition their interpretation of the events presented. The use of comics as a medium to convey information is particularly relevant to Sacco's Bosnia comics, as he is interested in places and subjects that are beyond the ambit of much journalistic and academic work on the war.[17] In a 2002 interview with Gary Groth, Sacco touches on the informative element of his work in Bosnia: "I wanted to convey very solid, factual information or atmospheric information, or stories of people, and . . . but I want people to read it."[18] Similarly, the insertion of maps into the narrative is a technique that situates the reader in the story and conditions their interpretation of the story. Sacco's maps are necessarily selective in their representation, though they do serve the baseline function of locating the reader in Yugoslavia's complex geography. I refer to these objects and the informative process of mapping in graphic narrative as maps-in-text.

Second, I consider the role that maps play in generating an aesthetic, and potentially critical, response in the reader. Mapping is a process with respect to both creation and interpretation, and Sacco uses mappings—as opposed to classically conceived maps—to create a depiction of the conflict experience for his readership.[19] The critical cartography literature discussed below is increasingly acknowledging the contingency of the map as a textual object. The critique is varied and comes from artists, hackers, and non-traditional map producers (and can be broadly classed as counter-mappings).[20] However, though Sacco's work can be viewed as a form of critical engagement, its communicative essence must also be acknowledged. Sacco uses visual techniques in the narrative that ground his maps in the construction of a particular reality as interpreted by the reader, while also getting across a set of orienting spatialities. In sum, distinct from map artists and other counter-mappers, Sacco as comics artist uses his mappings to blend critique and communication. While the implicit "challenge [to] received notions of space, knowledge and power" is present in Sacco's comics, the communicative element remains relevant.[21] I suggest that the appropriation of the essence of mapping—that is, how space becomes and is interpreted—by Sacco as an artist, as well as the use of these mappings to depict the experiences of his characters, can be referred to as mappings-in-text. Before expanding on this argument with respect to Sacco's work in Bosnia, I offer a brief summary of the central themes in critical cartography.

Cartography and the Representation of Space

I have distinguished above between maps and mappings in Sacco's comics. This distinction is also present in varied considerations and theorizations of cartography. Foundationally, the map is an object that claims to represent a portion of the earth's surface. This definition is generally agreed upon and, to an extent, epistemologically secure in the discipline of geography. At the least, it is functionally secure; the map "continues to be used as a standard item of geographical apparatus."[22] The coupling of cartographic representation and geography reproduces some of the foundational, yet problematic, assumptions about the discipline; these include entrenched notions of geography as static and unchanging. Yet maps remain a central element of geography both inside and outside the academy. The second term—mappings—underscores the processual nature of maps; the range of engagements and interpretations possible in any mapping necessarily means that their definition is not fixed. Mappings, in a fashion not dissimilar from comic books, are subject to emergent interpretations dependent on the notions of the viewer. Sacco's comics embody both notions—maps and mappings—in his representations of the Bosnia conflict.

Uniting the threads of maps-in-text and mappings-in-text is the ongoing retheorization of the map in geography. Increasingly, geographers have come to question the assumptions implicit in the use of maps. The map is more than "lines, colors, lettering, [and] symbols" as traditionally defined in the literature on cartography in the discipline of geography.[23] Arthur H. Robinson's aim of developing "a better cartography" through the refinement of map design, structure, style, and lettering was situated in a post-World War II positivist approach to geography. Though there have been further attempts at refining Robinson's approach, the retheorization of maps and mappings has generally been skeptical of any attempts to establish an essential cartography. Rather, recent critiques of maps and the practice of cartography revolve around the problematic notion that maps are faithful and objective representations of space. J. Brian Harley acknowledges the socially constructed nature of maps and employs Foucault to question the idea that representations of space can be objective; he views cartographic productions as fundamentally influenced by political actions such as "warfare, political propaganda, boundary making, or the preservation of law and order."[24] Jeremy Crampton has refined this argument to more broadly interrogate the ontology of the map—its relation to the world, its voice, and the consequences of its representation—and its security as both a product and practice.[25] The approach endorsed by Rob Kitchin and Martin Dodge—that "maps are of-the-moment, beckoned into being through practices; they are always mapping"—is inherently processual and extends the realm of the possible in which mappings occur.[26] It is this ontogenetic approach—which denies the epistemological or ontological security of the map—that informs my approach in this chapter to the mappings found in Joe Sacco's graphic narratives. Sacco's mappings are not cartographic in form; rather, their essence is of movement through space, a performative approach to the conflict experienced by Sacco as artist and journalist and an attempt to situate the reader in the experiences of war.

At the same time, the classic cartographic forms employed in Sacco's comics are, foundationally, informative. Maps play an important role in Sacco's comics, inserted at key points to provide the reader with background on the politics revolving around the conflict and attempts at its resolution. In "Christmas with Karadzic," Sacco inserts a map of the zones of occupation in Sarajevo, Bosnia's capital, in the interim between the Dayton Accords and the final withdrawal of Serbian troops from their positions around the city. Similarly, in *Safe Area Goražde*, Sacco's cartography explains the process of Yugoslavia's dissolution, emphasizing the country's territorial division into six autonomous republics (as well as the second-level divisions of Serbia). For the reader, this cartography situates Bosnia in historical and political context, providing a framework on which to construct an understanding of the atrocities associated with the 1992–95 war in Bosnia.

In attempting to reconcile Kitchin and Dodge's approach to mapping with the foundationally informative role that maps play in Sacco's graphic narrative, I am informed by one more recent theorization of mapping technology: the possibilities of interpretation and spatial experience available through Google Earth. In articulating these potential interpretations, Paul Kingsbury and John Paul Jones III differentiate between the Apollonian view from above—"composed of control, order, and calculation"—and the Dionysian pleasure made possible by the varied entities, objects, and representations available to the user in the Google Earth interface, which underscores the possibilities of maps in other media.[27] In Sacco's graphic narratives, there are attempts at reproducing the Apollonian perspective, in order to inform the reader and situate their interpretation within the complex geography of the Bosnian war; there are also opportunities—mappings-in-text, as discussed below—for the reader to negotiate the space of Bosnia's conflict landscape through a contingent reading, one which can as readily lead to feelings of empathy and pain as enjoyment. The affinity between Google Earth and Sacco's mappings of the conflict experience is further strengthened through the capability to perform flyovers in this geospatial technology. As Jakob Linaa Jensen writes: "Google Earth enhances the representation [of actual space] in powerful ways by allowing the user to change the views between traditional map views, satellite views of landscapes, and even three-dimensional flyovers from destination to destination."[28] This multidimensionality of the spatial experience is also present in Sacco's work, made possible by the comics medium. To make the case for maps, mappings, and the representation of conflict, I now turn to this interplay of cartography and cartographic interpretation in Sacco's work on Bosnia.

Maps-in-text: An Informative Cartography

Joe Sacco first turned his attention to Bosnia as he was completing *Palestine*. He traveled to Bosnia with the intent of doing journalistic pieces about day-to-day life at the end of the war. At the time, Sacco was also refining the way in which he told the stories of those affected by conflict. In his prior work, *Palestine*, Sacco had adopted what he refers to as an "organic" approach, one that laid out his story in a chronological order and embraced similarities across the stories told.[29] His work in Bosnia acknowledged the value of individual stories, while also recognizing the need to establish the historical and geographic context for the reader. Along these lines, in his interview with Gary Groth, Sacco makes plain the need to convey a baseline of information to the readership: "You do need basic information in there. As far as whether comics allow for [the communication of such information along with eyewitness reporting and personal stories] . . . they seem to have allowed for it in this case."[30] This, in turn, influences the organization of Sacco's comics. Regarding the structure of *Safe Area Goražde*, he continues: "I realized I had two tracks. There was the historical track that took the reader chronologically through the major incidents of the war. And there was the atmospheric track that was basically my impressions of the people I was meeting, people who had survived something terrible and weren't quite sure that the war was over."[31] In sum, Sacco is using the comics medium to simultaneously tell the history of Bosnia and the 1992–95 war and the story of his experience in country at the end of conflict.

As Sacco himself acknowledges, this history is complex. In "Christmas with Karadzic," the background elements in the narrative center on the actions of the Bosnian Serb political leader Radovan Karadžić. Karadžić's rhetoric, his explicit endorsement of the siege of Sarajevo, regardless of its consequences, and his relegation to persona non grata status during the peace negotiations held in late 1995 are all touched on in the narrative.[32] One of Karadžić's most infamous lines—that "Sarajevans will not be counting the dead . . . they will be counting the living" is a key element in the organization of the story; when Sacco and his two colleagues track down Karadžić in the town of Pale, it is this line that Sacco focuses on during the encounter.[33] Yet Sacco also makes clear that Karadžić is behind many of the atrocities experienced in Bosnia's capital of Sarajevo during the course of the war. From the beginning of the siege of the city in April 1992, Serb forces held the heights in the Grbavica district; they used the position—close to the city's center—as their redoubt for sniper attacks.[34] Further to the south, in the hills ringing the city, the Serbs stationed artillery used to bombard civilians in the city below. The Serbs also held a strategic area near Sarajevo's airport. This made transport to the airport dangerous and, potentially, deadly; Bosnian Muslim forces completed a supply tunnel running under the airport to the Dobrinja district in July 1993.[35] The peace agreement signed in Dayton, Ohio, in November 1995 ceded control of Serb-occupied territory around the city of Sarajevo to the Bosnian federation.[36] Karadžić, however, was not party to these negotiations; in the wake of the genocide at Srebrenica and the Western response, he was left on the sidelines at Dayton. Instead, Slobodan Milosevic, the president of Serbia proper, represented the Bosnian Serb position.

Safe Area Goražde, with its in-depth portrayal of Goražde, a city in southeastern Bosnia located on the banks of the Drina River, is centrally concerned with the lived experiences of war. The two tracks of the narrative are temporally distinguished between present and past, although the vignettes that make up the former often include the recollections and remembrances of Sacco's interlocutors. Goražde, with a population of just under 40,000 people at the start of the war, was an area of heavy fighting between Bosnian Serbs and Bosnian Muslims between 1992 and 1995. Fighting began there in late spring 1992 and at various points Bosnian Serb offensives washed over the city. During these campaigns, many of Goražde's residents were injured or killed; the town also served as a relocation point for refugees from other Bosnian Muslim communities in the Drina River valley. Cut off from Sarajevo and other areas under the control of Bosnian Muslim forces, during the first winter of fighting Goražde's residents were forced to make dangerous treks overland to a resupply point; the city later relied on airdrops for food and other vital supplies. When Sacco first visited in October 1995, an uneasy ceasefire held between the Serb and Muslim forces.

Maps underlie the process of communicating the history of the war in Bosnia to the readership in Sacco's graphic narratives, both as experienced in Sarajevo and Goražde. In "Christmas with Karadzic," the sole map in the narrative is placed at the end of the background section, following panels that depict Karadžić and the perspective of the siege of Sarajevo.[37] The map displays the intended political geographies of the capital after Dayton; the Serbs were required to cede both the Grbavica district and occupied territory near the city's

Figure 5.1. Sacco's informative cartography of Communist-era Yugoslavia. Detail of Joe Sacco, *Safe Area Goražde: The War in Eastern Bosnia, 1992–1995* (Seattle: Fantagraphics, 2000), 19.

airport. A buffer zone around Sarajevo, though outside of the city limits, was to be transferred to Bosnian control. The text that supports the map reinforces a set of key points in Sacco's background to the story of the Bosnian Serb leader. Despite his rhetoric regarding Sarajevo, Karadžić and his supporters failed to secure any part of the capital for their envisioned state.

The use of maps-in-text is more extensive in *Safe Area Goražde*. In the book's first historical interlude, Sacco inserts two locational maps, which are each supplemented by a written summary (see Figure 5.1).[38] The first of these two maps shows the Yugoslavian federation as demarcated under Tito, with its six republics (Slovenia, Croatia, Bosnia, Serbia, Montenegro, and Macedonia) and the two autonomous areas within Serbia (Vojvodina and Kosovo). The second map focuses in on Bosnia—as Sacco writes, "of the six Yugoslav republics . . . Bosnia was the most ethnically diverse"—and identifies key cities, the capital of Sarajevo, and the towns and cities in the Drina River valley in the republic's southeast.[39] By 1992, multiethnic Bosnia was one of three republics that remained in a downsized Yugoslavia; Slovenia, Croatia, and Macedonia had all declared independence the year before and Bosnia followed with its declaration in March 1992.

The remaining maps in the narrative focus on two scales: the republic level of Bosnia and the local level of Goražde and its environs in the Drina River valley. During the course of the war, as losses to Muslim forces mounted, the territory controlled by the Bosnian government was reduced to six pockets scattered throughout the country. In 1993, the United Nations (UN) extended safe area status to the Bosnian Muslim-held territory beyond Sarajevo. These safe areas included small pockets encircling Goražde and Srebrenica, as well as a larger area around the city of Tuzla. Some critics viewed these as ineffectual: the safe areas were "islands surrounded by hostile forces and represented messy territorial anomalies in what was effectively a Serb conquest."[40] This proved prophetic; in July 1995, 8,000 Muslim men and boys were massacred after the safe area of Srebrenica was overrun by Bosnian Serb forces under the leadership of General Ratko Mladic. Sacco's map of the safe areas identifies these areas and is supplemented by a discussion of the United Nations' plan, its endorsement by the United States, and the failure of the plan to stem the violence, with a renewed Bosnian Serb offensive against Goražde and other towns occurring shortly after the extension of safe area status.

With this background established and supported through the insertion of maps into the narrative, Sacco proceeds to recount the experiences of Goražde's residents during the war. Central to this portion of the story are local-level maps-in-text. One of the book's most harrowing scenes recounts the experience of Edin, Sacco's translator and main point of contact in the city, as he traveled from Goražde to a Bosnian army post located to the city's west for supplies during the winter of 1992–93.[41] Food supplies in Goražde tightened due to the influx of refugees and the failure of UN convoys to deliver adequate support. The city's residents were forced to travel overland, at night, through Serb-held territory to reach Grebak, the nearby army post. Sacco prefaces Edin's experience with a map that details the route of travel—by truck to a point outside of Zorovici and then further on foot through mountainous terrain. The return trip was particularly difficult given the heavy load that Edin was carrying, the snow and cold temperatures in the mountains, and the varied topography; to reinforce this last point, Sacco's map provides elevations along the route.

In both "Christmas with Karadžić" and *Safe Area Goražde*, Sacco uses maps-in-text as a stylistic and journalistic technique to communicate two elements central to his stories: the historical context of the war in Bosnia and the lived experiences of his interlocutors in the town of Goražde. These maps set the stage for telling the story of the 1992–95 war, providing a baseline for understanding what is a complex and multifaceted narrative.

Mappings-in-text: Process and Narrative

In contrast, the notion of grounded perspectivalism—mappings-in-text—is employed to different effect in the two comics under consideration. In his interview with Gary Groth, Sacco explains the creative process that underlies these mappings. Taking the example of Edin's winter trek through the mountains for supplies, Sacco states that the movement through space is drawn with the intent of capturing "the experience of climbing over mountains with heavy packs."[42] Edin moves to the left in the panels, the narrative text is sparse, and the setting for the trek is intended to be ominous.[43] This process of moving through space is characteristic of other scenes in Sacco's narrative, and is used in a particularly effective manner as Sacco attempts to depict and communicate the consequences and experiences of conflict.

In "Christmas with Karadzic," Sacco's most effective representation of space comes towards the end of the story, when he illustrates the view from his landlady Rada's apartment.[44] This includes the Serb-controlled heights of the Grabvica district, the Holiday Inn that was the de facto headquarters for the international press corps through the course of the war, and the no-man's-land between Bosnian Serb- and Bosnian Muslim-controlled areas. The mapping—not a formal cartography but rather a representation of space that situates the reader in the conflict landscape—is supplemented by text that details how snipers shot into Rada's apartment from the Serb-controlled heights above the city. Sacco then takes the reader through Sarajevo's streets, with its derelict cars and blown-out windows, past patrols of the international peacekeeping force, and up the eleven flights of stairs to the apartment of Rada's sister.[45] As with the depiction of Edin's experience, the narration here is sparse. Sacco mentions that Rada is an ethnic Serb, yet one who has remained loyal to the Bosnian state despite the three-year-long war. The reader is provided with a perspective on Sarajevo at the end of the war, and is left to wonder how people stand the winter's cold, where Sacco got the bag of food that he carries to the dinner, and when life in the Bosnian capital might return to normal. These questions are examples of the possibilities of graphic narrative, as readers can variously interpret Sacco and his subjects' negotiation of the conflict landscape.

Critical cartographic representations of space—mappings that are processual rather than formal—are found elsewhere in *Safe Area Goražde* beyond Edin's overland trek. In one of the most moving scenes early in the narrative, Sacco recounts the first attack by Serb forces on the town of Goražde. As is the

Figure 5.2. Izet crawls to the river in an attempt to escape the Serb attack. Detail of Joe Sacco, *Safe Area Goražde: The War in Eastern Bosnia, 1992–1995* (Seattle: Fantagraphics, 2000), 83.

case in "Christmas with Karadzic," the reader is first provided with a removed perspective of the violence; Edin, on patrol in the hills above Goražde, is helpless to intervene in the attack. The story that follows depicts various negotiations with conflict space as told by Sacco's interlocutors, and concludes with a single map that simultaneously relays both the formal and personal impact of that first Serb offensive.[46] One of these stories is that of Izet and his escape from the Serb troops. Along with a large group of Bosnian Muslims, he tries to move through Goražde with his wife and daughter; Sacco quotes Izet: "I had seen dead women, children, and men, and I thought it's better to be killed while running than to stay in the same place..."[47] What follows is Izet's attempt to reach the Drina River. Crawling though a wooded area, he passes the dead and wounded, is himself shot in the arm, and guides his daughter to safety. The reader is taken through the town, across streets and past buildings, wading through the Drina, and crawling along a road in the early morning hours, with the eventual success of reaching safety in Bosnian Muslim-held territory. The comics medium, and Sacco's artistic style, make possible for the reader an engagement with space that is simultaneously removed and embodied, a technique of representation similar to the flyover modules possible in geospatial technologies such as Google Earth (see Figure 5.2). This representation of space is not a traditional map; rather, it is a mapping that is created through the interaction of Sacco's art and the reader's interpretation. The comics medium allows for an ontogenetic—that is, processual and emergent—engagement with the conflict landscape.

Conclusion

The creative possibility of both comics and cartography depend on the contingent and varied nature of interpretation possible for each. Mappings-in-text underscore the processual and evolutionary nature of cartography. The mappings in Sacco's narratives are unstable, in part due to their ontogenetic nature and in part due to the contingency and varied interpretation made possible through the comics medium. These mappings allow readers to situate themselves in the experience; the aesthetic and emotional responses that result are representative of the critique of the geopolitical made possible through the comics medium.

While Sacco's graphic narratives offer a critique of mainstream interpretations of geopolitical events, their informative function should not be overlooked. Sacco's graphic narratives also employ a traditional cartography. The aim of these maps-in-text is to secure a foundational level of understanding regarding Bosnia's history and the background to the war. Sacco's maps and mappings, in turn, balance the critical and the informative, the dual role of graphic narrative as a journalistic and aesthetic medium.

NOTES

1. These have been published as Joe Sacco, *Safe Area Goražde: The War in Eastern Bosnia, 1992–1995* (Seattle: Fantagraphics, 2000); Joe Sacco, *The Fixer and Other Stories* (Montreal: Drawn & Quarterly, 2009); and Joe Sacco, "The War Crimes Trials," in *Journalism* (New York: Metropolitan, 2012), 2–7. *The Fixer and Other Stories* collects *The Fixer*, "Šoba," and "Christmas with Karadzic."

2. Gary Groth, "Joe Sacco, Frontline Journalist," *Comics Journal* Special Edition (Winter 2002), 72.

3. On the possibilities associated with the graphic narrative format as considered in geography, see Jeff Wilson and Jay Jacot, "Fieldwork and Graphic Narratives," *Geographical Review* 103 (2013): 143–52.

4. See Jeremy Crampton, "Cartography: Performative, Participatory, Political," *Progress in Human Geography* 33 (2009): 840–48.

5. Scott McCloud, *Understanding Comics: The Invisible Art* (New York: HarperPerennial, 1994), 4. McCloud uses the term "comics" inclusively with respect to medium, while the object itself can be differentiated depending on format (comic books as opposed to comic strips, for example). In this chapter, I use "comics" and "graphic narrative" interchangeably in reference to the medium.

6. McCloud, *Understanding Comics*, 9.

7. Jason Dittmer, "Comic Book Visualities: A Methodological Manifesto on Geography, Montage and Narration," *Transactions of the Institute of British Geographers* 35 (2010), 225.

8. Dittmer, "Comic Book Visualities," 226.

9. McCloud, *Understanding Comics*, 92.

10. Gearóid Ó Tuathail, *Critical Geopolitics: The Politics of Writing Global Space* (Minneapolis: University of Minnesota Press, 1996), 16.

11. Gearóid Ó Tuathail, "General Introduction: Thinking Critically about Geopolitics," in *The Geopolitics Reader*, eds. Gearóid Ó Tuathail and Simon Dalby (New York: Routledge, 2006), 1.

12. Ibid., 9. On popular geopolitics specifically, see Jason Dittmer and Klaus Dodds, "Popular Geopolitics Past and Future: Fandom, Identities and Audiences," *Geopolitics* 13 (2008), 439.

13. Jason Dittmer, *Captain America and the Nationalist Superhero: Metaphors, Narratives, and Geopolitics* (Philadelphia: Temple University Press, 2012).

14. Edward C. Holland, "'To Think and Imagine and See Differently': Popular Geopolitics, Graphic Narrative, and Joe Sacco's 'Chechen War, Chechen Women,'" *Geopolitics* 17 (2012): 105–29.

15. See Joe Sacco, "Chechen War, Chechen Women," *Journalism*, 29–69.

16. Edward C. Holland, "Post-Modern Witness: Journalism and Representation in Joe Sacco's 'Christmas with Karadzic,'" in *Comic Book Geographies*, ed. Jason Dittmer (Berlin: Franz Steiner Verlag, 2014), 114.

17. I have argued elsewhere that Sacco's work echoes that of Maggie O'Kane, the Irish journalist for the *Guardian* who reported from Bosnia during the war. On O'Kane's stories and their

challenge to mainstream interpretations of the geopolitical, see Gearóid Ó Tuathail, "An Anti-Geopolitical Eye: Maggie O'Kane in Bosnia, 1992-93," *Gender, Place and Culture* 3 (1996): 171–86.

18. Groth, "Joe Sacco, Frontline Journalist," 72.

19. The use of graphic narrative for the depiction of experience, and its relevance to cartography, has been considered in John Krygier and Denis Wood, "Ce n'est pas le monde (This is not the world)," in *Rethinking Maps: New Frontiers in Cartographic Theory*, eds. Martin Dodge, Rob Kitchin, and Chris Perkins (New York: Routledge, 2009).

20. Jeremy W. Crampton and John Krygier, "An Introduction to Critical Cartography," *ACME: An International E-Journal for Critical Geographies* 4 (2005), 25.

21. Ibid.

22. David N. Livingstone, *The Geographical Tradition* (Malden: Blackwell, 1992), 351.

23. Arthur H. Robinson, *The Look of Maps* (Redlands: ESRI Press, 2010), 3.

24. J. Brian Harley, "Maps, Knowledge, and Power," in *The Iconography of Landscape*, eds. Denis Cosgrove and Stephen Daniels (New York: Cambridge University Press, 1988), 279.

25. Rob Kitchin and Martin Dodge, "Rethinking Maps," *Progress in Human Geography* 31 (2007), 332–35.

26. Ibid., 343. By suggesting that Sacco's scenes are mappings, despite lacking any sort of traditional cartographic representation, I am following the diverse engagement with mapping endorsed in Kitchin and Dodge's call for rethinking maps.

27. Paul Kingsbury and John Paul Jones III, "Walter Benjamin's Dionysian Adventures on Google Earth," *Geoforum* 40 (2009), 503.

28. Jakob Linaa Jensen, "Augmentation of Space: Four Dimensions of Spatial Experiences of Google Earth," *Space and Culture* 13 (2010), 125.

29. Groth, "Joe Sacco, Frontline Journalist," 59.

30. Ibid.

31. Ibid.

32. Holland, "Post-Modern Witness," 115–17.

33. Joe Sacco, "Christmas with Karadzic," *The Fixer and Other Stories*, 158.

34. Louis Sell, "The Serb Flight from Sarajevo: Dayton's First Failure," *East European Politics & Societies* 14 (1999), 179.

35. On the geography of the siege and the construction of the tunnel, see Curtis S. King, "The Siege of Sarajevo, 1992–1995," in *Block by Block: the Challenges of Urban Operations*, ed. W. G. Robertson (Fort Leavenworth: US Army Command and General Staff College Press, 2003) 244, 268.

36. For a recent recounting of the origins of war, the negotiations at Dayton, and the Accord's mixed legacy, see Gerard Toal and Carl T. Dahlman, *Bosnia Remade: Ethnic Cleansing and its Reversal* (New York: Oxford University Press, 2011).

37. Sacco, "Christmas with Karadzic," 158.

38. Sacco, *Safe Area Goražde*, 19.

39. Ibid.
40. Richard K. Betts, "The Delusion of Impartial Intervention," *Foreign Affairs* 73 (1994), 33.
41. Sacco, *Safe Area Goražde*, 133–49.
42. Groth, "Joe Sacco, Frontline Journalist," 64.
43. Sacco, *Safe Area Goražde*, 139–42.
44. Sacco, "Christmas with Karadzic," 171.
45. Ibid., 171–73.
46. Sacco, *Safe Area Goražde*, 86.
47. Ibid., 81.

6. A Thousand Plateaus: Mining Entropy in *Days of Destruction, Days of Revolt*

Georgiana Banita

> Now there is no life there. Only dust.
> —Larry Gibson

Journalism in its best forms has been a pivotal tool for social change. In a period spanning over one hundred years, from fiction and nonfiction narratives at the turn of the twentieth century to contemporary activist writings, muckrakers have exposed industrial monopoly and marketplace capitalism's abuses of the democratic system. The unique collaborative work by journalists Chris Hedges and Joe Sacco, *Days of Destruction, Days of Revolt*, combines the factual density and stylistic elegance of Hedges's style with the narrative sparseness and affective investment of Sacco's comics. A chapter of *Days of Destruction, Days of Revolt* focuses on mining practices, especially mountaintop removal (MTR) and the resulting dust, grime, and coal slurry that engulf the landscapes of states like West Virginia and Kentucky. From its origins, muckraking journalism has been inextricably linked with the injustices of the energy industry; with Hedges and Sacco, muckraking returns to its roots.[1] Their book intervenes in this tradition by revealing not only the systemic damage inflicted by rampant extraction, but also the contribution visual culture can make to investigative reporting in the twenty-first century. While earlier muckrakers decried the human cost of industrial and political malfunctions, *Days of Destruction, Days of Revolt* encompasses the effects of surface mining on the environment. When it describes human suffering, it seeks to extrapolate from the fate of individuals involved in the mining industry to the fate of all citizens. It does so by (literally) drawing attention to how an energetic awareness of nature dovetails with an aesthetic engagement with the visual arts that foregrounds conspicuous consumption, resource exhaustion, and entropic time.

Muckrakers were often criticized for their sentimentalism, stylistic blandness, and nostalgic desire to rewind history to a preindustrial era of pastoral contentment. They are still associated with, and in many ways held responsible for, the emergence and persistence of a so-called "popular naturalism" that has negatively impacted the reception of naturalist writing to this day.[2] As we shall see, Hedges often veers toward a similarly melodramatic tone, which isn't at all confined to this report but permeates the genre of energy documentary as a whole. His writing is accessible though not always objective, occasionally heightening observations into stark moral pronouncements. Sacco counterbalances these tendencies and shows that nothing can be rewound at this point. His images revolve precisely around the impossibility of return to a recoverable Eden. Moreover, while "the point of a literature of exposé was razor-sharp incision through veils of ambiguity and obscurity,"[3] this kind of ruminative vagueness is precisely what Sacco restores to the narrative, while still making clear the need for organized and immediate response to abuses of human rights and ecological integrity in Appalachia.

Of course, the fate of these zones also resonates with that of others in Sacco's body of work. Their inhabitants face loss, displacement, and the dwindling memory of a peaceful, prosperous past. They are pocked by the deep gashes of strip mining and buried under heaps of refuse.[4] Yet *Days of Destruction* poses a challenge to Sacco that his other works don't; the backbone of the book is the proposition to empathize with people who are very different from the groups for whom Sacco has already served as a visual champion. Here, Sacco repositions ordinary Americans as victims of the economic oppression and indenture that his readers are otherwise accustomed to discover only outside the United States. *Days of Destruction* asks readers to be alive to the fragility of that stable core—their privileged status—that guarantees their empathetic response to Sacco's *Palestine* or *Safe Area Goražde*. It contains a provocation to contemplate the risks of giving short shrift to injustice at home while loudly bemoaning injustices elsewhere in the world. To that extent, the book functions as "the Other" vis-à-vis the works that Sacco produced single-handedly—partly because the writing and the drawings complement and question each other, but above all because the world Sacco describes corresponds to what anthropologist Kathleen Stewart has called an "Other America." Stewart sees in the coal-mining region of southwestern West Virginia a "space on the side of the road"[5]—a space on the side of progress, democracy, individualism, and civilization, on the side, in other words, of triumphant Western history naturalized into national myth.

Stewart's image resonates with Sacco's comics because it denotes "a place that insists on the necessity of gaps in the meaning of signs and creates a place for story—for narrativizing a local cultural real."[6] This is what Sacco's images juxtapose with Hedges's carefully honed accessibility and rhetorical order: "a poetics of deferral and displacement, a ruminative re-entrenchment in the particularity of local forms and epistemologies."[7] His illustrations hold seriality and sequence at bay, instead favoring texture, density, and ambiguousness. They contrast the vocal advocacy of the text with the failure of representation, throwing up a roadblock of entropic fatalism and decline to the utopian empowerment of journalistic prose. I argue that all of Sacco's images in this section—and especially his large-scale, wordless illustrations—open voids, gaps, and interstices in the narrative to give us pause, to alert us to the tension between coherence and interruption, both between words and images and within images themselves. The discourse of comics theory, especially on the function of the gutter and of the single image, provides fertile ground for exploring the book's encounters with the detail and imagination of the local. Integral to these encounters is an entropic interlude that elicits attention to the boom-and-bust structure of mining economies, to the postindustrial nostalgia of the regions afflicted by them, and to the potential of the graphic medium to encompass a visual poetics of ruin.

I will focus here on the chapter "Days of Devastation," which brings to light the pillage of landscapes and communities by strip mining and MTR in West Virginia. Two interrelated arguments emerge in this section and, to various degrees, throughout the whole book: labor communities suffer at the hand of a ruthless corporate class; and America's heartland is under ecological assault. Hedges is fascinated with how civilizations, whether Roman, Sumerian, Mayan, or American, "ossify and collapse"[8] as a result of profligate use of resources and energies. Entropy weaves itself through the entire book, from the scrap industry in Camden, New Jersey—where the main driveway has become "almost a bleakness"[9] and street signs signaling to cars to "slow" down are emblematic of how industrial development has stalled—to the disenchanted nature and spirit of the Pine Ridge Indian Reservation, an area beset by the same material and psychic devastation as the coalfields.

The nature of strip mining makes it especially malleable to a reading that emphasizes gradual decline and deterioration. A highly destructive form of strip mining, MTR differs from underground, contour, and area mining, which continue alongside it, by blasting off entire mountaintops, pushing down everything that isn't coal into the valleys below, burying streams, polluting wells, and dismantling wildlife ecosystems.[10] The damage often remains unseen because the devastation occurs in inaccessible areas. As writer and environmental activist Rick Bass notes, while the "scale of disorder" is overwhelming, it remains invisible: "The wide-open spaces shield the secrets from the rest of the world."[11] To heighten the impact of that damage, journalists and activists draw all sorts of creative parallels, for instance: "The tops of the mountains had been blasted away with the same mixture of ammonium nitrate and diesel fuel that Timothy McVeigh used to level the Murrah Building in Oklahoma City"; or (about the circuits of haul roads coursing through the rubble): "It looked as if someone had tried to plot a highway system on the moon." The idea that, for some Kentuckians, footage of the Apollo 11 moonwalk looked like astronauts hopping around on the barren tableland of a strip mine at night belongs in the same category.[12]

Even before MTR was introduced, the mining regions of Appalachia were textbook examples of economic and social decline. In 1963, Harry Caudill published *Night Comes to the Cumberlands: A Biography of a Depressed Area*, probably the most powerful plea for taking a stand against mining and its socioeconomic toll on Appalachia in the twentieth century.[13] Though important and effective, the book didn't trigger the reforms Caudill wanted, which prompted him to make embittered speculations about genetic decline in eastern Kentucky, and even about eugenic intervention to protect this area from brain drain and genetic impoverishment. Though sadly misguided, Caudill's diagnosis in the 1960s confirmed an important fact: the economic woes of the region were entangled with a sense of disillusion and powerlessness in its population. Hedges quotes a retired teacher, son of a coal miner: "This is the blitzkrieg. And someone wants you to fight back against an outfit that can take the tops off of mountains? You don't feel like you're a very big person."[14] It's important to bear in mind, however—and this is where both Hedges and Sacco can be said to tread on eggshells—that the book does not imply there is anything inherently wrong in the character and psychological makeup of these people. Ideas about a so-called Appalachian fatalism all too easily "constitute Appalachians as victims and obscure the possibilities for agency and empowerment, but are refuted by the rich history of struggle and resistance in the region."[15] In their controversial study *The Triple Package*, Jed Rubenfeld and Amy Chua insist that no cultural factors predetermine poverty and general decline in this region. When Rubenfeld and Chua examine other areas and groups, their focus is firmly trained on cultural and temperamental predictors of social mobility. Yet it's not culture, they claim, but a version of the resource curse—or what other scholars deplore as a form of internal colonialism—that should count as the chief cause of poverty in Appalachia.[16]

While preserving this distinction between how culture and resources impact Appalachia, I want to look at Sacco's work in *Days of Destruction* through the lens of graphic entropy. My aim is to outline a way of thinking about energy depletion and human exhaustion that brings the medium of comics into the proximity of other extraction narratives and aesthetics. I argue, quite simply, that Sacco transfers Hedges's often emotional, enraged accounts of America's sacrifice zones into a pared-down visual language whose main engine is the loss of power. Presented in static tableaus, the landscapes of formerly bustling industry and energy hubs are frozen into silence. That comics can visualize such drained, solitary moments especially well is no surprise. In Chris Ware we find perhaps the best example of how a series of panels can communicate stasis rather than motion, energy that bleeds away from a character as he drags himself from one corner of the page to another.[17] *Days of Destruction* is full of Jimmy Corrigans, drained not by masochistic impulses and a depressive temperament—and who but Ware can make comics into such an effective medium in embodying depression?—but by the social atomization, addictive disorders, and rampant despair left behind by the manufacturing and extraction juggernaut in West Virginia.

To make sense of Sacco's contribution to the book, we must negotiate the larger context of MTR representation in visual culture and make room for the kind of generic contamination that Sacco obviously intended with this unusual blend of comics and journalism. Hedges and Sacco conceived of this book as a genre-bending work that cuts across aesthetic traditions and raises questions about the relationship between art, reportage, and activism. I want to follow this legacy across four lines: first, a line of comics works that relate to other sacrifice zones of fossil fuel extraction—a line that also pursues entropy as theme and form in comics; second, documentary images of the same zones and social processes selected from films that resemble *Days of Destruction* in tone and visual style; third, the cinematic representation of mining strikes and riots, where stories of miners' struggle for unionization alternate with images of illness and physical exhaustion among the workers and often with nature imagery—a nature that was in a relatively pristine state at the time; and, fourth, the work of New Topographics photographers, known for their stylistically austere view of man-altered landscapes. Sacco's illustrations invoke and perhaps even emulate their large-scale images of ravaged extraction sites.

Still Life with Mountains: Entropy and Comics

Sacco and Hedges are not the first to use comics in making an activist appeal for a more responsible negotiation of the costs and benefits of fossil fuel extraction. But theirs is undoubtedly a uniquely thoughtful response, to the extent that it doesn't merely deliver accessible information, but also asks how images, so important in grasping the scale of destruction, can enhance written reportage. *Oil and Water* (2011), the title of the collaboration between journalist Steve Duin and cartoonist Shannon Wheeler, aptly summarizes the possibility that narration and visuals do not mix easily.[18] In that black-and-white book, where we are asked to imagine black crude and blue water as the core contrast, they don't in fact mix at all: the loud, wordy narrative clashes with the very basic, telegraphed visual style of the cartoons. In two page-size panels, for instance, the plume of smoke emanating from the rig looks the same as the plume of oil rising from the out-of-control well in the aftermath of the *Deepwater Horizon* blowout in April 2010. Most of the book consists of dense, flippant dialogue that doesn't pack much emotional punch beyond the moving account of oil-soaked pelicans in the Gulf of Mexico. The book too easily separates text and image, black and white (here even racially, with a focus on Louisiana as a particularly hard-hit sacrifice zone), lacking the filigreed detail of Sacco's more landscape-oriented view.

Similarly, for a book so vociferously invested in the plight of the underdog—"people who have no material worth, but who are worthy because of the life that flows through them in their various struggles for social justice"[19]—Seth Tobocman's *Disaster and Resistance: Comics and Landscapes for the Twenty First Century* (2008) stifles the material with sensationalist drawings and an imperious, self-important protest voice. The resistance of Nigerian women against a ruthless petrostate is worthy of exploration and praise, but the representation of the Ogoni versus Chevron is too emphatically cartoonish. Even more problematically, Tobocman doesn't just draw refineries; he draws himself drawing a refinery, then includes a photograph of the scene, too—which is perhaps one self-indulgence too many for the selfless agenda that his comic strips attempt to propagate. While the dynamic use of color evokes the work of African American painter Jacob Lawrence, generally the panels tell unmediated stories for immediate effect—and some of them were indeed handed out at protest rallies or circulated online. Sacco not only takes his time filling in detail, looking for the best angle and the most iconic scene; his art would not work as agitprop for a public audience. It demands individual reflection and time to absorb all the elements of the panels; and it leaves out the words, which often determine how long we gaze at a panel before we move on to the next speech balloon. Thus, it invites a formal decision about personal investment that might ultimately inspire an ethical response.

Sacco uses both panel sequences and single images in the text: the former mainly for historical accounts, the latter for eyewitness evidence of current destruction. The longer narrative sequences result from a process of *breakdown*, understood in the specialized sense it has in comics studies, as a splitting of the plot into images that the reader reassembles—an analysis familiar to us as *closure*.[20] But the single images are splinters of specific local systems and structures whose "breakdown"—to employ the negative meaning of the term—is irreparable, in the sense that their integrity cannot be recovered from their broken fragments. The lack of connectedness between images mirrors the disintegrating social fabric of mining communities. When Sacco does link non-narrative images in successive panels, they contain no sense of rhythm, expectation, or advance; they merely depict the same mutilated landscape from a different angle. The images don't support any motion, be it through the use of connective lines acting as "verbs" or through the depiction of unstable conditions whose impending shift or termination renders the image temporary in some way. And yet, as Elisabeth El Refaie points out, "it is the very *lack* of concrete activity that invites the reader to conjure up a sense of the passage of time, which, through the terror of meaninglessness, feels as if it will never end."[21] Indeed, Sacco's images don't emanate the fear that something awful is about to occur, but the acceptance that nothing else will happen here—ever again. The absence of action in these images fuels the *call* for action that the reportage and the illustrations want to issue. Instead of adding up to a story about entropy—which does denote a progression in the gradual loss of power or meaning—the solitary illustrations establish a subtle thematic nexus with the motif of drainage and fatigue. They don't propel an idea horizontally, as a narrative would do, across space and time; they allow it to seep down vertically, each illustration ruminative and ponderous with its own gravity and the gravitas of the situation. The fact that the drawings are always at the bottom of the page, under the writing and underneath it, as it were, confirms their role as an open pit, as the gaping mine hole into which we are asked to peer.

What's more, the single images show natural and human subjects in a state of rest. People don't move at all; mostly they stare blankly at the viewer, with resigned expressions rendered even more powerful by the knowledge that these individuals are either severely ill or heavily sedated (if not both). As these sluggish portraits demonstrate, the most chilling aspect of entropic decline in this area is psychological. Hedges writes about West Virginians who not only are out of work but avoid employment by having themselves diagnosed with mental disabilities. Many are addicted to painkillers and opiates. The state has the highest national rate of fatal drug overdoses. Hedges recounts his discussions with a group of young men who resort to prescription drugs to alleviate the depression caused by unemployment and by the utter lack of prospects, for themselves and their families. Sacco draws these men in poses that bespeak psychic atrophy without overdramatizing their affliction. His portraits of two military widows are equally subdued: their gloomy facial expressions clash with the cheery, chirpy patterns on the fabric of their clothes: flowers in bloom, dancing penguins. The outdoor equivalents of these zoned-out figures are the high-crane shots of the MTR sites. Their perspective is distant, and the rigorous detail they capture conveys the sheer drudgery of the crime being perpetrated against the mountains, together with a sense of weariness about it all—destruction and (barely existent) revolt.

It's also significant that the people we see in close-up rarely appear together. Isolated in their pain, they are unlikely to unite in a concerted response to the mining behemoth. The coal companies have managed to divide and conquer. The fact that people remain isolated from one another also aligns Sacco with a slew of American writers who found in the plight of miners the ideal peg on which to hang their disgust with what Theodore Dreiser called "giant and rapacious individualism here in America, now operating for the whim and the comfort of a few, and the debasement and defilement of the many."[22] One illustration depicts a man and his dog, both looking forlornly at the flatland left behind after the trucks have hauled the mountains away. Sacco draws this man, named Larry Gibson, atop an incline at the edge of his property and surveying the pits and rocks into which mountains have been ground, black coal seams, barren flatlands, and partly reclaimed patches unconvincingly sprinkled with topsoil that wind easily blasts away. Gibson and his dog rise above the plane of the illustration, unprotected, living substitutes for the dead forests that once carpeted these peaks. This individual might seem marginal to the broader narrative, but Sacco encapsulates in his pose the fate of many like Gibson, whose familiar rug (land, property, ownership, safety) has been pulled from under them. "The rise of large industry in the United States," Barbara Freese writes in *Coal: A Human History*, "was a stark challenge to the nation's image of itself as an egalitarian land of farmers. America, or at least those Americans most attached to the Jeffersonian ideal, celebrated the citizen-farmer as the solid foundation of representative government."[23] In the nineteenth century, the agrarian ideal was transformed by the image of the pioneer conquering the wilderness. In contemporary West Virginia the agrarian relation has become collective, anonymous, and fully mechanized. The solitary American colonizing the wilderness has given way to energy colonization.

So large are the solitary images that they bleed into the space of the page, as if they were not an image but another form of writing. When this happens, Scott McCloud explains, the open image "hemorrhages and escapes into timeless space."[24] Paradoxically, as McCloud's apt phrasing suggests, bleeding narratives both suspend time and retain a violent power. In other words, the image itself serves as a gutter, fulfilling the cryptic function reserved for this key compositional tool: both literally, as a "crypt" that collects bridging events whose "existence is known but unseen, locked away in the gap between the explicit elements of the story";[25] and formally, by creating a space of ambiguity in which the ostensible and subconscious affect invoked by the narrative can settle and grow. Indeed, the crypt/gutter is often the site that harbors unrepresentable events, violent acts too gruesome to visualize. As Roger Whitson writes:

> The events between the panels are not symbolizable, and the function of sequential art is to produce the illusion of motion through the absence of

what cannot be symbolized. The white space cuts through the consistency of the image, separating characters from each other, slicing off body parts, separating one moment from another with rivers of nothingness.[26]

In "Days of Devastation," the rivers of nothingness separate portions of the text rather than panels. Sacco uses them to almost entirely suspend the dramatic potential of braiding: the people we see appear only once—and not in the sense that the following panels stop featuring them: there simply are no following panels. Their stories are momentary and short-lived—even literally so, as the West Virginians we meet either die or expect to die. The different diegetic strands seem concurrent, but also entirely isolated from the passage of time, having reached an entropic endpoint where time no longer materializes as space, where space has withdrawn or has been violently pushed out of our field of vision, together with the detonated mountains. Importantly for my approach to this book, the disjointed illustrations cohere more with extratextual imagery (film and energy photography) than with other panels in this book or elsewhere, whether sequential or not.

"Days of Devastation" and Documentary Poetics

In the course of the twentieth century, changes in the fuel marketplace often led to the decline of capital, labor, and communities in mining areas. In particular, the rise of oil and gas as alternatives to coal left cities and counties in disarray, ravaged by poverty and demographic decline.[27] Hedges makes no bones about the drastic nature of this natural and human pillage. He curses those who initiated the destruction and those who allow it to happen, hoping they would not be spared by "the death they have unleashed."[28] Fittingly, Hedges recounts the efforts of coal companies to open up cemeteries for mining, which causes graves to sink into vast depressions beneath the earth. "The wide cracks and gaping holes that dot the landscape mark the earth collapsing in on itself,"[29] as the entire terrain drops into a deep sinkhole that doesn't engulf just cemeteries but people's nerves, health, and resolve. While deforestation shears the mountain ridges and residents abandon their homes, billions of gallons of slurry fill vast impoundments that stain the landscape with their improbable colors and spread anxiety about dam ruptures and leaks. Bill Haney's 2011 documentary *The Last Mountain* tracks the debris left behind by MTR extraction on Coal River Mountain, whose boom-and-bust cycles resulted in desolate ghost towns with long rows of abandoned houses too devalued to be sold; detritus piling up in the aftermath of floods caused by deforestation and topsoil removal; and evacuated schools at the foot of impoundment ponds prone to rupture. Several

Figure 6.1. Jenkinjones, West Virginia. Chris Hedges and Joe Sacco, *Days of Destruction, Days of Revolt* (New York: Nation, 2012), 146–47.

photographs of such depopulated towns feature in the film. The disarray and contingency of objects scattered among the ruins give off the ghostly aura of a past landscape, a past community, and past bodies dismembered and wiped away by visible blasts, invisible contaminants, and crippling dejection. Hedges and Sacco might as well be describing these documentary shots: "Joe and I see long rows of deserted and desolate structures in the twilight and long mudflats where buildings once stood.... Those who remain live amid the ruins."[30] Short-term employment and exhaustible resources, Haney's film warns, don't bode well for the future and sustainability of the region.

Hedges describes a very similar entropic environment in grisly detail:

> Rutted streets are lined by empty clapboard houses with sagging roofs. Porches fall away from the buildings. Wooden steps are rotted. Rusted appliances, the frames of old cars, tires, and heaps of garbage lie scattered in front of rows of deserted dwellings or clog the brackish water in the creeks, where low-lying branches are tangled with plastic bags and bottles.[31]

From electric appliances to plastics and discarded tires, the circuit of fossil fuel extraction and consumption has run full circle. Sacco's illustrations condense this cycle of decay in two images that capture a town in winter. The leafless trees behind the houses loom into view in compact ranks, as if to reclaim the landscape. Not a single house or vehicle is fully visible; those that remain intact are represented only partially, segmented by other unstable structures on the verge of collapse. Wooden sticks, half-covered in snow, protrude from the rubble, like grave crosses sucked in by a mining sinkhole. The neatly filled-in detail makes everything seem coated in grime. The second image adds some depth to the deserted Main Street as it winds through dilapidated housing under frail-looking wooden telephone poles whose usefulness under the circumstances isn't immediately obvious (see Figure 6.1).

Much like Haney in *The Last Mountain*, Sacco details not so much open violence (more prominently displayed in plot-driven feature films) as the rather insidious, "slow violence" perpetrated against entire communities.[32] The documentary film features interviews with residents whose neighbors perished with unsettling frequency from brain tumors and other diseases that don't routinely occur at such a rate. Also interviewed are representatives of Massey Energy, the chief mining corporation in West Virginia, who reasonably ask: Do enemies of coal begin by turning off their electricity before preaching about environmental hazard and climate offenses?

This is a key question in both "Days of Devastation" and the documentary film, because it entails identification patterns between the victims of mining practices and the reading or viewing audience. Clearly not all of us live in that war zone, but we are implicitly asked to identify with its direct victims by taking conservation measures that would reduce electricity demand and would make it less of an ineluctable fate for the mountains and their folk to endure incessant detonations. The path to empathy is now easier than it would have been one hundred years ago, because most of these people either are not involved in mining or they operate heavy machinery on the surface (rather than participating in the classic underground room-and-pillar mining). The gap between normal households and the shacks of old, in which miners used to live, would have been considerable in the days of unionization struggles; nowadays, victims are indistinguishable from regular consumers.

The closest that the two works come to a wake-up call, or to summoning our empathy, is in their morbid voyeurism as they observe and interview ailing people shortly before their demise. In film and book alike, the stories follow a similar structure: they introduce the characters and cement a certain intimacy with the audience before the subjects' lives are abruptly cut short. For instance, Neil Heizer, a gay painkiller addict, speaks over several pages of text and drawings about his recent brush with death following an overdose. Then Hedges tersely reports that "Heizer, seven weeks later, dies of a drug overdose, sitting on the living room couch in front of the big screen television."[33] Like Heizer and other residents of these coal communities, all of us, at a symbolic level, run the risk of a deadly overdose: of energy overuse, moral apathy, and the excessive ingestion of pollutants. Such toxicity is now claiming lives in Appalachia but soon enough, if the already poorly regulated mining bonanza goes out of control, it will extend far beyond the mountains of West Virginia. Returning to a time when violence among and around mining communities was more widespread than it is today, John Sayles's 1987 film *Matewan* doesn't shy away from showing us the high body count of victims in the mining wars, of which *The Last Mountain* and "Days of Devastation" are only a sketchy—albeit moving—thumbnail.

Between a Rock and a Hard Place: Comics and Miner Movies

Hedges explicitly evokes the struggle of miners to unionize through civil uprising and armed insurgency when he mentions the rebellions at Blair Mountain in 1921 and Matewan in 1920. It was the Ludlow Massacre of 1914—when striking coal miners were attacked by the Colorado National Guard and twenty-six were killed, women and children among them—that "exemplified the vulnerability of American workers to corporate rapacity, and the necessity of government safeguards to ensure working people's right to organize in defense of their lives and liberties."[34] Ludlow inspired works by Upton Sinclair, Woody Guthrie, George McGovern, and more recently parts of Thomas Pynchon's novel *Against the Day*. Yet visual renditions of miner strikes remain few and far between. Films that do recount miner strikes leave little doubt about the primacy of human interests over environmental concerns. In *North Country* (2005, dir. Niki Caro), mineworker Josey Aimes (Charlize Theron) stands up against sexist male coworkers and a community that turns a blind eye to domestic and workplace violence. Eventually, she succeeds in filing the first class-action sexual harassment suit in America (this account is based on the 1988 landmark case *Lois E. Jenson v. Eveleth Taconite Co.*). While there are breathtaking aerial shots of the steel mines of Minnesota, whose violent impact on the landscape sustains the film's focus on sexual abuse, it's the cruelty against the female body, rather than any abuse against nature, that holds our interest in this film. Similarly, *Harlan County War* (2000, dir. Tony Bill) features a dressed-down Holly Hunter speaking in a thick Kentucky accent as she bites her way through family bereavement (her father dies of black lung disease), poverty, and humiliation to rally the women of her mining community on the picket line alongside their husbands, until the mineworkers join UMWA (United Mine Workers of America) and their requests are met. This is a rare success story where, again, a woman embodies the vulnerability of the entire community. If nature is present at all, it is because Hunter's Ruby Kincaid is herself a force of nature: an inspiring leader, often seen in her garden or collecting rainwater and cavorting along railroad tracks. She doesn't simply resist the abuse of corporate greed, she implicitly stands up to the juggernaut of industrialization, which is making inroads into a world that the film idealizes in pastoral hues of twilight blue and ripe green, setting it against the darkness of the coalmines, of which we get only fleeting glimpses.

Oddly, even though independent filmmaker and novelist John Sayles, like Sacco, has always been attracted to the dramas of collective life, his film *Matewan* doesn't separate wilderness from corporate incursion as much as these other films do. *Matewan* portrays in grim, oppressive detail the substandard conditions miners were forced to live in. But Sayles's miners join forces with the wilderness to defy and even kill company men who try to evict them from their homes and to claim their belongings. Joe Kenehan (Chris Cooper) and Few Clothes (James Earl Jones), among others, respond with what they regard as "the law of nature," the only law they bow to—and one that inevitably ends in violence. Miners whose land has been stolen by the company retreat to the woods and resurface to fight the harassing company minions like "genuine hill people," armed to the teeth and carrying rifles passed down by forefathers who fought in the Civil War. A few key scenes (including the famous Matewan massacre) occur on the town's railroad track outside the station; the contrast between Ruby's diplomatic efforts and the bereaved mother who shoots endless loads into a dead company man—the man who murdered her son—could hardly be greater.

Sacco fuses the nature/industry contrast typical of miner films with the union of industry workers and landscape preferred by Sayles. In his illustrations, wilderness is at home on Main Street; it has recaptured some of what was lost when corporations came to town. This isn't simply nature, but a wild reversion to the beginning, a nature folding back into itself. Sacco shifts the focus from labor exploitation, effectively captured and castigated in various films, to natural and human devastation. He does so by switching between aerial views of the ruins left behind by the energy industry to close-ups of people coated in coal dust and choked by a sense of sorrowful powerlessness. Despite being obviously in awe of the environmental degradation, Sacco remains alive to the buoyancy of the human stories behind the landscapes, which prevents his drawings from sinking entirely into disillusion. Importantly, the panel sequences add to Hedges's report actual, authentic dialogue with the people whose lives the text describes. In Sacco's panels, these people are given a voice, or maybe I should say they assume a voice—because Sacco doesn't intercede as a filter—that allows them to speak for themselves. The restraint in his contribution to this book has a lot to do with his desire to record rather than process what Kathleen Stewart calls "just talk—talk that rises to the surface to overwhelm the merely referential with a rush of poetic forms and the living phantasm of a sociality embedded in remembered drama"[35]—remembered not by Sacco but by the protagonists themselves.

Comics and Eco-Photography

Sacco's drawing of the Alpheus Preparation Plant, once a thriving structure, projects a notable listlessness (see Figure 6.2). The feed belt conveyor is visible; and, even though we cannot see whether or not it is moving, we do notice that the upper end is engulfed by vegetation that wasn't meant to be there, but worked its way up during a long period of disuse. Leakage of some description streaks the earth. The railroad tracks, so essential to representations of coal-mining areas in film, are overgrown with weeds. The stub of one building and the crumbling edges of another frame the image, ironically recalling the structured efficiency of the now dilapidated coal handling plant. The image wouldn't draw special attention if it didn't look almost identical to hundreds of images taken by the German photographers Bernd and Hilla Becher at former mining sites in the US.[36] Many of Sacco's single illustrations in this book recall photographic representations of mining sites and deserve to be placed and read in this broader tradition.

The most striking aspect of *Colstrip, Montana* (2010)—Rick Bass and David T. Hanson's definitive photo book, which collects Hanson's images taken in the early 1980s in and around a coal-mining town—is the flatness of the area. The stark, straight horizon line separates the ruins in the foreground from the tipples of the coal plants looming in the background. Hanson pictures the same abandoned mines and houses, the same stripped land, smoke-enveloped coal plants, and waste ponds that not only Sacco but a number of photographers, from Emmet Gowin to Edward Burtynsky, have captured from high vantage points. Hanson's colors are rich, ripe, and above all dynamic. The sites are just as abandoned and quiet as Sacco's, but their colors throb with energy. Much like Sayles, who rejects the "diffuse golden cream" of many period films whose "gauziness would rob the images in *Matewan* of their solidity,"[37] Sacco emphasizes the tangibility and weight of machinery with sharp, spare lines. Taken together, his illustrations display a weary monotony; individually, they seem flat and inert. Nothing happens down there, certainly nothing that can be glimpsed (in sublime color) from high above. Even where the landscape is striated by mounds of overburden, the soil irregularities are strangely well-structured and carefully aligned. But the order seems intrinsic rather than imposed from the outside (indeed, there is no outside to these images; the plateaus they depict engulf the entire space of the image). Like Deleuze and Guattari's plateaus, they designate regions of intensity that don't point toward an external point of culmination.[38] What would give meaning to these images is the act of consumption toward which the mining processes are ultimately geared, but the pictures remain fragmentary.

Figure 6.2. The remnants of the Alpheus Preparation Plant, once the largest coal-cleaning facility in the world. Chris Hedges and Joe Sacco, *Days of Destruction, Days of Revolt* (New York: Nation, 2012), 131.

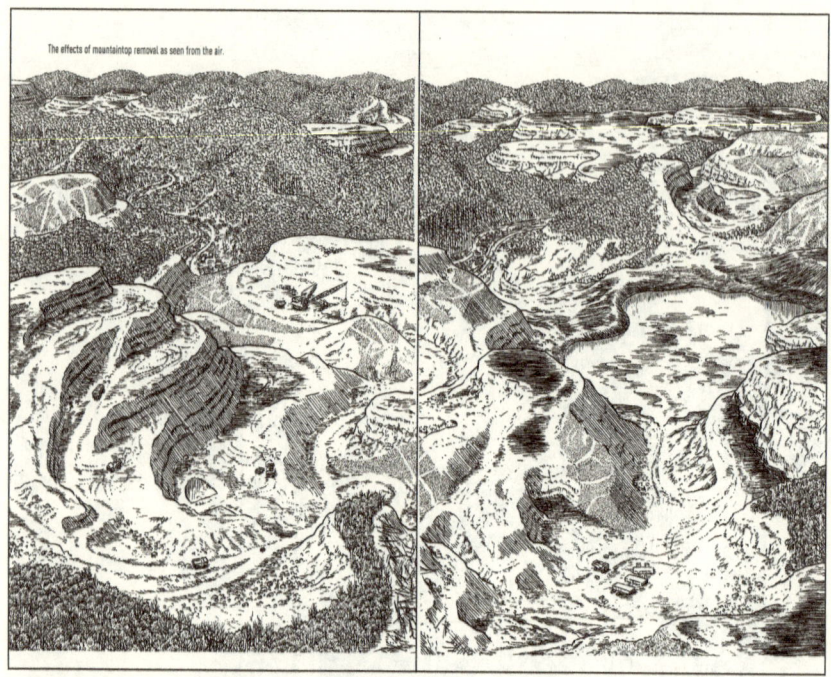

Figure 6.3. The effects of mountaintop removal as seen from the air. Chris Hedges and Joe Sacco, *Days of Destruction, Days of Revolt* (New York: Nation, 2012), 126–27.

One image in particular, spread over two pages, distills Sacco's photographic aesthetic (see Figure 6.3). Construction vehicles, draglines, coal haulers: it's unusual to see comics function on such a molecular level, especially in such inanimate detail—unlike, for instance, the much livelier and densely populated battlefield sequences in Sacco's other works. Certainly even those cluttered series—usually large, painstakingly crafted canvases of bloodshed as in *The Great War*[39]—occasionally included empty silent panels in which abandoned buildings or devastated cities testified to the failure of language and art to make sense of, or to give a voice to, violence and destruction.[40] Hedges himself draws attention to the parallels between mining areas and war zones seen from above:

> It was impossible to grasp the level of destruction in the war in Bosnia until you got in a helicopter and flew over the landscape, seeing village after village dynamited by advancing Serb forces into ruins. The same scale of destruction, and the same problem in realizing its true extent, holds true for West Virginia and Kentucky.[41]

The remains of houses, eviscerated buildings stripped of piping, and flat-roofed churches whose domes were stolen by crane-operating thieves "give the landscape the feel of a ravaged war zone."[42] In the aftermath of MTR, despite the silhouettes of monster trucks among piles of overburden, a post-apocalyptic landscape emerges that heralds the extermination of the human race. The destruction, as Hedges's use of the term *landscape* suggests, is also ecological.

Certainly animation, from *Bambi*'s forest fire to *WALL-E*'s garbage-strewn planet, has evinced a keen interest in nature as a realm of enchantment and cruelty, sensorial pleasure and pestilence. There is, however, very little in the way of environmental comics, and in Sacco's illustration we can see why.[43] The image almost doesn't work visually; indeed, it almost diminishes the chaos, because it simply lacks the definition of a photograph, the saturation of toxic colors, and the kind of earthy texture that makes photographs of such sites so magnetic and memorable. Sacco's unadorned, black-and-white drawing nonetheless succeeds—with simple dots and alternating straight lines and curlicues—in projecting a sublimity that breaks with conventional comics sequence and narration. Sacco abandons the strict temporality of comics to produce an image that seems both exhausted and inexhaustible. We cannot recognize much of what Hedges describes in detail—"weirdly-colored pools of water on the mine sites,"[44] for example, which we have already seen in aerial photos of extraction sites. This obliqueness is also a part of Sacco's effort to reproduce not a faithful image of reality but a "blasted moonscape"[45]—in other words, to use a fragmentary, corrosive visual language to convey the crumbling effect of strip mining on the land. The image doesn't draw the viewer in; there is little beauty in it (unlike, say, in Burtynsky's photographs, which are often reviled for their glamorizing aesthetics). It seeks to puzzle and alienate. Above all, it seems consumed by its own powerlessness—aesthetic and political—the kind of powerlessness induced by the sight of a long-lost paradise, stitched together from leftover sticks of a drawing rather than forming a comics tableau of operatic proportions. Sacco's lines have always been simple, but here their simplicity appears especially fitting because it delivers an effective antidote to the lavish photographic tradition of postindustrial energy landscapes.

Epilogue: Friends of Coal

Sacco and Hedges don't simply indulge in a nostalgic rehearsal of homilies about the brutal effects of mining on land and people. The socioeconomic and psychological entropy they delineate belies the notion that coal is cheap energy, forcing us to face the true ecological and human cost of extracting it.

Nothing can better rectify the illusion of long-term availability and sensible pragmatism that permeates coal rhetoric than the stark image of the drain and death that extraction leaves behind. To invoke Kathleen Stewart again, Sacco proves how a "low point in action could become the high point of cultural practice."[46] He does so by thrusting the audience out of the narrative and into "a scene that palpitates with vulnerability" due to its static composition, which makes its vulnerability even more insistent and contagious.[47] One could argue that any form of expression will do to make this point, but an amalgamation of verbal and visual means can impress especially well how the cost of extraction is externalized onto the land and the community: in the face of blasted mountains and uncontrollable levels of contamination and waste, neither words nor images are effective in themselves. One thing that doesn't give in to the entropic collapse of mountain ranges and of collective resolution is the resilience and creativity of the individual imagination.

As we learn in *The Last Mountain*, Joe Manchin, former West Virginia governor (and current senator), once introduced himself to a corporate audience as "a friend of coal." As Hedges mentions and is in fact well known, coal supplies the energy for half the nation's electricity, and about 70 percent of this coal is obtained by strip mining and MTR. Hedges and Sacco take us some way—though by no means all the way—toward wondering whether we, as consumers, should count as the most influential and destructive "friends of coal." Mountains are not destroyed "to make a few people rich,"[48] even though this income gap and class conflict between oppressed miners and greedy coal mongers may have been valid one hundred years ago. In our time, mountains are destroyed to make many people a little richer. The responsibility percolates much further than it did when miners took to their arms, which is why it is almost impossible for them to resort to the same measures today. The enemy is ubiquitous, the enemy is us. Sacco's drawings address us all, even though what these miners or descendants of miners consume (black grit and noxious coal dust) kills them, in stark contrast to the energy we ourselves consume to fuel our comfort and peace of mind. If Sacco's work elsewhere requires visual empathy with the victims of distant violence, here we need only identify with ourselves. But it is no less of a leap, a confession, an admission of duty and cowardice.

NOTES

1. Contributors to the pioneer muckraking *McClure's Magazine* often focused on labor conditions in the coal mine and oil industry. Precursors of the muckraking genre, among them Stephen Crane ("In the Depths of a Coal Mine," *McClure's*, August 1894) and Henry Demarest Lloyd

(*Wealth against Commonwealth*, New York: Harper and Brothers, 1894), along with self-identified muckrakers such as Upton Sinclair with his *King Coal* (New York: The Macmillan Company, 1917), Ida Tarbell with her "The Rise of the Standard Oil Company" (serialized in *McClure's*, 1902–1904), or Ray Stannard Baker with his seminal coal mine investigation "The Right to Work: The Story of the Non-Striking Miners" (*McClure's*, January 1903) exposed a wide range of social and public policy concerns that set investigative standards and still influence the work of journalists and activists today.

2. Christopher P. Wilson, *The Labor of Words: Literary Professionalism in the Progressive Era* (Athens: University of Georgia Press, 1985), xi.

3. Cecilia Tichi, *Exposés and Excess: Muckraking in America, 1900–2000* (Philadelphia: University of Pennsylvania Press, 2004), 12.

4. I am not the first to draw this comparison: "I imagine a resemblance, too, between these doubly occupied American places and the countless other tensely occupied places in other parts of the world like the Palestinian home deep in the heart of Israel." Kathleen Stewart, *A Space on the Side of the Road: Cultural Poetics in an "Other" America* (Princeton: Princeton University Press, 1996), 42.

5. Stewart, *A Space on the Side of the Road*, 3.

6. Ibid.

7. Ibid., 4.

8. Chris Hedges and Joe Sacco, *Days of Destruction, Days of Revolt* (New York: Nation, 2012), 150.

9. Ibid., 87.

10. On the controversy over and resistance to MTR, especially in the larger context of opposition to strip coal operators, see Chad Montrie, *To Save the Land and People: A History of Opposition to Surface Coal Mining in Appalachia* (Chapel Hill: University of North Carolina Press, 2003), 197–200; and Rebecca R. Scott, *Removing Mountains: Extracting Nature and Identity in the Appalachian Coalfields* (Minneapolis: University of Minnesota Press, 2010).

11. Rick Bass, "East of Billings," in Rick Bass and David T. Hanson, *Colstrip, Montana* (Fairfield: Taverner Press, 2010), n.p.

12. All three examples are taken from Erik Reece, *Lost Mountain: A Year in the Vanishing Wilderness: Radical Strip Mining and the Devastation of Appalachia* (New York: Riverhead, 2006), 17–18, 24.

13. Harry Caudill, *Night Comes to the Cumberlands: A Biography of a Depressed Area* (Boston: Little, Brown, 1963).

14. Ibid., 152.

15. Dwight B. Billings and Kathleen M. Blee, *The Road to Poverty: The Making of Wealth and Hardship in Appalachia* (Cambridge: Cambridge University Press, 2000), 13.

16. Jed Rubenfeld and Amy Chua, *The Triple Package: How Three Unlikely Traits Explain the Rise and Fall of Cultural Groups in America* (New York: Penguin, 2014). For the most influential

discussion of this issue, see Helen Lewis, "Fatalism or the Coal Industry?" *Mountain Life and Work* 46.11 (1970), 4–15.

17. On stasis and wordless panels in *Jimmy Corrigan*, see Georgiana Banita, "Chris Ware and the Pursuit of Slowness," in *The Comics of Chris Ware: Drawing Is a Way of Thinking*, eds. David M. Ball and Martha B. Kuhlman (Jackson: University Press of Mississippi, 2010): 177–90.

18. Steve Duin and Shannon Wheeler, *Oil and Water* (Seattle: Fantagraphics, 2011). Another comics work that includes a fossil fuel narrative is Rich Tommaso, *The Cavalier Mr. Thompson (A Sam Hill Novel): Sam's Early Days: 1924* (Seattle: Fantagraphics, 2012). As the title suggests, this graphic novel features the 1920s' oil boom (and the exploitative labor conditions it fostered), viewed through the lens of genre fiction—in this case, a kind of *noir* dime novel of a Texas brimming with swindlers and wildcatters.

19. Mumia Abu-Jamal, "Introduction: Joy Amidst 'Disaster . . . ,'" in Seth Tobocman, *Disaster and Resistance: Comics and Landscapes for the Twenty First Century* (Oakland: AK Press, 2008), 1.

20. On the complementary relationship between breakdown and closure, see Charles Hatfield, *Alternative Comics: An Emerging Literature* (Jackson: University Press of Mississippi, 2005), 41.

21. Elisabeth El Refaie, *Autobiographical Comics: Life Writing in Pictures* (Jackson: University Press of Mississippi, 2012), 119.

22. Theodore Dreiser, "Introduction," in *Harlan Miners Speak: Report on Terrorism in the Kentucky Coal Fields*, ed. Theodore Dreiser et al. (Lexington: University Press of Kentucky, 2008), 16.

23. Barbara Freese, *Coal: A Human History* (London: Heinemann, 2005), 127.

24. Scott McCloud, *Understanding Comics: The Invisible Art* (New York: HarperPerennial, 1993), 103.

25. Julia Round, *Gothic in Comics and Graphic Novels: A Critical Approach* (Jefferson, NC: McFarland, 2014), 58.

26. Roger Whitson, "Panelling Parallax: The Fearful Symmetry of Alan Moore and William Blake," *ImageTexT: Interdisciplinary Comics Studies* 3.2 (2007), §15. Other critics have referred to motionless comic panels outside a diegetic sequence as "tableaux" and linked them directly to the motif of death. See Mario Gomes and Jan Peuckert, "Memento Mori: A Portuguese Style of Melancholy," in *Comics as a Nexus of Cultures: Essays on the Interplay of Media, Disciplines and International Perspectives*, eds. Mark Berninger, Jochen Ecke, Gideon Haberkorn, and Donald E. Palumbo (Jefferson, NC: McFarland, 2010), 116–26. In Sacco's mining strips, death isn't just a symbol. A panel shows a coal truck heaving into view around a sharp turn in a mountain road, forcing a smaller vehicle only inches from the shoulder as it hurtles by. This is by no means an exceptional sight: coal truck accidents occur frequently and often result in fatalities when the trucks cannot slow down in time and smaller cars get crunched. See Michael Shnayerson, *Coal River* (New York: Farrar, Straus and Giroux, 2008), 5.

27. The economic collapse and social disintegration of the anthracite region of northeastern Pennsylvania is an example of this; see Thomas Dublin and Walter Licht, *The Face of Decline: The Pennsylvania Anthracite Region in the Twentieth Century* (Ithaca: Cornell University Press, 2005), 3–4. Literature about coal mining consequently portrays a world that suppresses resistance and

the hope for a better future among people whose "lives are regulated by economic determinants that . . . corral generations of such miners by the fatalistic attitudes that have been fashioned for them." Tom Frazier, "Coal Mining, Literature, and the Naturalistic Motif: An Overview," in *Caverns of Night: Coal Mines in Art, Literature, and Film*, ed. William B. Thesing (Columbia: University of South Carolina Press, 2000), 201.

28. Hedges and Sacco, *Days of Destruction*, 130.

29. Ibid., 119.

30. Frazier, "Coal Mining," 145.

31. Hedges and Sacco, *Days of Destruction*, 132.

32. I am borrowing the term from Rob Nixon, *Slow Violence and the Environmentalism of the Poor* (Cambridge: Harvard University Press, 2011).

33. Hedges and Sacco, *Days of Destruction*, 158.

34. Thomas G. Andrews, *Killing for Coal: America's Deadliest Labor War* (Cambridge: Harvard University Press, 2008), 7.

35. Stewart, *A Space on the Side of the Road*, 31.

36. See especially Bernd Becher and Hilla Becher, *Coal Mines and Steel Mills* (Munich: Schirmer/Mosel Verlag, 2010).

37. John Sayles, *Thinking in Pictures: The Making of the Movie* Matewan (Cambridge: Da Capo Press, 2003), 57.

38. Deleuze is always subliminally present in discussions of Sacco's inertial work in this book. His panels echo what Deleuze, in his analysis of cinema, called *the time image*, in which nothing happens at the narrative level but a lot is going on in terms of perception and style, decoupling the experience of time from an external trajectory and latching it on to subjective consciousness. A careful application of Deleuze's "movement image" and "time image" cinematic taxonomies to comics and animation remains to be undertaken. At least one critic, using Chris Ware as an example, has taken an interest in such a project. See Scott Bukatman, *The Poetics of Slumberland: Animated Spirits and the Animating Spirit* (Berkeley: University of California Press, 2012), 93.

39. Joe Sacco, Adam Hochschild, and Chin-Yee Lai, *The Great War: July 1, 1916: The First Day of the Battle of the Somme: An Illustrated Panorama* (New York: W. W. Norton, 2013).

40. On the political significance of silence in Sacco's wordless panels, see Georgiana Banita, "Cosmopolitan Suspicion: Comics Journalism and Graphic Silence," in *Transnational Perspectives on Graphic Narratives: Comics at the Crossroads*, eds. Shane Denson, Christina Meyer, and Daniel Stein (New York: Bloomsbury, 2013), 49–65.

41. Hedges and Sacco, *Days of Destruction*, 130.

42. Ibid., 132.

43. A remarkable exception is Paul Chadwick, *Concrete*, Volume 5: *Think like a Mountain* (Milwaukie: Dark Horse, 2006). This unique book not only criticizes the oil business and its impact on the environment, but also encourages us to experience nature more viscerally and thus to be less removed from its destruction. As human fingers and tree roots merge underneath the ground, we read: "Do soil minerals have a taste? Would there be a heightening, a swelling, after a soaking rain?"

(124). The title is misleading: although Chadwick seems to propose a non-anthropocentric approach to environmental ethics, his work relies on human figures who absorb ecological violence, and thus also the interest of ecological care and preservation. I would also argue that it would be difficult to create a comic work without an anthropocentric element, simply because it seems unimaginable to predicate a comic narrative on a nonhuman (and entirely nonhumanoid) central consciousness. For an analysis of Chadwick's environmental vision, see Kevin de Laplante, "Making the Abstract Concrete: How a Comic Can Bring to Life the Central Problems of Environmental Philosophy," in *Comics as Philosophy*, ed. Jeff McLaughlin (Jackson: University Press of Mississippi, 2005), 153–72.

44. Hedges and Sacco, *Days of Destruction*, 125.
45. Ibid., 128.
46. Stewart, *A Space on the Side of the Road*, 34.
47. Ibid., 37.
48. Hedges and Sacco, *Days of Destruction*, 175.

7. The Politics of Space in Joe Sacco's Representations of the Appalachian Coalfields

Richard Todd Stafford

In *Days of Destruction, Days of Revolt*, Joe Sacco collaborates with journalist Chris Hedges to explore and expose conditions of extreme poverty, political marginalization, and ecological destruction in communities across the United States. Hedges and Sacco describe these conditions in terms of a proliferation of "sacrifice zones."[1] A "sacrifice zone," as the concept is used in the book, is an area that has been set aside as an exception to democratic expectations of economic, ecological, and social protection, generally subordinating the well-being of residents and their environment to capitalist imperatives. By making these sacrifice zones visible, Hedges and Sacco generate counter-publicity for issues that are typically set beyond the pale of political discourse or deliberation. But it is clear that the goal is not merely descriptive or an attempt at consciousness-raising for its own sake. By tracing out geographically distinct locations in which similar patterns of intolerable conditions have emerged—and by highlighting the moments of resistance within each community—Hedges and Sacco encourage a sense of solidarity among politically engaged readers, especially those who may be in structurally similar positions of economic or political marginalization. Quite explicitly, Hedges and Sacco call on the reader to act alongside the subjects represented in their account to address the underlying causes that limit access to the institutional apparatus of the state, lead to disparities in socioeconomic status and political power, and entail environmental destruction and abuses of civil liberties.

Describing these areas as sacrifice *zones* focuses their intervention on a dimension of political engagement that has long been seen as problematic: the relationships between *a territory* (or *the land*) and *a people* (or *the folk*). On the one hand, conceptualizing political action in terms of localism, bioregionalism, or nationalism has ideological, practical, and organizational functions for those opposed to currently dominant economic and political formations; on the other hand, the left is (and should be) haunted by Romantic nationalisms which strategically asserted relationships between a land and a people, but underwrote the advancement of political and economic processes that worked against egalitarian aims.² Even so, in political struggles marked by geographically differential environmental, economic, and public health impacts, the problem of *the territory* emerges with force and cannot be ignored. Departing from this observation that the "sacrifice zone" trope brings these questions of space and collective action into the foreground, this exploration seeks to translate vexing questions about the political and ethical potential of comics' advocacy into questions about how space is constructed, performed, and complicated by Sacco's illustrations of Central Appalachia. In brief, *Days of Destruction, Days of Revolt* explicitly treats the impacts of the coal industry as an often unnoticed, but particularly egregious consequence of uneven development; anticipating the reading process, Sacco implicitly entangles this uneven development of space with the problematic relationship between his audience and the geographically distant subjects of his illustrations.³ The question underlying this inquiry, then, is how Sacco's illustrations address an audience in order to generate the conditions of possibility for subsequent political action.

Though much of the analysis I perform here could be repurposed to read Hedges and Sacco's examination of other sacrifice zones, this chapter focuses specifically on Sacco's representations of coal mining. Given this, it will be helpful to begin with a very brief account of the contemporary political and economic developments that come to bear on the text, as the salience of Hedges and Sacco's provocations will be much more obvious with this context. While the painful effects of poor employment prospects, the immiseration of many of the region's residents, and the long-term environmental and public health legacy of the coal-mining industry described in Hedges and Sacco's chapter on Appalachia will likely persist for some time, it appears that mining may cease being a profitable regional industry in the foreseeable future.⁴ This industry has defined the culture and economy of the region since before the turn of the twentieth century, but has begun to exhaust access to economically recoverable coal, with larger mines in the Powder River Basin and abroad becoming increasingly competitive suppliers for the international market.⁵ Meanwhile, domestic electricity generation has begun to shift towards natural gas as a fuel source.⁶ Consequently, the current historical conjuncture calls on both the region and the nation to answer several related questions: What kind of infrastructural, economic, environmental, and cultural residues of the formerly dominant industry will structure future developments? And, as the energy industry moves to other regions and/or fuel sources, what tactics on the ground will help constitute a new economic and cultural order? Against what new strategies of accumulation and political power will they be posed? And, how does the desire to shape a new order enact, complicate, or resist the articulations between "the people" and "the land" that emerged under the long reign of "King Coal"? These are the kinds of questions that provide background for Hedges and Sacco's chapter on the Appalachian coal industry.

Reading Sacco's illustrations against this background, this chapter first examines how the impacts of the coal industry are deployed to frame the Appalachian landscape as a problem to be addressed through the generation of "new geographies of solidarity" which might enable collective political agency, even at a distance: the Appalachian landscape is treated not just as a site for intervention by the resisting agents introduced in the text, but as an occasion for political intervention by the distant reader.[7] Following this examination of the Sacco's landscapes, this analysis turns to the agents that populate this terrain, examining the ways that Sacco's portraits help to generate the conditions of possibility for ethical and political engagements alongside or on the behalf of Appalachian communities. This essay unpacks the narrative techniques Sacco uses to link landscapes and their residents, making visible stories typically left at the periphery of mainstream political discourses that have accepted the logic of the "sacrifice zone."

Sacrificial Landscapes from Above and Below

One characteristic shared by "sacrifice zones" and exemplified by the coal-mining regions of the Central Appalachian Basin is that they are constructed as "other" places. These "other" places are positioned conceptually as outside of the spatial regime of a national imaginary that ostensibly offers political protections against wholesale destruction to all within its borders. Frequently, such sacrifice zones are referred to as "internal colonies" to mark the way that they are positioned as "elsewhere" and "subject to" even as they fall within the national borders.[8] Outside of the immediate experience of locals, such spaces are constructed in terms of an exclusion from community consensus about what locations can be considered or spoken for within political discourse. Given the way that this positions the sacrifice zone as a kind of absence within political "common sense," it is significant that Sacco opens his contributions to the chapter on West Virginia with the comics equivalent of the establishing shot (see Figure 7.1). In this image, we view the site of an active mountain-top-removal mine alongside the gaze of Larry Gibson, a local opposed to the practice, to whom we have been introduced in Hedges's prose leading up to this illustration. Gibson's visage is provided in profile, gazing over a bluff at the manufactured landscape below, while his dog gazes across this scene of destruction at his side. On these side-by-side pages, Sacco's work illustrates the unfolding narrative provided by Hedges; indeed, the majority of the text above the illustration serves as a quasi-word balloon: it is mostly direct quo-

Figure 7.1. Larry Gibson surveys mountains shaved for coal near his property. Chris Hedges and Joe Sacco, *Days of Destruction, Days of Revolt* (New York: Nation, 2012), 122–23.

tation from Gibson. In this passage, Gibson explicitly calls for revolutionary action with a paraphrase from Thomas Jefferson; while Hedges often positions himself as an advocate for nonviolent revolutionary action, here he leaves his position as a sort of lacuna within the text, allowing Gibson to speak for himself.[9] There is something undoubtedly incongruous and unsettling about the juxtaposition of Gibson's appearance in the illustration and his call to violent action. This tension encourages a certain kind of distant or almost voyeuristic relationship to the text. Even so, as readers, we gaze across the landscape *with* Larry; though we may not agree with his prescription, our literal visual position is "at his side." As readers, we are positioned as Hedges and Sacco may have been; the presentation of Gibson's words positions us as an audience to a direct address, but in the illustration, our gaze directed outward at a devastated landscape. This juxtaposition of direct address and indirect gaze links Gibson's political call-to-action to a precise place that is already marked by a kind of violence.

Given the translation of politically charged relationships into questions about the perception of space that I am attempting to perform here, it is important to note a crucial problem with assessing scale in this illustration. Seen in-person, a mountaintop-removal site is of almost unimaginable vastness, but in this image, the sense of scale is difficult to establish. Gibson and his dog fill the foreground on the right-hand page, while the mountaintop-removal site is positioned at a considerable distance in the background on the left. The image thus offers a reversal of a more familiar or generic way of representing distant natural spaces—photographs taken by tourists in national parks and forests. In such photographs, the gaze of the camera captures a friend or family member in profile as they stand on an overlook; such snapshots ordinarily attempt (and fail) to capture some scene of the natural sublime by positioning it at a distance as an object of contemplation and appreciation. These snapshots, as I am reading them here, are a kind of performance of the impossibility of capturing the natural sublime, constructing it as an excess that evades photographic representation. Little of the lived experience translates from the scene of photography to the photograph itself, other than the human image framed within, for which the intended subject of the photograph becomes mere background. In Sacco's illustration of Gibson at Kayford Mountain, rather than the natural sublime at the foot of a waterfall or at a mountain overlook, we are presented with a kind of capitalist sublime—an incomprehensible and almost unrepresentable destruction that seems to be the intended subject of the illustration, but which appears paradoxically primarily as a background for the human agent that appears at the image's edge. Where national parks are geographically cordoned off as special sites where those whose everyday lives are "outside" of nature can cultivate a relationship to the natural sublime, the Appalachian sacrifice zone is likewise cordoned off as "outside" of the everyday. Indeed, mountaintop-removal sites are exceedingly difficult to see, since they are typically remote and rarely visible from public roads. Gibson, then, is making visible to Sacco a relationship to the capitalist sublime that is not available within the everyday experience of most readers. In turn, Sacco is attempting to transport this relation to the capitalist sublime to his readers through the illustration. But, just as the natural sublime exceeds the technologies of representation through which tourists attempt to capture it, Sacco's illustration makes visible the way that Gibson's relationship to the capitalist sublime exceeds the limits of representation.

In the next movement of Hedges's prose, the problem of representing or even sensing the scale of these mountaintop-removal sites becomes an explicit issue. In this portion of the narrative, Hedges and Sacco fly in a small private airplane over active mountaintop-removal sites and waste ponds. In Sacco's illustration of this flyover, the breathtaking destruction is obvious (see Figure 6.3), but again, the scale is not: one of Hedges and Sacco's guides is quoted to underscore this point. Speaking about the huge dragline equipment, loaders, and dump trucks that appear like dots in this moonscape, she says: "Your eye tricks you from up here . . . Those are some of the largest machines on earth. They have twelve-foot tires."[10] In an equally difficult-to-visualize passage, Hedges says that the dragline "can fill the back of a truck with sixty tons of bituminous coal rock in a few minutes."¹¹ Hedges's descriptions frame the scale of ecological destruction represented in Sacco's illustrations, while implicitly linking the extreme poverty in the region to the increasing mechanization of the industry, which has in recent decades transitioned from mostly labor-intensive deep mining and small-scale surface mines towards increasingly vast mountaintop-removal mines.¹² Even so, as readers, it remains extremely difficult to imagine the relationship between sixty tons of coal and Sacco's representations of the devastated landscapes. Rather than pointing to a shortcoming in the text however, this draws attention to the fundamental difficulties involved in making this sacrifice zone visible as a topic for debate within political discourse. Neither Hedges's words nor Sacco's landscape illustrations are adequate to the task.

A strong suspicion towards this kind of symbolic realism-from-above has been influential in both the visual culture and critical cultural geography literature. In Michel de Certeau's poststructuralist account of "walking in the city," knowledge generated by the "strategic" overhead view is associated with managerial power and its instantiation in built space, while the lived space of those whose everyday lives are thus structured is understood as the site of "tactical" resistance.¹³ Similarly, in the humanist Marxism of Henri Lefebvre, space is understood as a production of particular economic and power relations.¹⁴ For Lefebvre, like de Certeau, symbolic "spaces of representation" are associated with a managerial or instrumental production of space. Lefebvre suggests that these official "spaces of representation" tend to neglect or collapse the diversity of lived spaces and their cognitive correlates. In the visual culture literature, scholars like John Tagg have suggested that realism is fundamentally conservative, that it in some sense always serves the state or the power bloc, especially insofar as it contributes to the panoptic knowledge of a disciplinary society.¹⁵ Postmodern theorist Jean-Francois Lyotard has argued that realist aesthetics are fundamentally conservative insofar as they reproduce and normalize actuality while neglecting potentiality.¹⁶ Likewise, the aesthetics advanced by philosopher Jacques Rancière offers a strikingly suspicious account that contrasts the representative regime of art and characteristic strategies of mimesis and realism to the aesthetic regime, which enables potentially liberatory disruptions to the "distribution of the sensible."¹⁷

But here, realism serves as a sort of revelation: West Virginia is a distant site for many of Sacco's readers. There is little potential for mobilizing this kind of realism-from-above as a kind of managerial gaze in the service of capitalist power; instead, these moments of realism offer a necessary corrective. On the one hand, these images are an attempt to make visible conditions that are occluded from the perspective of those who consume electricity generated from the coal mined at such sites. On the other hand, to the extent that the juxtaposition of Hedges's text and Sacco's illustrations draw attention to the failure of the representational arts in the face of the capitalist sublime, this is a realism that highlights the limited knowledge that most readers will bring to the text. Rather than a mode of conservative realism that accepts things as they are, duplicating the managerial perspective that positions the region as a "sacrifice zone," this is a realism that acknowledges its own limitations and draws attention to the politically significant gap between representation and experience. Since seeing the destruction of a mountaintop-removal site is excluded from possibility for most readers by legal and geographical mechanisms, public understanding of the relationships between economic (and geographical) privilege and cheap electrical power cannot, without such interventions as these, adequately consider mountaintop removal. As a realism that knows its own limits, it marks itself very clearly with its inadequacy in relation to what I have called the "capitalist sublime": a scale of destruction that escapes the possibilities of visual representation.

From here, however, Sacco scales down his representations to more human dimensions, symbolizing precisely the kind of anthropological perspective that de Certeau, Lefebvre, and the like suggest is flattened or occluded by a managerial realist representation "from above." In the illustration following the flyover view, Sacco shows the stakes of unsustainable industry: eventually, the coal companies will be done in the region (see Figure 6.2). According to many estimates, the coal industry will begin to exhaust economically recoverable coal within the next three decades[18]—and will leave behind a legacy of abandoned sites. In Figure 6.2, despite the Alpheus Preparation Plant's formerly superlative status, it is markedly dwarfed by the scale of the landscapes to which we have been just attending. We look on this facility from a dirt path or road. In the background, we see the thin coverage of grasses, scrub, and/or small trees that passes for reclamation under the Surface Mining Control and Reclamation Act of 1977.[19] The landscape appears completely evacuated of human agents. The rendering of this evacuated space contrasts detailed and orderly crosshatching with more organic applications of curves and nearly pointillistic textures.

More than the overhead views, this rendering is in some unnerving sense aesthetically pleasing. Formally, the image fits the rule of the thirds, framing a coal elevator for maximum visual interest and balance; in the foreground, the road or path curves away out of view, establishing a strong sense of perspective. The coal facility fills the mid-ground, while the stubble-covered mountainside disappears into the distance. As I look at the image, the pleasure I feel as I gaze at Sacco's representation of this postindustrial landscape disturbs me. Many critics following Theodor Adorno have critiqued representations of suffering and destruction in general, wondering whether the risk of extracting aesthetic pleasure from these representations poses an undue and unacceptable ethical problem; equally, by circulating these representations as commodities, this critical stance enables us to attend to the ways that such representations facilitate indirect but systematic extraction of economic value from political, economic, and social problems by creative professionals and media industries.[20] Despite the transformations of the comics form into a space for politically significant communication that is represented in different ways by nonfiction comics artists and contemporary adult comics fiction, the salience of this reservation here should be obvious. These images confront us with the tensions between the seduction of aesthetics, the commodification of suffering, and the desire to document and intervene in intolerable situations. The absence of human subjects in Sacco's illustration of the Alpheus plant suggests a peaceful silence that contrasts with the doubtlessly noisy atmosphere that characterized the site in operation. Those whose lives were structured by its operations, whose livelihoods depended on the industry, and who ultimately have been dislocated from the lives that unfolded here are just as absent from this image as those who live near active coal sites are from the everyday experience of using the electrical commodity.

Later, Sacco will offer illustrations of a less benign-seeming ruin: Jenkinjones, West Virginia, which is a coal town that was damaged by flooding (see Figure 6.1). Though it is not articulated explicitly within the text, these landscapes are linked through the mechanism of public policy—the flooding in Jenkinjones is far from atypical in the region and was likely exacerbated by the removal of tree cover and topsoil along creeks upstream by the coal industry.[21] So, the scrub and grasses in the background of the Alpheus plant and the destruction in Jenkinjones are articulated together through a public policy that originally sought to mitigate the negative impacts of the coal industry, but which has proven to be an inadequate check on contemporary mining practices, has provided legal cover for malign neglect, and ultimately became an institutional site at which the logic of the "sacrifice zone" is most visible. In Jenkinjones, like Alpheus, the landscape is completely evacuated of human life but marked with the impacts of human action; again, the images are well-composed—beautiful even. And, like the illustration of the Alpheus plant, they bear immediate witness to the destructive legacy left behind when the coal industry moves on to another place.

In both the overhead landscape views and these more human-scaled representations of the postindustrial landscape, Sacco shows the way that the demands of capitalism have literally emptied the land, evacuating it of both "natural" and "human" inhabitants. The political function of these representations is clear: a significant portion of the electricity that powers everyday technologies comes from coal, and a significant percentage of it comes from mountaintop-removal mining practices in the Appalachian region—but the violence done to the nexus of relationships between individuals, their communities, and the land on which they depend by this electrical commodity is completely occluded from the everyday perspective of the consumer. In the landscape illustrations in *Days of Destruction, Days of Revolt*, Sacco draws attention to some of the barriers that make this violence invisible to his often-distant audience. Again, this militates against a too-quick dismissal of realism. While it is, perhaps, an obvious observation with respect to nonfiction comics, this is a realism in which the human hand selects, frames, and decides what is before our eyes. The effect of this acknowledged subjectivity is a realism that is always "honest" and resists the temptation to present and occlude the conditions of its own production through an illusion of "transparent immediacy."[22] But, at the same time, as we move into a discussion of how Sacco positions agents within these distant landscapes, I want to underscore a synergistic relationship between the overhead and anthropological realisms Sacco has deployed here. Sacco's illustrations implicitly acknowledge the problems involved with a representation of the capitalist sublime from above; likewise, his illustrations of a postindustrial beauty at a more human scale make visible the logic of commodity fetishism: where the fetishism of the commodity occludes the social relationships that produced the landscape and sustained the industry, Sacco's illustration of postindustrial beauty shows these landscapes evacuated of the agents whose actions shaped them.[23]

Faces at a Distance

As the preceding analysis has suggested, Sacco's illustrated landscapes may be read as an attempt to make visible conditions that are not simply outside the experience of his readers, but at the edge of representability. In this section, I will argue that Sacco's narrative portraiture establishes relationships with the residents of the region that take a comparable logical form. These portraits make visible agents and social relations that are occluded in the networks of exchange associated with coal and coal-generated electricity, while creating conditions that could enable feelings of solidarity. Simultaneously, these portraits mark the limits to this visibility by drawing our attention to particularities that exceed the limits of representation and call for a politics that acknowledges fundamental differences between the Self and the Other.

In the "Days of Devastation" chapter, the empty landscapes previously analyzed are matched with a number of highly personal portraits; in addition to Larry Gibson, these portraits offer glimpses of the faces of an ex-miner named Rudy Kelly, whose employment has afflicted him with black lung, three young men whose health and livelihoods have been adversely impacted by the ecological and economic impacts of the industry, and some older women who confronted the negative impacts of a coal facility on their small town. Here, I want to focus on just one portrait: that of Rudy Kelly, the ex-coal miner whose life provides the subject matter of an extended conventional comic narrative at the heart of this chapter.[24] His story personalizes and dramatizes the narrative of twentieth-century transitions in the political economy of coal and will be the focus of the next section; here, however, I want to focus strictly on the portrait that offers a sort of prelude to this narrative as a way to theorize the political possibilities opened by what I will call "faciality at a distance."

In one of the most striking and now-familiar passages in *Understanding Comics*, artist Scott McCloud suggests that the iconicity of the comic face is a kind of invitation for readerly identification; that is, he posits a positive relationship between the level of "cartoonishness" of the comic face and the availability of this illustration for identification.[25] This reading of the iconic or cartoonish face doubtlessly makes sense in many circumstances, but as a frame for reading Rudy Kelly's portrait, it may deserve some examination and qualification. First, as Judith Butler argues in *Precarious Life*, the condition of possibility for identification is non-identity: the aim of identification "is accomplished only by reintroducing the difference it claims to have vanquished."[26] So, while the relationship of iconicity and identification may, at times, operate as McCloud suggests, a critical analysis of this identification should highlight the resistance put up by the illustrated image. Obviously, all illustrations will be selective about what they represent and will provide a particular perspective on a scene that is both less dynamic and less detailed than the image that might have presented itself to the artist's eye or imagination. Though Sacco's modulations of detail and rendering style may, at times, function as a rhetorical strategy for making characters more or less available for identification, let us identify the limit cases for McCloud's account before we apply it blindly. Limit cases like a sketch of a smiley face, to cite McCloud's example, and a photorealist illustration fail to fully demonstrate the limits of readerly identification and disidentification: as Judith Butler, Susie Linfield, and Ariella Azoulay have observed, even the photograph can, under some circumstances, be made available for readerly identification.[27] Quite simply, discerning the conditions under which McCloud's hypothesis might be applied to Sacco's portrait of Rudy Kelly requires that we first acknowledge that there are other aesthetic choices that shape the possibility of readerly identification.

As a phenomenon that problematizes McCloud's simple frame, we might consider the role of essentializing iconic caricature in visual rhetoric intended to "other" the subject, to render the subject as more animal, less human, physiologically retrograde, or in some other way beyond the pale of readerly identification. Given the long history of racist stereotyping in comics genres, this seems to be a crucial observation to make. Caricature may be a simple and obvious counter-example to simplistic applications of McCloud's hypothesis, but I want to use it to stage a more nuanced critique of his claims. Sacco's earlier works on Bosnia and Palestine provide many sophisticated examples of a dimension of identification not marked so much by extent as by quality.[28] In these comics, Sacco often positioned a representation of himself within the unfolding narrative as a somewhat more cartoonish "subject" whose rendering contrasted with a more realistic or "objective" landscape and relatively more realistic secondary characters. This artist-character gives visibility to Sacco's role as the artist, determining the principles of selection and the patterns of inclusion and exclusion in both the visual frames and their textual inscriptions. It is Sacco-the-artist whose representational choices articulate the narratives he chooses to tell using a visual rhetoric that innovates on familiar norms from other comics. Given this shaping hand, the presence of a cartoonish illustration of Sacco within many of the frames contributes to a sense of identification with not just the Sacco-the-illustration, but with Sacco-the-artist's gaze. Interestingly, Sacco often used this cartoonish artist-within-the-narrative (that is, Sacco-the-illustration) to encourage a sense of critical distance at the same time that it encouraged identification: the ethical, empathetic, and political limitations of Sacco's privileged subject position in relation to the unfolding stories were often quite intentionally foregrounded. As Butler observed, identification presupposes a lack of identity—that with which we identify puts up a resistance. By creating this critical distance, Sacco encourages the reader to take a reflexive relationship to the narrative, to consider her own position of privilege, and her own role as a spectator in relation to subjects represented. Importantly, Sacco often undermined the strict relationship of cartoonish subject (e.g., Sacco-the-illustration) and realistic object (e.g., the characters and landscapes with whom Sacco interacted in the course of the research) by simultaneously modulating the cartoonishness of these other characters, informants, and sources. This tended to grant these characters varying degrees of unique subjectivity within the narrative space—a subjectivity that was at times inflected with particularity and specificity through "realistic" representations of the face, while it was at other times inflected with the weight of cultural ideology through more "stereotypical" or iconic representations. What this demonstrates is that we should not take on board a too-easy understanding of identification, as tempting as this might be as we try to establish portraiture in *Days of Destruction, Days of Revolt* as an aesthetic intervention that could condition the possibilities for political intervention.

In *Days of Destruction, Days of Revolt*, Sacco's visage is absent. For Sacco's longtime readers, this absence is conspicuous. And though each of the portraits in the book might stand in for a "type," it is difficult to identify the kinds of over-the-top subjective renderings we can see, for instance, in some of Sacco's early drawings of IDF soldiers or residents of occupied Palestine.[29] In *Days of Destruction, Days of Revolt*, we are faced with relatively realistic portraits that bear witness to the uniqueness and particularity of the characters they represent: their suffering, their struggles, their movements through the landscape. Often, these characters speak directly to us—we are positioned as the audience of their stories. Judith Butler's *Precarious Life* deploys Emmanuel Levinas to examine the problem of representing the faces of suffering and oppression. In the image of such a face, Butler argues, we see the irreducible otherness of the represented subject; we recognize him as a subject. According to Butler, this image calls on us to imagine ourselves from the perspective of this other subject, whose position is fundamentally different than ours and whose experience we understand to be profoundly incommensurable with our own: paradoxically, the face of the Other allows us to see ourselves as subjects. The difference and incommensurability between the Self and the Other then calls into question the narcissistic action of the Self's gaze. In Butler's reading of Levinas, this "resistance" posed by the face of the Other provides the foundations for a relationship characterized by something that I will provisionally call here "justice": an engagement that exceeds the regimes of representation and discourse, which positions the other as an Other. This, in turn, places the Self in a relation to the particularity of the Other that calls for a human response that appreciates, rather than flattens, difference.[30] For Butler, representations of the Other's suffering can thus reveal the "precarious life" that we share—which, in turn, can provide the precondition for political action on the behalf of the Other.[31] So, returning to *Days of Destruction, Days of Revolt*: when we look on the face of Rudy Kelly, his image calls on us to see the unbridgeable gap between us and him. We are asked to identify with Sacco's eye and Sacco's imagination. In this way, Sacco's illustration calls on us to appreciate not just Kelly's historicity, but also a unique subjectivity that is incommensurable with our own.

Without embracing the ontological and metaphysical claims that subtend Levinas's account, I think Butler's deployment of his philosophy with respect to representations of the face helps us articulate the political possibilities latent in Sacco's portraits. On the one hand, McCloud is undoubtedly right that the iconicity of illustrated faces can, under some conditions, contribute to a visual rhetoric that makes a character more available for readerly identification; this iconicity may even set the conditions for a certain kind of relation of solidarity across difference on the basis of a shared experience of humanity. But, on the other hand, the realism of Sacco's rendering of Rudy Kelly resists a simple narcissistic identification, positions Kelly as a subject, and provides grounds for a politics attentive to difference. Much of post-Enlightenment political theory is predicated on an ideal of public, rational debate grounded in a consensus about what counts as relevant and real.[32] But the radical *difference* we can dimly perceive through our relation to Kelly's face in Sacco's portrait suggests the limits to this consensus. As agents, our lived spaces and times are profoundly disjunct from those experienced by others. Typically, we bridge these incommensurabilities by articulating lived spaces in terms of overarching representations of space. Reading the Other through these homogenizing representations of space, rather than on the basis of the way that individual experiential worlds are organized, underwrites types of violence that we take as normal or beyond notice—for instance, the setting aside of some places as sacrifice zones to national or commercial gain and some subjects as exceptions to the guarantees of fundamental political and social protections. Here, engagement with Kelly's portrait provides a precondition for calling this way of understanding space into question by putting the reader in proximity to an Other whose difference resists identification.

Institutionalized as a sacrifice zone, the Central Appalachian Basin is a site where relationships-at-a-distance are constructed, even necessary, and Sacco encourages us to call this into question. As we see in the traditional comic narrative at the core of Hedges and Sacco's chapter on Appalachia, Kelly's experiences are, indeed, quite different than the largest majority of their readers. By dramatizing Kelly's life as an Other to his audience and by positioning Kelly's life within a spatial regime that has been previously excluded from consideration by many in his audience, I want to suggest that Sacco calls on the reader to think carefully about what it means to act on the basis of solidarity-at-a-distance and on the basis of radical difference. Taken together, these themes raise important questions about what preconditions exist for making a claim of "equality" on the behalf of those who are positioned differently.

Sacco's comics and Hedges's prose seek to make the sacrifice zone of the Appalachian coalfield visible and thinkable. This makes it possible, but by no means certain, that we might make a claim for equality on the behalf of—or alongside—individuals like Larry Gibson and Rudy Kelly. Such action or political speech would, of necessity, be articulated from our own positions within global and national networks of capital and state power; in agreement with curator Ariella Azoulay, I am suggesting that we must cultivate a "civil imagination" of that which is outside of our normalized modes of representation in order to effectively take action.[33] Sacco's self-reflexive comic realism calls on us to imagine what is beyond the frame, including the parts of the narrative that are more immediately within the spaces we experience in our everyday lives.

This essay has established the ways that Hedges and Sacco make ethical, representative, and aesthetic interventions into an unspoken consensus that the concerns of the Appalachian sacrifice zone are peripheral to the everyday operations of power and economic exchange. In doing this, my overarching project has been to trace out the ways that they attempt to construct conditions of possibility for the kind of political action they explicitly advocate towards the end of *Days of Destruction, Days of Revolt*. I have, I hope, done so while registering my reservations about the limits to such an analysis: it is quite impossible, I would argue, to establish the political effectiveness of a text beyond these conditions of possibility without *post hoc* contact with audiences involved in identifiably political action. That said, I have advanced three points here about *Days of Destruction, Days of Revolt* that I think may be generalizable to many politically engaged nonfiction comics. *Days of Destruction, Days of Revolt* has

> 1. Attempted to make visible to us places or landscapes against which our own commodity consumption does a kind of violence while drawing attention to the problems of representation that encourage us to ignore these landscapes.
>
> 2. Created the conditions of possibility for identification of common ground between the reading Self and the represented Other as a foundation for a sense of solidarity across spatial distance.
>
> 3. Generated the possibility of a richly reflexive appreciation of the incommensurable differences between the reading Self and the represented Other.

This evident contradiction between solidarity and a politics of difference, I would argue, is not the grounds for political inaction, but provides a foundation for just interventions in our own spaces on the behalf of others who are situated differently.

NOTES

1. Chris Hedges and Joe Sacco, *Days of Destruction, Days of Revolt* (New York: Nation, 2012), xi.
2. See Roger D. Abrahams, "Phantoms of Romantic Nationalism in Folkloristics," *Journal of American Folklore* (1993): 3–37.

3. See Neil Smith, *Uneven Development: Nature, Capital, and the Production of Space* (Athens: University of Georgia Press, 2008).

4. For public health and economic impacts of coal in the region, see Paul R. Epstein, Jonathan J. Buonocore, Kevin Eckerle, Michael Hendryx, Benjamin M. Stout III, Richard Heinberg, Richard W. Clapp, et al., "Full Cost Accounting for the Life Cycle of Coal," *Annals of the New York Academy of Sciences* 1219.1 (2011): 73–98. See also Appalachian Voices, "The Human Costs of Coal," *iLove Mountains.org*, http://ilovemountains.org/the-human-cost.

5. For a history of early twentieth-century mining in the region, see David Alan Corbin, *Life, Work, and Rebellion in the Coal Fields: The Southern West Virginia Miners, 1880–1922* (Urbana: University of Illinois Press, 1981). For an account of the region today, see Ken Ward, Jr., "Coals Decline Forewarned: Minable Seams Running Out, Experts Say," *Charleston Gazette*, October 13, 2012, http://www.wvgazette.com/News/201210130087.

6. See "Annual Energy Outlook 2014 Early Release Overview," Energy Information Administration, December 16 2013, http://www.eia.gov/forecasts/aeo/er/index.cfm.

7. See Barbara Ellen Smith, "The Place of Appalachia," *Journal of Appalachian Studies* 8, no. 1 (April 1, 2002): 49.

8. For a critique of the "internal colony" framing, see David S. Walls, "Internal Colony or Internal Periphery? A Critique of Current Models and an Alternative Formulation," in *Colonialism in Modern America: The Appalachian Case*, eds. Helen Matthews Lewis, Linda Johnson, and Donald Askins (Boone: Appalachia Consortium Press, 1978), 319–49.

9. Hedges and Sacco, *Days of Destruction*, 122–23. For Hedges on nonviolence, see, for example, Chris Hedges, "The Cancer in Occupy," *Truthdig*, February 6, 2012, http://www.truthdig.com/report/item/the_cancer_of_occupy_20120206.

10. Hedges and Sacco, *Days of Destruction*, 128.

11. Ibid.

12. See Paulette Young, "Annual Coal Report 2010," Energy Information Administration, Office of Oil, Gas, and Coal Supplies, July 2010.

13. See Michel de Certeau, *The Practice of Everyday Life*, trans. Steven F. Rendall (Berkeley: University of California Press, 2011).

14. See Henri Lefebvre, *The Production of Space*, trans. Donald Nicholson-Smith (Malden: Blackwell, 1991).

15. See John Tagg, *The Burden of Representation: Essays on Photographies and Histories* (Minneapolis: University of Minnesota Press, 1988), 60–102.

16. See Jean-Francois Lyotard, *The Postmodern Condition: A Report on Knowledge*, trans. Geoff Bennington and Brian Massumi (Minneapolis: University of Minnesota Press, 1984).

17. See Jacques Rancière, *The Politics of Aesthetics*, trans. Gabriel Rockhill (New York: Continuum, 2004).

18. For a conservative projection of declining production, see Randall A. Childs and George W. Hammond, "Consensus Coal Production Forecast for West Virginia 2009–2030," West Virginia Department of Environmental Protection, Office of Special Reclamation, September 2009.

19. See Chad Montrie, *To Save the Land and People: A History of Opposition to Surface Coal Mining in Appalachia* (Chapel Hill: University of North Carolina Press, 2003); and Bryan T. McNeil, *Combating Mountaintop Removal: New Directions in the Fight Against Big Coal* (Urbana: University of Illinois Press, 2011).

20. See, for example, Theodor W. Adorno, "Cultural Criticism and Society," *Prisms*, trans. Samuel Weber and Sherry Weber (Cambridge: MIT Press, 1981), 17–34.

21. For another example, see Kai T. Erikson, *Everything in Its Path: Destruction of Community in the Buffalo Creek Flood* (New York: Simon and Schuster, 1976).

22. For a discussion of "transparent immediacy" and media, see J. David Bolter and Richard Grusin, *Remediation: Understanding New Media* (Cambridge: MIT Press, 2000).

23. For the classic account of commodity fetishism, see Karl Marx, "The Fetishism of the Commodity and Its Secret," *Capital: A Critique of Political Economy*, trans. Ben Fowkes (New York: Penguin, 1977), 163–77.

24. Hedges and Sacco, *Days of Destruction*, 133–42.

25. Scott McCloud, *Understanding Comics: The Invisible Art* (New York: HarperPerennial, 1993), 44.

26. Judith Butler, *Precarious Life: The Powers of Mourning and Violence* (New York: Verso, 2006), 145.

27. See Butler, *Precarious Life*; Susie Linfield, *The Cruel Radiance: Photography and Political Violence* (Chicago: University of Chicago Press, 2011); and Ariella Azoulay, *The Civil Contract of Photography*, trans. Rela Mazali and Rubik Danieli (New York: Zone, 2008).

28. Joe Sacco, *Safe Area Goražde: The War in Eastern Bosnia, 1992–1995* (Seattle: Fantagraphics, 2000); and *Palestine* (Seattle: Fantagraphics, 2001).

29. See Sacco, *Palestine*, 2, 270.

30. Along with Butler, *Precarious Life* on identification, see Alison Landsberg, *Prosthetic Memory: The Transformation of American Remembrance in the Age of Mass Culture* (New York: Columbia University Press, 2004) on proximity.

31. For a related argument, see Linfield, *The Cruel Radiance*, 36–37.

32. For a foundational account of the public sphere, see Jürgen Habermas, *The Structural Transformation of the Public Sphere: An Inquiry into a Category of Bourgeois Society*, trans. Thomas Burger and Frederick Lawrence (Cambridge: MIT Press, 1991). For other influential accounts, see Charles Taylor, *Modern Social Imaginaries* (Duke University Press, 2004); Hannah Arendt, *The Human Condition* (Chicago: University of Chicago Press, 1958); and Neil Postman, *Amusing Ourselves to Death: Public Discourse in the Age of Show Business* (New York: Penguin, 1985).

33. See Arielle Azoulay, *Civil Imagination: A Political Ontology of Photography*, trans. Louise Bethlehem (New York: Verso, 2012).

Section III
The Politics and Aesthetics of Joe Sacco's Comics

8. Little Things Mean a Lot: The Everyday Material of *Palestine*

Ann D'Orazio

It has become something of a critical consensus that Joe Sacco does not adhere to the conventions of traditional, objective journalism. He eschews one-dimensional reportage, pretensions to neutrality, and the imperative to provide audience members with both sides of an issue, as if there were only two sides to a given issue. Sacco's works of comics journalism rely upon techniques that objective journalism typically resists: slow-paced collection and delivery of information, personal involvement, pathos, and long meditations upon the subjects of a work. Sacco himself has critiqued objective journalism in various interviews, stating that "the problem with modern journalists is they truly believe they are objective. They believe that they are in the service of some platonic idealism of journalism. I would rather try to be as honest as possible and source information as accurately as possible but admit that by meeting and befriending people, they respond to you. I want all of that to go into my story; I want to be upfront about it."[1] Interpreters of his work have maintained that Sacco accomplishes this critique through various means, one of the most salient being the outstanding attention he gives to visual and verbal detail, and the everyday events and things that make up his subjects' lives.[2] In this essay, I argue that Sacco's use of quotidian material things comprises an integral part of his divergence from conventional journalism because things themselves are polysemous in his work; things function in a variety of ways in his texts. The multivalence of things throughout Sacco's work helps him accomplish nuanced, at times messy, reportage while avoiding the repetition and valorization of narratives that flatten and binarize conflicts.

Thing Theory and Vital Materialism

Recent work on thing theory and materialism provides a useful inroad to understanding how and why a comic about human beings, war, and politics depends as much upon the presence of stuff as people. Bill Brown's thing theory creates a framework for thinking about how things function simultaneously as objects and things. What may first appear to be a subtle semantic difference or even an improbability—aren't things and objects the same?—lies at the heart of thing theory. According to Brown, *objects* are inert material goods, important only in how human subjects conceive of and use them: "As they circulate through our lives, we look *through* objects (to see what they disclose about history, society, nature, or culture—above all, what they disclose about *us*), but we only catch a glimpse of things."[3] In other words, the object's detectable presence often sits in a kind of secondary relationship to the human subject, and the subject's drive for meaning-making fills the object with meaning, not vice versa. *Things*, of course, function differently but they do not abandon objecthood; things hold onto object behavior and do more. Things embody and represent themselves while encompassing the relationship among subjects and objects; as Brown asserts, "*the thing seems to name the object, just as it is, even as it names something else.*"[4] Things also contain and exude "what is excessive in objects . . . their force as a sensuous presence or metaphysical presence, the magic by which objects become values, fetishes, idols, or totems."[5] Things, then, are at once physical material objects with use value defined in relation to people and are simultaneously sites of meaning and power. Sacco's *Palestine* features a variety of objects, and these objects resonate as things, with constitutive power over and crucial involvement in culture, place, history, the market, and the realities of living in a war zone. Thing theory provides a way into my analysis of Sacco's comics because it corroborates Sacco's departure from the journalistic standard of objectivity by fixing meaning in things; therefore, things' many functions and meanings help Sacco bring to light the realities of living in a war zone.

Jane Bennett goes further than Brown's thing theory and finds a living, vibratory nature in all matter. In *Vibrant Matter: A Political Ecology of Things*, Bennett details her iteration of vital materialist theory, which conceives of humans, nonhuman animals, organic and synthetic objects, and environments existing in a network of interactions that affect and push the course of human (and nonhuman) existence.[6] Since Sacco's comics chronicle people's stories of living under occupation and in war, such an emphasis on the vitality and primacy of the nonhuman may seem counterintuitive or even disrespectful; however, as Bennett asserts, things, places, animals, and people exist as actants in a field.[7] Thus, things play a significant role in any given event, much like people. Bennett neither allots complete agency to humans nor does she assign complete power to nonhumans.[8] This is not to say that Bennett reduces or ignores human responsibility for imperialism or violence, but rather understands action as a conglomeration of forces:

> Autonomy and strong responsibility seem to me to be empirically false, and thus their invocation tinged with injustice. In emphasizing the ensemble

nature of action and the interconnections between persons and things, a theory of vibrant matter presents individuals as simply incapable of bearing *full* responsibility for their effects... The notion of a confederate agency does attenuate the blame game, but it does not thereby abandon the project of identifying (what Arendt called) the sources of harmful effects. To the contrary, such a notion broadens the range of places to look for sources.[9]

Bennett's notions of distributive/confederate agency can be traced throughout Sacco's work because he portrays his subjects and their environments in great detail. The reader rarely, if ever, finds hard binaries or easy answers in Sacco's work—much of this has to do with the way he visually renders minutia in his journalism. Sacco's deliberate concern with interrelated networks of *things* and people develops a more holistic picture of regions and peoples in conflict, demonstrating a complex system rather than grand, epochal shifts and prominent individual actors upon which to lay all praise or blame. By combining Bennett's and Brown's theories, then, one can see the powerful nature and shifting meaning of things throughout Sacco's work. Sacco's emphasis on minutia demonstrates the ways in which the journalistic standard of objectivity can only lead one to fail to account for multiple agencies—not just human, but also nonhuman—in the events represented in *Palestine*.

Tea

In *Palestine*, Sacco's first major work of comics journalism, glasses of tea appear throughout the narrative. The tea is not only everywhere in the text temporally—appearing over forty times in illustrations, verbal descriptions, and dialogue—but also everywhere in the text spatially, crossing boundaries of public and private spaces, gendered spaces, and even locales as different as living rooms and prisons. The first appearance of tea also marks the first series of counters to objective journalism's tendencies: it demonstrates that individual people comprise groups and that journalists have agendas and biases rather than neutral, blank slates from which they collect and disseminate unaltered information. When Sacco encounters a vendor in a Nablus market who makes tea for him (with a lot of sugar), the reader sees that Palestinians have salient cultural practices around food and hospitality—a notion reinforced by tea as an in-text constant (see Figure 8.1).[10] The bottom panel, depicting a large quantity of sugar going into the glass accompanied by Sacco's inner assessment of the beverage and situation, shows the tea operating as itself and more. The glass of sweetened tea acts as a point of bonding and a catalyst for evidence-gathering. Also, despite the oppression and deprivation Palestinians must endure, the

Figure 8.1. Joe Sacco, *Palestine* (Seattle: Fantagraphics, 2001), 4.

man's very friendliness and eagerness to tell his story pushes back against the notion that Palestinians are people whose lives are governed by violence and barbarism and are therefore violent and barbarous themselves. In other words, the terrorist mass is unlikely to serve its guests tea. The guest-host exchange between Sacco and the vendor over tea opens an opportunity for the vendor to bring others to meet Sacco and tell their stories. The tea and conversation bring a sense of intimacy, as Sacco wryly remarks: "But now my buddy on the West Bank wants to make some introductions, to set me up, he wants me to shake hands with his people's pain."[11] By taking time to share refreshment and conversation—in this case, the ritual of sharing tea—Sacco gathers more information, and the people's pain becomes less of an abstraction and more of a present, lived experience attached to individual people.

Tea appears in many domestic spaces as itself (a refreshment) and a reiteration of cultural ritual and hospitality. It also carries different contextual meaning within domestic spaces; sometimes tea serves as a welcome and an entry point into conversation and at other times tea acts as a gesture of apology or a habitualized way to commiserate or share sorrow. As often is the case throughout *Palestine*, tea arrives before Sacco gets his story from each family he meets in a village near East Jerusalem ("The Bucket"), from Khaled's friend's family in Kalandia ("Brother for a Day"), in Jabril's home ("Moderate Pressure"), in the rooms of Nuseirat ("Rooms" and "Black Coffee"), in the tomato farmers' home ("Tomatoes"), and in the woman's home in Rafah ("Pilgrimage"). Tea's ubiquity and Sacco's comments such as, "The cold, the men, the tea. . . . That's the Essence of the Palestinian Room . . . this could be almost every room I've ever sat in in Palestine . . ."[12] and his statement that he momentarily cannot remember the names of the men he has just met may seem to enact the flattening tendencies of objective journalism. Instead, Sacco's admissions provide his subjective point of view while serving to underscore the consistency and totality of suffering in Palestine. The ever-present glasses of tea are always juxtaposed with individuals and their stories, reminding the reader that cohesion and unity both in cultural practice and the comic itself do not necessarily equal an erasure of people's individuality, their stories' significance, or the multivalence of tea. In the vignette "Rooms," for example, as Sacco begins to listen to Ibrahim, Masud, and the other men in the room discuss armed struggle, he remarks upon the "hundred times before" the conversation must have occurred in similar rooms, "with the tea coming and coming, year after year . . ."[13] The upper right and lower left panels on the page show the current scene—the same men talking over the same tea, yet they are positioned next to images of violent struggle and underneath captions that complicate simplistic interpretations of armed struggle. This positioning's effect highlights the tea as a prop in habitualized commiseration, but it again reminds the reader that despite any perceived homogeneity due to the reoccurrence, and perhaps even drudgery, of the situation, there is no monolithic Palestinian experience. This mundane scene along with its depictions and analysis of revolutionary acts works carefully to build a picture of survival and adaptation as an everyday reality. The pace and detail of Sacco's accounts impresses upon the audience that, for his many interview subjects, the struggle to survive is a constant mode of existence, almost banal, rather than being an aberration.

In the vignette "Pilgrimage," Sacco and his friend Sameh travel to a woman's home in a refugee camp near Rafah. There, Sacco records the woman's harrowing account of a gas attack, the brutality of Israeli soldiers, the soldiers' responsibility for the beatings she receives, and the deaths of her sons and husband at their hands. Though her narrative forms the center of the vignette, tea announces its start and punctuates its end. Before the woman begins to relate the tragedies she has endured, tea is served as refreshment, but it also reiterates tea's ritual function and marks an entry point into conversation. In the top panel of the anecdote's beginning, representing present time, the glasses of tea sit on a small table in the bottom center of the panel, and Sacco renders the scene from his point of view. As readers, we see how Sacco takes part in the scene via the tea ritual. His partially disembodied presence in the panel—we see just his hands and notepad—reminds us that he is only a guest and not a permanent fixture, able to depart whenever he wants. At the same time, the tea visually links him to his interview subjects. The rendering of this opening tea-sharing subtly foreshadows the woman's skepticism about talking to Sacco or any other reporter. Journalists do not impress her, as she has talked with many before and sees only impotent words in place of actions. When Sacco flounders and cannot answer her understandably skeptical questions, he attempts to make for the door. Surprisingly, she thanks him, offers more tea, and then brings her son out to show his scar from a head wound. She offers further hospitality, but Sacco wants to keep moving. After she expresses her disillusionment with journalists, the significance of the tea shifts to show her apology or perhaps a desire for Sacco to stay and listen more despite the offense other journalists may have caused in the past. Here, the tea itself, as a thing, is not inert; it acts in concert with the woman to pull Sacco back into the house and her story, thereby disrupting the journalist's pattern of mechanistic, cursory story collection. Sacco wants to leave, but the woman and her tea behave as obstacles to his flight.

When Sacco recalls the statements of a few of the many men who spent a significant amount of time in Ansar III prison, we see that tea plays a significant part in humanizing the prisoners intratextually as well as extratextually. Like the above examples, the tea maintains object behavior as sustenance or refreshment, but it also gives the prisoners something around which to organize (the tea-distribution committee), to show the Israeli soldiers that they are humans, not animals. As one of Sacco's subjects explains, "Prisoners working in the kitchen would bring the tea in a big pot. The tea committee had to make sure that the distribution of tea was fair, so that no one complained, and fast, so that the tea was served hot. The tea committee served everyone once, and then began serving from the beginning of the line again until the leftover was gone. The tea monitor in the tent would take note of who was next in line for tea so that he would be served first next time. There's a problem the moment you start goofing with fairness. Prison is a small world where a cup of tea is something, a piece of soap is something."[14] Sacco's repetition of "is something" underscores the everyday objects' (tea and soap) transition to powerful thing-status; the men in Ansar III maintain control, albeit in a small way, over their routine through the organization and distribution of the tea. Sacco uses tea to exemplify the time, dedication, and perseverance the prisoners have in the face of their predicament. In its relation to the prisoners—as an agent among other agents, following Jane Bennett's notion of confederate agency—the tea marks another force working against the dehumanization that the Ansar III inmates experience. The tea and its organized distribution counters the Israeli propaganda dissected by one of the prisoners: "It [the Israeli guard duty] serves the ideological purpose of exposing Israelis to conditions where they don't see Palestinians as humans. . . . They see people, first of all, dressed like animals, who, until recently, didn't have spoons to eat with . . . people who are dirty, who have no access to proper hygiene, with hundreds of different flies and mosquitoes around their faces. And it sticks in their minds—'Those are my enemies.'"[15] Any humanizing mode of being—the tea committee, songs, lectures and other educational activities—critiques and resists the logic of dehumanization. Furthermore, the tea and its organized, equal disbursement contributes to *Palestine*'s complication of a monolithic image of Palestinian men and prisoners in general. Rather than interpreting the tea as a basic necessity given to the prisoners by the guards, its pivotal role in Ansar III—arguably as pivotal as hydration—is to be another actant in the men's struggle to retain their humanity and individuality in the face of the prison's horrible conditions.

The Keffiyeh and the Hijab

A recognizable symbol of the Arab world and especially Palestine, the keffiyeh does not immediately indicate complexity in the context of Western depictions of the Middle East. Instead, to the consumer of typical Western journalism, it is an artificial marker of Arab-ness and various binaries—Western/non-Western,

Arab/Israeli, or Arab/non-Arab. The keffiyeh first appears prominently in the same place tea appears prominently. The keffiyeh-wearing vendor welcomes Sacco to "his country."[16] Sacco's initial objection—"*his* country?"—repeats a conventional and widespread association of the Palestinian with the category of terrorist or interloper rather than the category of citizen. In *Palestine*, though, the reader quickly sees that the garment plays a role in individualizing the vendor and, in a way, letting Sacco and the reader know that this *is* his country, that he is a citizen, an individual, a Palestinian. Sacco himself avoids wearing a keffiyeh until he has spent some time in Jabalia camp in Gaza. Though he never indicates to the reader explicitly why he dons the scarf, his adoption of such a symbolically loaded accessory shows his increasing embeddedness among and implicit identification with the Palestinians. This seemingly unimportant omission underscores the very human inconsistency and possibly shifting allegiance of the journalist through whom this whole story is mediated. The reporter's presence is made palpable, not just in the obvious way—Sacco represents himself throughout the narrative, and we read much of his inner monologue—but also in the understated but intentional visual detail of when and where he wears his own keffiyeh.

Inside a crowded ward of Nablus's hospital, Sacco talks to patients, many of whom were wounded by Israeli fire. A young man posing for a photograph wraps on a keffiyeh, "For Palestine!" and flashes a peace sign. Here, the keffiyeh is not the accessory de rigueur of a young terrorist, but a comforting thing for a boy who physically suffers the realities of living under an occupation. He passes the keffiyeh to another young man who pulls back his blanket to reveal a foot cast. Like his hospital companion, the second young man also wears the keffiyeh proudly; the material thing displays national pride despite the continuous risk to life and limb these young men experience. The piece of cloth itself moves among bodies and genders—a little girl gets to wear a keffiyeh—subverting commonly held notions about patriarchal oppression in Palestine and other Middle Eastern nations. It's not just strong young men who get to wear textile markers of pride and political participation, nor is it just women and children who are injured and displaced by war. The visual repetition and sharing of the keffiyeh places the little girl into the group of wounded and worthy subjects, and gives her as much importance as the young men in the hospital.

The keffiyeh signifies devotion to political factions as well, which is as problematic as it is important for many of keffiyeh-bedecked men Sacco encounters. This is a particularly interesting *thing* in the comic because Sacco must verbally describe the colors and their respective associations—black for Fateh, red for the Popular Front—as the comic itself is in black-and-white. A verbal explanation reminds the audience of Sacco's presence in the narrative as journalist, artist, and writer, while also intimating the limitations of an external audience's ability to know or understand the situation completely. We see black-and-white, but we need someone to reveal and explain the details. Sacco also relies upon his friend Sameh to elucidate the constitutive power of the keffiyeh. Because of the danger associated with openly showing one's political alliances, Sameh prefers not to wear the keffiyeh. He neither wishes to mark himself nor to be damned by association. He objects to the thing's binarizing, fractious power. Sameh seems to want his people to be unified, and he certainly wants to maintain his physical safety. The keffiyeh does not just identify varieties of Palestinian political factions, then, but it also gets tied up in inter-sectarian violence, as described by Firas, a young member of the Popular Front. Despite the perceptions or opinions of outsiders, oppressed peoples do not necessarily present a homogenous, united group, and the keffiyehs found throughout this text make an artifact of that often-messy heterogeneity.

The hijab behaves much like the keffiyeh in that it comprises a recognizable invocation of the male/female and Arab/non-Arab binaries, but it complicates a much more widely known and potentially polarizing conversation. The hijab's role in the comic also creates a space in which Sacco talks directly to and about women and their varied opinions on wearing the hijab. Since the hijab has acted as, and frequently been misread as, such a potent signifier of Arab oppression of women, especially to Westerners, Sacco's use of the hijab is particularly enlightening. The thing itself is not just a veil to hide women, but it is also a shelter women can take up against the outside world and a symbol of faith and respect. Some of Sacco's interview subjects echo the sentiments of women in the more contemporary Egyptian Women's Mosque Movement, as documented by Saba Mahmood in *Politics of Piety: The Islamic Revival and the Feminist Subject*. Mahmood's fieldwork within Egyptian women's religious movements reveals teachers and faithful women who enact agency through obedience, wherein donning the veil represents a ritual, behavioral step that enacts and embodies true belief. Mahmood relates Hajja Nur's, a dā'iya (Islamic religious teacher), critique of current practices surrounding the hijab in Egypt:

> It is the project of the government and the secularists ('almāniyīn) to transform religion (al-dīn) into conventions or customs ('āda). . . . An example of this is the use of the veil (hijāb) as a custom ('āda) rather than as a religious duty (*fard*). When you . . . as a foreigner look at Egyptian society right now and see all of these women wearing the hijāb you must remember that a lot of them wear it as a custom rather than as a religious duty that also entails other responsibilities. These people are in fact no different than those who

argue *against* the hijāb and who say that the hijāb is [an expression of] culture [and therefore a matter of personal choice], rather than a religious command. So what we have to do is educate Muslim women that it is not enough to wear the veil, but that the veil must also lead us to behave in a truly modest manner in our daily lives, a challenge that far exceeds the simple act of donning the veil.[17]

Nur's understanding of the veil calls for a movement beyond its objecthood; in other words, the thingness of the veil, its ability to assist in building behavior, belief, and identity make it more than a religiously significant garment. Some of Sacco's interview subjects express similar sentiments, as one young woman states, "I *want* to believe strongly enough to wear the hijab always. . . . Not just in the streets. . . . I want to really believe in wearing it . . ."[18] For this young woman, the hijab has constitutive power that she is responsible for eventually attaining through her faith. The hijab comprises not only a significant site of faith and feminine agency, but also a variety of complex historically and socially situated subjectivities, as Sacco's work demonstrates, in relation to the Intifada and larger Palestinian society.

In the vignette "Hijab," Sacco collects testimony from a variety of women on their relationship to the hijab. Sacco literally objectifies the hijab-clad women in the vignette's beginning and reinforces the Western/non-Western binary, stating, "Let's face it, I'm from the West, I've seen plenty of leg, orange hair, too, and other fashion statements. . . . But *this* getup, it's nondescript, I blank out most all the women who wear it, they're just shapes to me, ciphers, like pigeons moving along the sidewalk . . ."[19] Sacco objectifies the women here in the same way that Bill Brown understands *objects*; they are a passive, unindividuated part of the scenery. The larger top panel on the section's first page depicts a scene of faceless, similarly shaped bodies all moving away from Sacco (see Figure 8.2). Here, the hijab, and the women wearing it, are objects, but in the bottom panel, the hijab becomes a *thing* that demonstrates a concrete identity attached to a real person. In the bottom panel, Sacco reacts with surprise when the woman who shares a taxi with him speaks. Their interaction and his response show the hijab's movement from object to thing and the woman's movement in Sacco's mind from a flat type to a real person. Their exchange exemplifies the potency and polysemy of the hijab, as Sacco's initial descriptors, "just shapes," "ciphers," "pigeons," and "life-forms" give way to a whole chapter that explores the nature of the hijab and its relationship to women's identity, Palestinian politics, and Islam.

Sacco's careful and detailed portrayal of a variety of women's opinions and, visually, a variety of hijabs and hijab-less women, undercuts the totalizing tendency of Western journalism's depiction of Islamic women. Rather than paint-

Little Things Mean a Lot: The Everyday Material of *Palestine* 151

Figure 8.2. Joe Sacco, *Palestine* (Seattle: Fantagraphics, 2001), 235.

ing Islam or men solely as repressive forces or women solely as passive victims, the vignette shows how the garment itself creates and participates in aspects of the Palestinian struggle. In this way, Sacco renders the hijab as part of a confederate agency, one piece of a long cultural narrative that also includes other significant forces and actors. The second page of "Hijab" visually exemplifies the vexed relationship some contemporary Palestinian women have to the attire through an inset panel.[20] Muna, a non-practicing Muslim who does not wear a hijab, appears at the top of the inset panel while traditionally garbed women appear behind the inset. The visual contrast between Muna's uncovered head and the traditionally garbed women underscores Muna's explanation that the emphasis on traditional dress has been a political strategy. Whether or not women were freely choosing to don the Palestinian attire, the attire still marked them as Palestinian Muslims, neither Christians nor Israelis. Muna's historicizing continues to reveal the multivalence of the hijab and the force it exerts on relationships among political groups and between men and women. As Muna explains, Hamas members threatened and sometimes attacked women who appeared in public without the hijab, eventually resulting in public denouncement by the Unified Leadership of violence against women who chose not to cover their heads. In this context, the hijab constitutes a central point of political dispute that influences the actions of both men and women. Rather than understanding the hijab as a static piece of cloth, we see how the accessory-as-thing has its own role in the development of Palestinian policies for women, and men's reactions to those policies. Sacco's detailed account of the historical and political dimensions of the hijab make it clear that the garment is not solely a sign of patriarchal oppression or religious fundamentalism. In contrast, when the hijab is recognized as a thing in itself, its meanings and functions multiply exponentially. Sacco's exposition of the Palestinian women's wide-ranging opinions and beliefs surrounding the hijab demonstrate the potency and lack of fixity of the thing itself.[21]

Tomatoes

Just as the hijab becomes a complex thing, enmeshed in and integral to networks of meaning, so, too, do the "Produce of Israel" labels on Gazan tomatoes. In *Palestine*, Sacco examines how the labels mark and conceal the conditions surrounding the tomatoes' growth. In the vignette "Tomatoes," Sacco speaks to a group of Gazan tomato farmers about their produce and the Israeli policies that control their access to water for, transportation of, sale of, and profit from the tomatoes. The tomatoes themselves are inexorably linked to questions of labor, self-sufficiency, and systemic Israeli oppression; reading the tomatoes as things provides an understanding of an economic chain that binds the Palestinian growers. Their deceptive labeling reveals the complicity of European nations economically—the Carmel produce company profits from European consumers' purchase of Israeli-labeled tomatoes, while Gazan-labeled tomatoes are often left to spoil before reaching their target markets. Sacco renders the tomato cartons in detail; the Gazan tomatoes sit in plain-looking cartons with Arabic writing while the same tomatoes labeled "Israeli Tomatoes" have Carmel-branded cartons and fancier design. Further complicating the situation, the Gazan farmers are forced to participate in their own exploitation because of the difficulty of getting permits to work in Israel. They know the problems plaguing their farming, their tomatoes, and the inaccurate labels, but they must provide for themselves and their families. Here, Sacco's revelation of what exists underneath the tomatoes' labels and the stakes attached therein concretizes abstract notions of trade and market. The tomatoes perform as actants in a field that includes the farmers, the crooked Palestinian and Israeli middlemen, Israeli policy makers, and European consumers. Sacco's focus on the labels and the tomatoes themselves links multiple participants to the produce, and the tomato itself—as sustenance and commodity—functions as the rationale for why the farmers choose to continue to work under policies and conditions that yield little profit.

Sacco's microcosmic approach allows him to experience the thingness of the tomatoes, the quality of their flesh, their smell, the farmers' meticulous quality control, and their pride in their produce. His account carries an affective and sensual dimension eschewed by objective journalism. After relating the bureaucratic, legal, and financial obstacles the Gazan farmers face, Sacco comments, "Despite all this, these guys want to prove that Palestinians know how to grow a tomato . . ."[22] On this same page, the tomatoes loom large in the center; the man's hands holding the tomatoes break the boundaries of the panel, displaying their perfect shape and consistency. The visual weight accorded in the panel to the tomatoes and the farmers' hands emphasizes the centrality of the produce to these men's very existence, but also their emotional investment in growing and nurturing the plants. Sacco matches this central illustration with a detailed verbal rendering of the scarcity of resources the farmers face, noting that access to water is a major problem—the little water available to Palestinians is so saline that it is dangerous to people and crops.[23] Because resources are not only tightly controlled but also potentially poisonous, the tomatoes are more than consumable food-objects. They are material testaments to the persistence of Palestinians who have been pushed into a tiny corner of their own land and denied access to natural resources. These farmers still manage to continue producing food that can sustain them physically and, at least somewhat, financially. The care Sacco takes in rendering the fruits and their growers creates a nuanced, root-like picture, which reveals a web of relationships among the various actants and their relative levels of complicity in the situation. Despite the material and financial obstacles the growers face, "Tomatoes" maintains an overall feeling of perseverance, exemplified by the high-quality tomatoes' visual and verbal centrality in the vignette.

Family Trees—the Olive Tree

One of many far-reaching Israeli policies has been the systematic destruction of olive groves to facilitate the movement, market growth, and settlement of Israeli people, which simultaneously cuts down the livelihood of Palestinians dependent upon the trees. In the vignette "The Bucket," Sacco interviews a family in a small village east of the Green Line which has lost a number of their trees. The elderly patriarch explains that cutting down the trees is more than losing money or labor opportunities; it is like killing your own children. The old man experiences pain as a result of policies that sanction filicide in the form of violence directed at his children and grandchildren, and silvicide in the forced removal of his trees. Sacco renders his account of the loss of his trees with equal visual significance to his daughter's account of his grandson's beating at the hands of Israeli soldiers. Both narratives appear in panels of the same shape and size. Though one could argue that Sacco illustrates the trees as objects, a mere part of the scenery, they are only shown in their cut-down and uprooted state, thereby emphasizing their thing-status. As the trees cease to function in a typical way, Sacco is able to show their myriad roles and their crucial position in these people's lives. Here, the political and the material are tied to intimate domesticity; we see an affective and familial connection among the human and nonhuman.

The trees themselves are old, some a century or more, and they testify to the enduring presence and persistence of Palestinians in the land claimed by Israelis.[24] The trees, like the Palestinians, were there before the Israeli settlement of 1914. They are tied back to family and progeny because they are living proof of ancestry. Family trees, in this context, have a dual lineage, both as trees and as evidence of the generations of Palestinian people who have lived and grown alongside the olive trees. Though the trees' growth is slow, the grandfather says that it takes "many years to grow, six or seven years for a strong tree,"[25] their destruction is quick. Sacco relates that "The Israelis uprooted 120,000 plus in the intifada's first four years ... 'for security reasons' like in these cases ..."[26] Sacco's slow and deliberate account of the trees' various functions and crucial emotional (as well as financial) importance to the Palestinians shows that the trees sustain and constitute a part of Palestinian families. The old man informs Sacco that "a good Roman tree can produce 20–30 liters [of olive oil] in a year . . ."[27] In this case the living, nonhuman thing produces saleable goods while also supporting Palestinian people's claim to a long and rooted history. The evocation of Rome, albeit brief, carries a significant amount of cultural weight. The ancient and often understood as Western empire reads as a point of linking and reference in a similar manner to the invocation of the Bible in justifications of Israeli settlement, but the trees—the physical presence of trees—strengthens this idiomatic expression of time and rooted authority. This also ties back to Sacco's particular style of deliberation in that a monument can be flashed over quickly as a recognizable symbol of a people's long presence or a nation's existence or history. When the living memory of a people is present, however, the generational testimony of families and trees takes the place of such monuments or symbols. Additionally, the trees need not be cut down to prove their age; the peoples' collective memory of both trees and place testifies to the ongoing presence of the Palestinians in their homeland. As the ancient trees and their longtime stewards get destroyed to make way for new roads and new settlements, both the human and nonhuman experience dispossession and violence. Simple images or brief reports on the systematic removal of trees points to the problem, but such strategies do not promote a subtle understanding of the significance of the trees nor the full range of ways in which the policy affects Palestinian people.

Though people often seem to be the prime movers in any report of conflict, they are always enmeshed in a multiplicity of things, nonhuman actants that often subtly and quietly influence and exemplify the events surrounding them. Conventional journalism typically erases the nonhuman or sees it only in terms of objects—passive, inert stuff with little significance beyond fixed meanings and external appearances. Sacco effectively counters and critiques the usual information-gathering and reporting techniques of objective journalism through his long forays into areas of conflict and his detailed accounts of both people and things in sites of conflict. The people who share their stories, time, food, and homes are certainly memorable in *Palestine*, but Sacco never removes them from a real context, a context that includes both human and nonhuman agents. Time and time again, the audience sees multiple agencies at work through not only the unfolding of human events in acts of violence and perseverance, but also the detailed illustrations of tea, clothing, tomatoes, and olive trees. By focusing visually and verbally upon *things* as much as people, Sacco renders a nuanced picture of Palestinian life after the first intifada, and demonstrates that little things influence and shape large events.

NOTES

1. Alex Burrows, "The Myth of Objective Journalism—Joe Sacco Interviewed," *Quietus*, 2012, http://www.thequietus.com/articles/10196/joe-sacco-journalism-interview.html.

2. See Andrea A. Lunsford and Adam Rosenblatt, "'Down a Road and into an Awful Silence': Graphic Listening in Joe Sacco's Comics Journalism," in *Silence and Listening as Rhetorical Arts*, eds. Cheryl Glenn and Krista Ratcliffe (Carbondale: Southern Illinois University Press, 2011), 138–43; Adam Rosenblatt and Andrea A. Lunsford, "Critique Caricature, and Compulsion in Joe Sacco's Comics Journalism," in *Rise of the American Comics Artist: Creators and Contexts*, eds. Paul Williams and James Lyons (Jackson: University Press of Mississippi, 2010), 69–73 and 81–84; Brigid Maher, "Drawing Blood: Translation, Mediation, and Conflict in Joe Sacco's Comics Journalism," in *Words, Images, and Performances in Translation*, eds. Brigid Maher and Rita Wilson (New York: Continuum, 2011), 123–25; and Tristram Walker, "Graphic Wounds: The Comics Journalism of Joe Sacco," *Journeys* 11.1 (2010), 75–81.

3. Bill Brown, "Thing Theory," in *Things*, ed. Bill Brown (Chicago: University of Chicago Press, 2004), 4.

4. Ibid., 5 (emphasis in original).

5. Ibid.

6. Jane Bennett, *Vibrant Matter: A Political Ecology of Things* (Durham: Duke University Press, 2010). Brown is not a vital materialist like Bennett, but the two authors' theories dovetail extremely well for the purposes of my analysis.

7. Ibid., 8-10. Bennett uses "actant," a term coined by Bruno Latour "for a source of action; an actant can be human or not, or, most likely, a combination of both" (9).

8. Ibid., 20–38.

9. Ibid., 37.

10. Joe Sacco, *Palestine* (Seattle: Fantagraphics, 2001), 4–5.

11. Ibid., 8.

12. Ibid., 152.

13. Ibid., 155.

14. Ibid., 87.

15. Ibid., 92.

16. Ibid., 4.

17. Hajja Nur, quoted in Saba Mahmood, *Politics of Piety: The Islamic Revival and the Feminist Subject* (Princeton: Princeton University Press, 2005), 50–51.

18. Sacco, *Palestine*, p. 140.

19. Ibid., 137.

20. Ibid., 138.

21. For more on agency, custom, and faith in relation to the hijab, the khimar, the niqab, and other Islamic women's garments and their larger role in the Women's Piety movement and feminine subjectivity in Islam, see Mahmood, *Politics of Piety*, 23–24, 41–57. On the hijab and "self-cultivation," see Mahmood, *Politics of Piety*, 155–61.

22. Sacco, *Palestine*, 171.
23. Ibid.
24. Ibid., 62.
25. Ibid.
26. Ibid.
27. Ibid., 61.

9. John's Story: Joe Sacco's Depiction of "Bare Life"

Øyvind Vågnes

Originally published in the winter and spring 2010 issues of the *Virginia Quarterly Review* and collected in his book *Journalism*, "The Unwanted" is one of several comics in recent years to reflect Joe Sacco's increasing interest in reporting on pressing global issues such as poverty and migration. In *Journalism*, "The Unwanted" follows stories about conflicts in Chechnya and Iraq and precedes "Kushinagar," a story about poverty in India.[1] Whether he has been reporting from war-torn countries or other global conflict areas, a central component of Sacco's work has been the plight of civilians, of human beings who for various reasons outside of their own control find themselves living under desperate life conditions. "The Unwanted," a story about an African migrant trying to reach Europe through Malta, describes how such conditions urge equally desperate measures, as individuals place themselves in danger in order to try to change their lives for the better elsewhere.

Every journalist or documentarian attempting to address the problem of what is often referred to as "undocumented migration" is faced with very specific representational constraints. The following essay will address the ways in which "The Unwanted" comes to terms with these challenges, and will argue that the story represents an intervention into the visual culture of migration. It is in the nature of so-called "illegal immigration" that the individual who crosses national borders is a violator of the immigration laws in the country of destination, and neither these individuals, nor those who support them, are interested in being identified in the media or elsewhere. Most of the problems of telling the stories of undocumented immigrants come from this simple, decisive fact: photographic or audiovisual records are difficult to produce, as well as potentially hazardous for the subjects they strive to depict and give voice to. A journalistic account of an undocumented immigrant's story in comics form thus inevitably invites the reader to attend to questions of visibility. The notion of the immigrant as "a guest" is, in Mireille Rosello's striking formulation, "a metaphor that has forgotten that it is a metaphor": "Immigration issues are a symptom of how profoundly the citizens of a modern European state can disagree about the definitions of hospitality."[2] In a book where she explores how immigration is historically and theoretically linked to hospitality, Rosello distinguishes, with reference to Jacques Derrida, between an ethics and a politics of hospitality. An ethics of hospitality is "infinite and beyond any human law," whereas a politics of hospitality "involves limits and borders: calculations and the management of finite resources, finite numbers of people, national borders and state sovereignty."[3] This essay will argue that telling the story of "The Unwanted" in drawn words and images enables a form of visibility that is essential for generating a shift to a politics of hospitality that does not have to be radically distinguished from an ethics of hospitality.

The Face of Migration

The heterogeneous population of the island of Malta, which is located in the Mediterranean Sea, south of Italy, east of Tunisia, and north of Libya, is a typical example of what Ariella Azoulay describes as a "differential body politic," whose forms of being are governed by one regime, but where the living conditions of citizens and noncitizens reflect the differentiation of that regime.[4] In reporting from this body politic, Sacco, who was born in Malta, and who remains a Maltese citizen and knows the language fairly well, chooses to begin by presenting interviews with Maltese women and men, ministers and officials. The first twelve pages of "The Unwanted" give voice to a number of opinionated citizens of the country, all of them ranging from skeptical to hostile with regard to the increase of uninvited guests to their shores. There are the fishermen off the coast who claim that it is not their responsibility to pick up refugees from the many crowded boats they come across while fishing bluefin tuna. There is the government communications coordinator who says that "Italy can absorb the numbers; we just can't."[5] Then there are the interviewees who speak for the general population, people Sacco happens to encounter during his visit to the island, giving expression to various misgivings over what the future might bring when the country has to accommodate even more refugees. Gradually we are introduced to public figures, such as Francis Debono, the mayor of Marsa (the capital of Malta), and William Lowell, imprisoned head of the ultra-nationalist party Imperium Europa, who describes himself as a "racialist," both of them adding to the impression that the Maltese born and raised on the island are overwhelmingly resistant to the massive influx of largely African refugees.[6]

When we are introduced to what is arguably the focal point of "The Unwanted," an immigrant from Eritrea, then, we are well into the story, and very familiar with the governing sentiments of the population, one of the most dense in the world, with around 400,000 people sharing its 122 square miles. The first panel to depict the Eritrean is a portrait against a black background.[7]

The mode of address might seem paradoxical: the man, while expressing the wish to retain anonymity, is facing the reader. Even though he will be telling his story under a pseudonym, we are presented with a drawing with a visual form of identification. The panel thus invites us to reflect on the fraught visibility of the story's subject. To most readers, this is likely to be the first image that they come across that depicts an illegal immigrant as a single individual addressing them. Illegal immigrants are often made invisible as individual human beings in mass-media depictions; either they are pictured as part of a threatening mass, suggesting that immigration is a form of invasion, or they are depicted as one passive victim among many (and nowhere are these stereotypes more evident than in what Francesca Falk refers to as "the icon of the threatened border"—the image of the crowded boat).[8] The rise of so-called grassroots media has not effected a transformation of this state of affairs, and this is in part due to the complexities of representing migrants in contemporary political discourse. In spite of the rise of a variety of new social-media platforms, the illegal immigrant is often rendered faceless because people often wish to speak out and to "be seen," but still wish to conceal their face. Videos posted online, for instance, threaten the principle of what is somewhat paradoxically referred to as "visual anonymity," as there are a number of ways in which the individuals involved can be identified, whether by older techniques such as facial recognition tools, or by the metadata embedded in the image, which can often lead back to location and creator.[9] In the cases where journalists and documentarists tell the stories of immigrant subjects, they have established a diversity of verbal-visual strategies to work around the impasse of facial recognition, including various ways in which to avoid showing the subject's face (views from the back, forms of masking), while allowing her or his voice to come through, in audio or print.[10]

Accordingly, the non-citizens of the differential body politic are rendered faceless, a fact that urges us to reflect on the relationship between visibility and human rights. The identity of the undocumented immigrant is reduced to what Giorgio Agamben has described as "bare life," a life deprived of the rights of the citizen. In an article published in English translation in 1993, "Beyond Human Rights," Agamben argues that every time that refugees seem to represent a mass phenomenon rather than individual cases, as between the two world wars, or indeed at the moment in which we presently live, neither organizations such as the United Nations nor single states are capable of resolving the problem or even dealing with it adequately, leaving the refugee question to the police and humanitarian organizations. According to Agamben, this is in part because the Universal Declaration of Human Rights falls short of describing the rights of "all human beings," a formulation that echoes the mottoes of the French Revolution, because in reality it propagates the rights of the citizen rather than the human being. In *Homo Sacer: Sovereign Power and Bare Life*, his book-length exploration of how natural or bare life vanishes into the figure of the citizen, refugees break the continuity between the "natural" human and the citizen. "In the system of the nation-state," Agamben writes, "the so-called sacred and inalienable rights of man show themselves to lack every protection and reality at the moment in which they can no longer take the form of rights belonging to citizens of a state."[11]

The way in which John's portrait occurs throughout Sacco's story allows for a form of direct address within the inevitable parameters of anonymity. The reader recognizes a human being telling his distinct yet representative story in the pages. Sacco's usual use of ad verbatim quotations in balloons and captions places John's narrative within the realm of witnessing. Through what Thierry Groensteen has called "iconic solidarity," the image of his face represents the central vocalization around which "The Unwanted" revolves.[12] Hand-drawn and hand-lettered comics thus enable a narrative of bare life which is hard to imagine in any other verbal-visual form. By drawing John's face, Sacco can represent the immigrant as an individual, while at the same time avoiding photographic and possibly incriminating depiction in the story.

In *Precarious Life*, her timely interrogation into the ethics of representation, Judith Butler observes that the use of the face within the media often effects a form of dehumanization. Writing about the plight of the media in the era of perpetual war against terror, Butler argues that the photographed face of media portraits fails to represent its subject as a human being. Instead, these portraits propose a metonymical relationship, as in the case of Osama bin Laden, "the face of terror itself," or, alternatively, the human individual remains faceless to us because we do not see a photographic or visual depiction at all. To Butler, the philosophy of Emmanuel Levinas offers critical reflections that can help us rethink "the face" as something that produces affect; for Levinas, she writes, "the human is not *represented by* the face":

> Rather, the human is indirectly affirmed in that very disjunction that makes representation impossible, and this disjunction is conveyed in the impossible representation. For representation to convey the human, then, representation must not only fail, but it must *show* its failure. There is something unrepresentable that we nevertheless seek to represent, and that paradox must be retained in the representation we give.[13]

As Joseph Darda observes in an attentive reading of Butler and Marjane Satrapi's *Persepolis*, comics can potentially lend itself to this ethical work.[14] Through its approximate visualization of the illegal immigrant, the mode of witnessing in "The Unwanted" is such that it escapes the constraints of the audiovisual and photographic representations of bare life. The portraits of John, a human being who is known to the readers by means of Sacco's hand-drawn depiction, but who is afforded human identity through it, differ from those of official figures in "The Unwanted." Unlike the refugee, these characters will be easily recognizable from the several photographic records readily available on the Internet and elsewhere. When figures such as minister Carmelo Mifsud Bonnici and Debono go on record towards the end of "The Unwanted," they are thus made accountable for their views and actions, not entirely unlike the way they would be in a story in a newspaper or a television report.[15] The effect of the story is thus to provide insights into the mechanisms and machinery of the differential body politic by contesting the invisibility of its non-citizens and retaining the visibility of its regulators.

In the lingua franca of the media and humanitarian organizations, the phrase "the face of migration" is often used to describe the nature of migration, as in the expression "the changing face of migration," which often relates to shifting notions of the migrant individual—her or his identity, background, and various reasons and motives for attempting to relocate elsewhere. "Face" in this context promises to humanize immigration, when in fact the singular "face" serves as a way of referring to immigrants as an abstract, undifferentiated mass rather than individuals. "Images go before the immigrant," W. J. T. Mitchell observes, "in the sense that before the immigrant arrives, his or her image comes first in the form of stereotypes, search templates, tables of classification, and patterns of recognition."[16] But the term "refugees," Azoualay reminds us, "does not constitute a visual category, although the people it denotes might have visual characteristics." Instead, she writes, it is "a political category at the heart of the regime that imposes it upon those people."[17] The first time the reader is introduced to John, she is likely to think of him as the Eritrean refugee; however, as the story develops, she will think of him as John. If he is remembered by the reader as the face of migration, then, it is also the face of a human individual who has suffered tremendous hardship, and whose trials and tribulations are, however traumatic, now knowable to us.

The Space of Migration

Migratory movement, Francesca Falk observes, is often described as if it were a natural disaster; the global and local conditions that make people leave are often not shown in mainstream media coverage.[18] "The Unwanted" takes the time to report in detail what happened to John before he boarded a boat to

Figure 9.1. Detail of Joe Sacco, "The Unwanted," in *Journalism* (New York: Metropolitan, 2012), 133.

cross the Mediterranean Sea.[19] He was one of thousands of students from the University of Asmara who in 2001 refused an Eritrean government order to work the whole summer without pay. More than 2,000 of these students were arrested, loaded onto trucks and transported to prisons in the eastern part of Eritrea, where they were mobilized for national service. John was ordered into the army, and three years went by; he then ended up in prison. He managed to escape when he was on leave, and crossed the border to Sudan, to a desolate UN refugee camp in Kassala, and on to Khartoum, where he lived in constant danger of deportation because he did not have a residence card. For a period, he was traded back and forth by Sudanese, Libyan, and Ethiopian smugglers, before he ended up in Tripoli—and, finally, in July 2006, on a crowded boat which took him to Malta, where he, along with others who arrived with him, was locked up and guarded in a closed detention center. The final pages of "The Unwanted" describe what these individuals can hope for while they wait there: after a lengthy review process, about half of the asylum seekers can expect to be approved for some sort of humanitarian status; the rest are deported. When finally released from detention, those who can stay move on to so-called "open centers" resembling refugee camps, from where an overwhelming majority move out into unemployment in Maltese society.

As John moves through these series of locations he is subject to ever-new forms of isolation and alienation while living in constant fear of being identified by authorities as paperless. We see him hiding in apartments in Khartoum and in Tripoli, where daily life goes on outside open windows, or crammed into a concealed compartment in a tomato truck on a desert road, fearing for the next checkpoint. We see him making his dangerous oceanic crossing, moving into what scholars have referred to as "exterritority," "the transient dwelling of refugees," where so many boat immigrants disappear in the waves.[20] Yet the most devastating conditions described in "The Unwanted" are arguably those in the detention centers of Malta, where John and other immigrants like him are no longer on the move, but are caught, instead, in a seemingly endless standstill (see Figure 9.1).[21]

The very first image of detention in "The Unwanted" suggests that however fearful John's journey has been up to that point, his courage has been motivated by a sense of hope that now has left him. The four individuals in the image, each looking in different directions and not communicating among themselves, have nothing to cling to but despondency. The barbed wire on the wall makes the detention center look like a prison, and in the pages that follow, "The Unwanted" indeed describes how illegal immigrants are treated like criminals. Here, comics description works very much against a form of euphemism that is characteristic of a particular type of political language that obscures human suffering. This making visible of what euphemism obscures is a strategy Sacco has made use of memorably in the past, notably in stories such as "Moderate Pressure, Part Two" in *Palestine*: the images show us something that is not reflected in the descriptions made by those in authority.[22] The European Commission, Petra Mayrhofer observes, describes the Lampedusa camp as "an accommodation centre"; the detention center at Malta is referred to as "a community centre" in the Commission's press material.[23] Euphemism, Marianne Hirsch has suggested, is "the linguistic equivalent of obstructed, censored, vision," "an assertion of the power and danger of language."[24]

The system of detention described and visualized in "The Unwanted" can be understood with reference to Agamben's notion of what he calls "the camp" in *Homo Sacer*: "In the camp, the state of exception, which was essentially a temporary suspension of the rule of law on the basis of a factual state of danger, is now given a permanent spatial arrangement, which as such nevertheless remains outside the normal order." According to Agamben, the camp is thus "the space that is opened when the state of exception begins to become the rule."[25] As Mitchell observes, the detention camp represents "a new form of legal limbo where persons may be detained indefinitely in a situation that is de jure 'temporary' but de facto 'permanent,'" a space where the illegal immigrant is "subject to the law and excluded from it at the same time."[26] It is a space, Mitchell points out, which is placed well out of sight; as Francesca Falk observes, it is often located in the periphery, where it is more likely to receive marginal press coverage, to remain, in the words of Almut Rembges, "well out of sight from the public eye."[27]

Perhaps the most lasting impression of what we might call the space of migration in "The Unwanted" is of a regulated system where the various places in which John finds himself come to resemble each other. For even if he and others like him make it out of the open center, the living conditions that await most of them are not unlike those he lived through in Kassala or Khartoum. As Eyal Weizman has pointed out, there is a systemic quality to how humanitarian spaces grow and solidify, and then give rise to camps. These camps then go on to "form a material link between humanitarianism and a massive and rapid process of migration, construction and quasi-urbanization."[28] Unlike the urban spaces they resemble, camps are strictly governed, and whereas Sacco, like the aid workers, is free to come and go in and out of the zone, the refugees do not have that choice. However, the panels depicting the immigrants who have finally made it out of detention and into the crammed rented flats, as unwanted there as they have been anywhere, suggest that the logic of the zone extends beyond its material manifestations. Ultimately, what characterizes the space of migration is the persistent inhospitality that gave Sacco the name to his story. "The most salient fact about migration in our time," observes Mitchell, "is the way it has become, not a transitional passage from one place to another, but a permanent condition in which people may live out their lives in a limbo of illegalized immigration, perpetual confinement in a refugee camp, or a perpetual motion and rootlessness, driven from place to place."[29]

In the final panel of "The Unwanted," Sacco invites one of his relatives in Malta to join him in comparing the reception of St. Paul, who according to the Bible was shipwrecked there and "struggled through the raging surf onto the island where the natives showed him and the other survivors 'unusual kindness,'" with that of the Africans.[30] "But St. Paul was here for a while and left," she responds.[31] "Making the asylum seeker visible as the guest who was denied hospitality," Mireille Rosello holds, "is a first step toward a politics of hospitality that does not have to be radically distinguished from an ethics of hospitality."[32] Ultimately, the achievement of "The Unwanted" is precisely that act of making visible.

NOTES

1. Joe Sacco, *Journalism* (New York: Metropolitan, 2012).

2. Mireille Rosello, *Postcolonial Hospitality: The Immigrant as Guest* (Stanford: Stanford University Press, 2002), 3, 6.

3. Rosello, *Postcolonial Hospitality*, 11.

4. See Ariella Azoulay, "Regime-Made Disaster: On the Possibility of Nongovernmental Viewing," in *Sensible Politics: The Visual Culture of Nongovernmental Activism*, eds. Meg McLagan and Yates McKee (New York: Zone, 2012), 30.

5. Sacco, "The Unwanted," in *Journalism*, 112.

6. Ibid., 117.

7. Ibid., 121.

8. Francesca Falk, "Invasion, Infection, Invisibility: An Iconology of Illegalized Immigration," in *Images of Illegalized Immigration: Towards a Critical Iconology of Politics*, eds. Christine Bischoff, Francesca Falk, and Sylvia Kafehsy (Bielefeld: Transcript-Verlag, 2012), 89.

9. Sam Gregory, "Human Rights Made Visible: New Dimensions to Anonymity, Consent, and Intentionality," in *Sensible Politics: The Visual Culture of Nongovernmental Activism*, eds. Meg McLagan and Yates McKee (Cambridge: Zone, 2012), 554.

10. Olaf Berg and Helen Schwenken, "Masking, Blurring, Replacing: Can the Undocumented Migrant Have a Face in Film?" in *Images of Illegalized Immigration: Towards a Critical Iconology of Politics*, eds. Christine Bischoff, Francesca Falk, and Sylvia Kafehsy (Bielefeld: Transcript-Verlag, 2012), 112–113.

11. Giorgio Agamben, *Homo Sacer: Sovereign Power and Bare Life*, trans. Daniel Heller-Roazen (Stanford: Stanford University Press, 1998), 126.

12. To Groensteen, the relationship between panels is the central element of comics, and the first criteria of its foundational order what he calls "iconic solidarity." Interdependent images, he writes, are "plastically and semantically over-determined by the fact of their coexistence *in praesentia*." See Thierry Groensteen, *The System of Comics*, trans. Bart Beaty and Nick Nguyen (Jackson: University Press of Mississippi, 2007), 20.

13. Judith Butler, *Precarious Life: The Powers of Mourning and Violence* (New York: Verso, 2004), 144.

14. To Darda, Marjane Satrapi's *Persepolis* offers an alternative to how Western media, according to Butler, allows the face either "capture" or "erasure." See Joseph Darda, "Graphic Ethics: Theorizing the Face in Marjane Satrapi's *Persepolis*," College Literature, 40.2 (Spring 2013): 31–51.

15. Sacco, "The Unwanted," 155.

16. W. J. T. Mitchell, *Seeing Through Race* (Cambridge: Harvard University Press, 2012), 127.

17. Azoulay, "Regime-Made Disaster," 41.

18. Falk, "Invasion, Infection, Invisibility," 97.

19. Sacco, "The Unwanted," 121–32.

20. Ruti Sela and Maayan Amir, "Exterritory Project," in *Solution 196–213: United States of Palestine-Israel*, ed. Joshua Simon (Berlin: Sternberg Press, 2011), 82.

21. Sacco, "The Unwanted," 133.

22. For more on this, see Øyvind Vågnes, "The Unmaking of the World: Trauma and Testimony in Two Stories by Joe Sacco," *Afterimage: The Journal of Media Arts and Cultural Criticism* 39.1–2 (2011), 60–62.

23. Petra Mayrhofer, "Fortress Europe?: Iconographical Aspects of European Borders," in *United in Visual Diversity: Images and Counter-Images of Europe*, eds. Benjamin Drechsel and Claus Leggewie (Innsbruck: Studien Verlag, 2010), 172–73.

24. Marianne Hirsch, "Editor's Column: Collateral Damage." *PMLA* 119.5 (2004), 1214.

25. Agamben, *Homo Sacer*, 168, 169.

26. Mitchell, *Seeing Through Race*, 134.

27. See Mitchell, *Seeing Through Race*, 141; Falk, "Invasion, Infection, Invisibility," 92; and Almut Rembges, "Who is a Refugee? Strategies of Visibilization in the Neighborhood of a Refugee Reception Camp and a Detention Centre," in *Images of Illegalized Immigration: Towards a Critical Iconology of Politics*, eds. Christine Bischoff, Francesca Falk, and Sylvia Kafehsy (Bielefeld: Transcript-Verlag, 2012), 167.

28. Eyal Weizman, *The Least of All Possible Evils: Humanitarian Violence from Arendt to Gaza* (New York: Verso, 2011), 58.

29. Mitchell, *Seeing Through Race*, 132.

30. Sacco, "The Unwanted," 156.

31. Ibid.

32. Rosello, *Postcolonial Hospitality*, 26.

10. Sacco with Badiou: On the Political Ontology of Comics

Alexander Dunst

Over the last decade, literary and cultural critics have taken increasing note of Joe Sacco's perceptive portrayals of trauma, hailing his dispatches from the world's conflict zones that have few equals in any medium. Sacco's harrowing images of poverty and destruction not only communicate the suffering of distant Palestinian villagers or Bosnia's war-ravaged generations, but also "restore a sense of humanity to those dehumanized by the pace of globalized media."[1] Scholarly opinion depicts Sacco as a witness to global suffering and contends that as readers of his graphic reportage we too become witnesses, in the process bridging the gap between rich and poor, between the West and what it perceives as the rest.

It seems difficult to disagree with such a beautifully uplifting narrative, but nonetheless we should. For this ethical reading fails to critique the elements of Sacco's work that remain mired in an exoticism of difference and mask imperial power as humanitarian intervention. As a consequence of this oversight, critics have paid little attention to Sacco's steady distancing from the ideological gaze of *Safe Area Goražde* and *Palestine*. In its conflation of politics with ethics, ethical criticism overlooks Sacco's explicitly *political* aesthetic and the formal innovations specific to his medium that govern *Footnotes in Gaza* and some of his shorter recent pieces. In addition to an ethics of witnessing, this essay identifies two additional registers in Sacco's work to date: what I describe, building on Alain Badiou's cultural and political philosophy, as visual investigations into the situation of contemporary politics, and a militant art in fidelity to Palestinian grassroots struggle.

Badiou's thought also provides the basis for my understanding of the narrative structure and visual ontology of comics in general, and Sacco's comics in particular. My suggestion is that we cannot seriously evaluate Sacco's engaged journalism without paying close attention to its formal characteristics. At base, this means that we need to account for how comics produce a visual presentation of the *being* of our world. Traditionally hand-drawn, comics possess a remarkable material quality, their visual aesthetic producing an "effect of immersion and absorption" that goes far beyond storytelling.[2] Yet scholars have so far spent little time thinking about the specific ontology of comics. Thus, part one of this essay adapts Badiou's ontological philosophy of art to this particular medium.

Part two reads Sacco's earlier volumes on Bosnia and Palestine alongside Badiou's *Ethics*. Badiou's essay functions as a vehement critique of the ways in which Western governments and academia, both in their own specific ways, hide the pursuit of their interests behind the smokescreen of ethical intervention. This section contrasts Sacco's narrow focus on the evil of ethnic cleansing with the realities of imperialist politics that were a major, perhaps *the* major, cause of the barbarities of the Yugoslav wars. Like *Goražde*, *Palestine* professes a love of the other that masks its logical inversion: an imaginary objectification that finds expression in the voyeurism of the tourist. The remainder of section two traces the ambivalences of the tourist gaze and identifies Sacco's gradual evacuation of this ideological position, epitomized in his account of the outbreak of the first Intifada and taken to a new level in *Footnotes*.

Applying my earlier discussion of comics ontology, part three contends that there is something insistently political about the world created by Sacco's *Footnotes*.[3] This politics exists precisely insofar as it escapes the common-sense opinion and visual ideology of corporate journalism. In presenting the recollections of the people of Rafah and Khan Younis, Sacco wagers that the incidents he investigates are not consigned to the dustbin of history but constitute the foundation of a living present—and can thus be described as what Badiou terms a political truth procedure. Leaving behind a purely ethical perspective for a self-consciously political aesthetic, Sacco questions history's givenness and explores the future the past may yet become.

My pairing of Sacco with Badiou throughout this essay comes despite the fact that, with the exception of occasional essays on cinema, Badiou has had little to say about popular culture, and, to the best of my knowledge, has never written about comics.[4] Thus, their purposeful conjunction in these pages may benefit from a few words of explanation. Sacco's complex oeuvre has been ill served by the singular focus on ethics, producing readings with a narrow focus on trauma and witnessing. At the same time, much scholarship on comics remains overly textual, when it would appear that the medium is one of visual presentation over narrative *re*presentation. The pages that follow suggest a new way of understanding this hybrid medium and argue that, Badiou's silence on the matter notwithstanding, his thought has much to tell us about popular culture, Joe Sacco, and comics as an art in the Badiouian sense of the term.

Sacco with Badiou: The Visual Ontology of Comics

For years, Badiou's philosophy of art received little attention in Anglophone cultural and literary studies. This has started to change, with book-length studies of *Beckett & Badiou* and *Badiou and Film* appearing alongside an increasing number of articles, but Badiou is still primarily understood as a political philosopher.[5] While not false in itself, this view can be traced to his initial reception within that academic field. However, the concentration on political philosophy overlooks Badiou's ongoing dialogue with poetry, theatre, film, and visual art, and thus a considerable part of his oeuvre.

Badiou himself has summarized his thinking on culture by the neologism "inaesthetics." Inaesthetics rejects didactic, cathartic, and romantic conceptions of culture and affirms it as an autonomous thought practice, the occurrence of ideas in the realm of the senses, and the construction of a truth specific to art. For Badiou, the transformative rupture that opens up the possibility of such truths, or the event, stands at the center of his philosophy. Art then forms one of four procedures—alongside politics, love, and science—that to him are capable of constructing such truths. Badiou's essays on culture thus all share a similar aim: to show how the arts, with the help of their respective formal operations, lay bare the inconsistency of ideological knowledge and allow us to perceive what formerly we could not—from the invention of cubist painting to twelve-tone music. An artistic truth procedure can then be described as the step-by-step construction of such a novel aesthetic practice. For all its conceptual precision, however, Badiou's reflections on culture always remain an application of his existing philosophy to art and never open themselves up to an artistic practice they might be unable to accommodate.[6]

For the simplicity of argument I have so far spoken of art and culture as if Badiou used the two terms indiscriminately. That is not the case. In fact, the relationship between them is part of the ongoing evolution of his thought. In attacking a liberal identity politics in *Saint Paul*, Badiou had conceived of culture simply as "the subjective or representative glue for the group's existence" and lamented the supersession of concepts of art by such communitarian fictions.[7] Equally, the essays in *Handbook of Inaesthetics* are concerned with establishing clear boundaries between art and nonart, as well as *between* the arts. At the same time, Badiou's work on cinema conceives of film as a "mass art," whose power lies in a purification of the ideological image and a destabilizing juxtaposition of the older media upon which it builds.[8] Implicit here is already the notion that cinema draws its vitality from the promiscuity of the popular. Badiou has since moved towards a generalization of this thesis: art exists in a constant dialectic between a constitutive impurity and its formal purification.[9]

This leaves us with the question of art versus culture. Contrasting his polemical identification of culture as a tool of communitarian identity, Badiou has also put forward a much more instructive conception of the term: "In the end, a culture, to the extent that it can be thought or identified by philosophy, is a singular interconnected configuration of truth-procedures."[10] This understanding is taken up in his recent reflections on the possibility of activist or "militant art" today, described as the artistic configuration of an emancipatory politics.[11] While holding onto the narrower term of art in this context, in effect his thought has moved from an understanding based on clear boundaries to a necessary impurity.

In the case of comics, this impurity can be traced to its emergence from the cheap mass publishing of the industrial age, traditions of political caricature, the partial overlap and transformation of working-class, migrant, and youth cultures in the US, popular science, mid-twentieth-century modernization, and the Sixties counterculture—to name just a few causes. As a consequence, the formal procedures of comics are not exclusive to it. As Badiou has said of film, the art of comics does not simply add itself to existing media: "It operates on the other arts, using them as its starting point, in a movement that subtracts them from themselves."[12] Equally, comics subtract themselves from—put at a distance or disrupt—painting, drawing, photography, drama, narrative prose, lyrical poetry, film, and television.

Like film, comics are arguably split by a rupture that distances commercial entertainment from an art form propelled by a specific truth procedure. This is not to denigrate commercial comics or to erect absolute distinctions but to wager that the medium is transformed by an event designated by the name *comix*. Given the focus of this essay, I will be unable to provide the critical investigation necessary to establish this claim in detail. But its contours can already be gleaned from Jean-Paul Gabilliet's cultural history of American comics and its description of the scandalous novelty of the first underground publications: as he shows, *comix* should be understood as a radical subtraction from the profit-motive of the entertainment industry and a distancing from a cultural product geared towards character identification and nationalist mythology.[13]

If we accept this argument for the time being, then what are the formal processes that allow for the emergence of ideas in comics? I have drawn on Badiou's account of cinema to stress the similarities between the two forms, but their differences are as revealing. These distinctions relate to what Groensteen describes as "the unique ontological foundations of comics," namely their "relational play of a plurality of interdependent images," which is usually said to establish a continuity of time and meaning.[14] "The image is first cut from the visible. Movement is held up, suspended, inverted, arrested. Cutting is more essential than presence," Badiou writes about film.[15] The opposite can be said of comics: where cinema feigns movement, its successive still images combining to reimagine the passage of time on which it feeds, comics begin and end with the static image. In comics, all movement is thought alone. As importantly, comics do not cut but frame.[16] They establish, or present, images that do not preexist in this form. This is true even where comics draw on photography, painting, drawing, or the video still. The comics image reduces and typifies. It is concerned not so much with verisimilitude as with the idea, and thus is defined by an act of subtraction from other visual media.

Of course, the comics image is usually supplemented by text. But this juxtaposition establishes a differential logic that enacts another subtraction. As in film, the co-presence of different media interrupts their respective independence and totality—the power of the image to arrest and trap the gaze, and the lure of narrative suspense. The subtractive ontology of the single comics panel finds its analogy in the logic of sequence. Sequence in comics means that a visual scene is never singular, that it is preceded and succeeded, and thus sequential art always subtracts from the autonomy of the single, still image. It may seem that something similar occurs in the succession of stills that establish the movement and temporality of cinema. Film projects static images for a split second before they disappear before our eyes, thus enacting a "perpetual past" that inverts the eternal present of painting. In contrast, the constitutive co-presence of images in comics falls on neither side.[17] When Sacco merges past and present in adjoining or single panels—placing a survivor of the Rafah massacre simultaneously in 1956 and the early 2000s in *Footnotes*—it is not sufficient to characterize the effect as a complex temporality.[18] Rather, he destabilizes past and present as much as stable meaning. Film establishes the idea as passage and ultimately loss, Badiou argues, whereas painting presents the idea as fully given.[19] In comics, in contrast, the idea emerges from a compositional space that interrupts linear time and delimits what is given.

It is in an attempt to defuse the tension inherent in this potential disruption that scholars have invested the "gutter" with the certainty of meaning and the passage of time. Neil Cohn is surely right when he insists that these gaps between panels, in and by themselves, provide neither.[20] Rather than guaranteeing linear temporality, the sequential construction of comics constantly threatens the continuity of time and gives rise to a spatial and reconstructive understanding of their visual narratives. In comics, images are never fully present and never fully past. Sacco's formal inventiveness subtracts from an assumed continuity of represented time and thus lies at the core of what comics as an art form are capable of. Something very similar can be said with regard to the gutter's lack of meaning. The fact that it is only by way of the gap, the radical lack of image and text, that sequential comics are inaugurated, announces the radical discontinuity of the *real*—of raw experience in its unmediated intensity—as the artistic truth of comics. That this empty space presents no meaning as such does not entail that it cannot *re*-present meaning for readers. But its subtraction from sense once again indicates the fundamental potential of the comics image to interrupt knowledge: to construct truth, as Badiou writes, as "a *hole in sense*."[21]

The term "potential" is decisive here. As in any other medium, formal characteristics are one thing, and their implementation is quite another. The artistic disruption of established norms, art's exposure of the inherent "instability of being," is easily captured by established opinion, by conventional modes of representation.[22] The pervasive impact of film and video on comics often means that the ideology of Hollywood cinema or TV news trumps the power of subtraction. In what follows, I explore how this potential is at times reigned in, at times realized to its fullest, in Sacco's comics.

Goražde to Palestine: From Difference to Sameness

Sacco's three major volumes of graphic journalism to date—*Safe* Area *Goražde*, *Palestine*, and *Footnotes in Gaza*—have usually been read within an academic framework known as ethical criticism. Thus, Hillary Chute writes that "*Footnotes* is about the situation of testimony—which is to say, it is a book about memory and about the transmission of trauma."[23] Similarly, Aryn Bartley argues that *Goražde* accepts "a pre-existing responsibility for the other" and "records the stories of those who are positioned as victims."[24] There are a number of acute political and philosophical problems with this approach. Interpretations such as the above adopt a perspective that privileges the transfer of memory to a Western audience via a Western interpreter. But do Gazans depend on American or European visitors or academics to remember and communicate their suffering? As Sacco's literary alter ego discovers in *Footnotes*, most of his subjects have already been interviewed about their experiences and a history of the Rafah massacre has already been written by a local historian.[25]

Thus, it is not so much Palestinians who rely on outsiders to mourn and remember but a Western audience that depends on similarity, the translation of the other's experience into their own language and cultural framework by one of their own. In this way, liberal ethics incessantly slides between a reiteration of non-identity and a yearning for its opposite, a passage that ultimately can only be stabilized by the recourse to religious metaphysics.[26] Politically, the emphasis on suffering and its transmission to the West does very concrete ideological work. As Bartley notes, this discourse understands Bosnians, Palestinians, or other war-torn populations, as victims. In the process, it reduces them to passive recipients of violence, and symbolically robs them of subjective agency at a time when they are desperately trying to build a better future. In return, an ethical perspective offers the recognition of their suffering by the West. But this comes at a high price: the offer of recognition institutes a Western figure of authority that often privileges symbolic acknowledgment or psychological healing over material recovery, which would necessitate wholesale economic and political change.[27]

The combination of imagined passivity, victimhood, and dependence on the West's benevolence makes for a highly unstable mixture. In *Goražde*, the protagonist's deep sympathy for the town's inhabitants goes hand in hand with condescension at the petty desires of its "silly girls" and at times outright disgust at their "pathetic prospects."[28] Sacco's honesty is as admirable as it is revealing. For our ethical valuation of the other is always undercut by less noble sentiments: love by narcissism, friendship by jealousy, respect by voyeurism. Badiou comments on the latter aspect, when he writes: "Ethics feeds too much on Evil and the Other not to take silent pleasure in seeing them close up."[29] Once again, Sacco is remarkably frank in the depiction of his voyeuristic desire for suffering—after all, he is a foreign journalist visiting a war zone in search of spectacular images and stories—and his fascination with psychological and physical wounds motivates large parts of *Goražde*.

This voyeurism both derives from Sacco's status as an outsider in Bosnia and constantly threatens to condemn him to the periphery. But what shines through the depiction of his friendship with the town's inhabitants is Sacco's attempt to nevertheless make himself one of them. That this ethical imperative remains utopian should not be seen as an individual failure but can be traced back to the historical situation Sacco confronts. To return to Badiou's terminology, the Balkan wars, fought by Bosnian, Croat, NATO, and Serb forces for nationalist and imperialist gain, lack a political truth procedure that would sustain an ethics in service of such a truth. Yet Sacco's willingness to make himself equal to his hosts indicates a much more forceful alternative to a liberal ethics of alterity. In fact, it is this alternative that the violent imposition of ethnic difference during the Balkan conflicts sought to bury but which can still be glimpsed under the rubble in *Goražde*. As the protagonist's friend Kimeta explains to Sacco about her youth in a unified Yugoslavia: "I didn't pay any attention to whether someone was Serb or Muslim. Everybody was the same."[30] Ethical value then resides in the construction of sameness, not in an insistence on difference that is always liable to induce fear or even hatred. As Badiou argues in *Ethics*, difference is simply what there is. That is to say, "infinite multiplicity is the very medium of being itself," and therefore of no intrinsic value.

In contrast, ethics consists in an indifference to differences and in producing what is not yet but comes to be.³¹

However, such an ethics of sameness depends on a truth procedure for its realization. Or rather, ethical practice lends consistency to the construction of a truth, whether it may be in politics or love, science or art. I have already remarked upon truth's absence from the political situation of Bosnia in the 1990s, and the same must be said of *Goražde*. Unlike Sacco's books on the Israel-Palestine conflict, *Goražde* more or less reproduces the mainstream account of the Yugoslav breakup, which begins with Serb nationalist aggression, continues with Croat and Bosnian resistance, and, after some dithering by European powers, ends with decisive US action. Politically, Sacco remains in thrall to the ideology of humanitarian intervention. Ignoring the wider causes of the conflict he covers, he constructs a narrative frame that falls into a dichotomy of good and evil—and can only understand the actions of the Serb population with reference to the latter.

Even a rough sketch of the breakup of Yugoslavia lies beyond the limits of this essay. But given its importance for *Goražde* and the fact that Sacco's account of it has so far escaped criticism, a few brief comments seem called for. The initial cause of the breakup was an economic crisis, which was the consequence of a debt-restructuring plan imposed by the International Monetary Fund (IMF).³² Mass unemployment ensued, undermining the link between the Socialist state party and the working class. To counter this threat, politicians in the federal republics of Slovenia, Croatia, and Serbia resorted to nationalist rhetoric, creating an opening for countries with long-standing interests in the region, notably Austria, Hungary, and Germany. Individually and in concert, they agitated for Slovene and Croatian "self-determination," ultimately recognizing their independence, despite polls indicating that a clear majority of the population was committed to a unified Yugoslavia. In addition, the Yugoslav constitution stipulated that no national group in the ethnically mixed republics could break away without the agreement of all the others—a consequence of the fact that large parts of the majority Serb population lived outside of Serbia. A reunified and ascendant Germany rode roughshod over these objections in Croatia, driving local Serbs into the hands of ruthless nationalists when Croatian leaders refused to recognize their minority rights. In 1992, the US entered the fray to do the same in Bosnia. Where Germany had sought to expand its sphere of influence, the Clinton administration was determined to stem it. Ignoring repeated warnings by the State Department and the CIA about the inevitable outcome, the US government persisted, reasserting its hegemony over Europe with the help of NATO's military might but plunging Bosnia into war. The rest of this history is on display in *Goražde*, but its fundamental causes are obscured. And so the book's Serbs appear as the epitome of evil and the US as Bosnia's savior.

Sacco's captivity to the narrative of humanitarian interventionism finds visual parallels in the pages of *Goražde*. The potential of his graphic reportage lies in the freedom from the institutional and formal constraints of corporate journalism with which it provides its author. Even Sacco's partial distancing from mainstream reporting in *Goražde* remains unthinkable for most of his colleagues, who must present what they have learned within ever-shorter news cycles and on ever-tighter budgets. As I argued in the preceding section, comics may function as a subtraction from the cultural forms and media on which they build—and this applies as much to journalism as to photography or film. Yet of all of Sacco's major works, *Goražde* remains closest to the conventions of news photography and commercial cinema. Sacco has said that he sketches little on his research trips and instead relies on photographs taken on site when he returns to the drawing board.[33] But where *Palestine* withdraws from photography by means of the skewed angles and the satirical abstraction of caricature, *Goražde*'s striving for journalistic veracity doubles as quasi-photographic perspective and mise-en-scène. This is particularly pronounced when Sacco, who adapts the performative authenticity of the New Journalism to comics, cannot personally vouch for his facts: in its recreation of zooms and close-ups, shots and counter-shots, his account of Serbian militia attacks at points resembles the storyboard for a Hollywood war movie.[34]

Even the first page of *Palestine* establishes a striking contrast with *Goražde*. Abandoning sequence in the single panel of the splash page, Sacco impresses a scene on his readers that speaks of his confusion upon the first arrival in Cairo and aims to similarly affect his readers. In its drawing style as much as in its page design, Sacco's approach in *Palestine* is far looser, indulging in caricatural dramatization and absurdity. Yet one can't help but detect a certain orientalism in the book's introductory chapters: a Western tourist's ambivalent fascination with the perceived chaos and charm of the Middle East. As in *Goražde*, Sacco is acutely aware of his own gaze, both as a tourist and a journalist, two identities that at times become nearly indistinguishable. Ultimately, however, the protagonist's ironic self-reflexivity can only problematize, not break through the logic of difference in either narrative. Distancing himself from the conventions of war reporting, Sacco mocks its tired formula and rejects the subject positions it offers to journalists and their subjects. But, as Andrew Gibson writes in his Badiouian reading of Beckett, irony is symptomatic of a present for which a substantially different future remains unthinkable, and its language as yet unavailable.[35]

The decisive rupture with a liberal ethics only comes in the final third of

Palestine. Yet it is prepared throughout much of the book by the author's interest in the everyday struggle of ordinary Palestinians. Sacco's account of "Ansar III," an Israeli prison built to house those accused of participation in the First Intifada, details the impressive levels of self-organization achieved by inmates, including literacy programs and lectures. Increasingly, Sacco's alter ego, ever-present in measuring his cultural distance from Palestine's inhabitants in early chapters, fades into the background.

Another episode, innocuously titled "The Boys, Part One," begins under the shadow of a military surveillance tower but establishes a sudden absence of state control. Here, local acquaintances take Sacco to the site where the First Intifada began in 1987. The sudden eruption of political struggle after more than two decades of occupation is described as an event that inaugurates a new present radically distinct from what existed previously. In a territory handled by the Israeli military as an uncontrollable excess of people, Palestinian resistance erupts without prior indication. Sacco writes: "It was a spontaneous popular explosion, and it caught everyone by surprise, including the PLO."[36] What emerges, Sacco's acquaintances explain after their return from the original site of the uprising, is a novel and previously unimaginable idea. The power of the Israeli state is put at a distance and becomes amenable to strategic analysis. This distance enables a newfound faith in the possibility of self-determination and a previously unimaginable future.[37] A decade later, Sacco returns to Gaza to investigate the history of this future. Visualizing the massacres that took place in the Palestinian towns of Rafah and Khan Younis in 1956, *Footnotes* is lifted by a political truth that it formalizes as an artistic procedure intrinsic to the medium of comics.

History's Future: *Footnotes in Gaza* and Beyond

In ways similar to *Goražde*, the absence of a political truth procedure conditions Sacco's recent shorter pieces.[38] Yet several of these comics can be seen as pertinent analyses of contemporary politics. Two chapters in *Days of Destruction* focusing on the struggle of Native Americans and industrial workers during the twentieth century may be seen as attempting what Badiou terms "resurrection." Extending and refining his account of the event and its consequences with *Logics of Worlds*, Badiou has argued that an earlier truth procedure can be revitalized and incorporated into a new present.[39] "The Unwanted," on African migration to Malta, as well as comics on African American politics in Camden, New Jersey, and the Occupy camp in Manhattan's Zuccotti Park, seek to identify "evental sites," situations that are defined by weak state power and political upheaval, and at which an event may therefore take place.[40] Badiou once may have dismissed the role such "pre-eventual assessment" can play in preparing the truth procedures that arise in fidelity to an event but now seems more willing to accord it political importance—and art its specific role in this process.[41]

This returns me to the question of militant art, a phrase I used at the very beginning of this essay to describe Sacco's *Footnotes*. Such creative activism constructs its truth as art but is equally determined by politics. Phrased differently, militant art expresses a political becoming in the cultural sphere. As the term "becoming" indicates, such art presents us with the formalization of novelty. It is thus, by definition, the art of an ongoing process and marked by the uncertainty of results. Or, as Badiou argues, "art can be a . . . subjective preparation for the reception of a political event."[42] Badiou is quick to distinguish between an earlier mode of militant art, associated with twentieth-century party politics, and its possibility today. In the absence of a strong ideology, or the state institutions under whose power it often turned into a celebration of past achievements, militant art must renew itself to become contemporary again. Never shy of programmatic statements, Badiou offers four guiding principles. Firstly, art should create a common space with local political struggles. Secondly, it must "organize progressively the return to a strong idea" and transform itself, thirdly, from an art of representation into an art of presentation."[43] The final aim of this artistic practice will be to synthesize these prior elements.

The only example Badiou gives of such local struggles is Palestine, which Sacco revisits a decade after his first stay. *Footnotes* is a very different book from the earlier foray. Absent are the aimless wanderings of a young artist at the center of his own images; gone the voyeurism of the earlier volumes. Upon his return in the winter of 2002–2003, Sacco finds the inhabitants of the Gaza Strip betrayed by their own leadership as much as by Israeli promises of peace. The truth of the First Intifada, however, the faith in the necessity of equality and self-determination, lives on in the collective existence of working-class Gazans. Sacco chooses a lateral access route into exploring this resistant subjectivity—conditioned by his long-standing interest in warfare. Throughout its 400 pages, *Footnotes* details the present-day consequences of the two massacres of civilians that took place almost fifty years earlier.

Yet *Footnotes* is not simply a book about "memory" in the sense in which it is used by adherents of the ethical turn. *Palestine* had already made this point upon the protagonist's visit to the site of the First Intifada. As Sacco recalls, the protest that inaugurated the Intifada led the participants back from a funeral. Here, memory and mourning motivate political action, and the obligation to history consists in the realization of a different future rather than in preserving the past. Sacco's decision to visualize local people's recollections of the massacres constitutes the book's great wager: that the incidents he investigates are not consigned to history but constitute the past of a living present. His artistic transposition of this insight, its sensory presentation as an idea, consists in a visual breaking-apart of history as closed, empty time—the violent destabilization of temporal planes. This takes form in two distinct subtractions, which may be termed isolation and interruption. Taking up my earlier argument that comics, like film, operate on the basis of established media, I appropriate these concepts from Badiou's discussion of the poetry of Stéphane Mallarmé and Arthur Rimbaud.

Badiou defines isolation as "bringing forth a contour of nothingness" in order to pass to "that which is subtracted from the count, inexistent"—that is to say, that which is not recognized by society and remains invisible to it.[44] Sacco brings forth such glimpses of raw experience as ontologically inconsistent by way of the withdrawal of image or text. The effect thereby achieved must be understood against the dense narrative and visual texture of Sacco's work, an image world of panoramic background bleeds, dramatic dialogue, and highly irregular panel shapes. But once in a while in *Footnotes*, this sensory intensity is abruptly displaced, and expectations deceived. Thus, on the final panel of one right-hand page, Sacco provides a textual description of Palestinian men lined up against a wall by Israeli forces. As an expectant reader turns the page, Sacco refuses to provide an image and the imagination of their deaths is completely left to the mind. Elsewhere, a splash page yields nothing but the utter silence of relatives coming to collect their dead, their speechless grief visible in the almost black crosshatching of Sacco's drawing.[45] These acts of authorial refusal insist on the insufficiency of vision and textual meaning. Isolating one of comics' constitutive media, they make the *real* appear in its radical absence, subtracting from what is acknowledged by the state to lay bare that which does not count.

Where isolation withdraws, interruption subtracts by the sudden opposition of the incongruent. As Badiou writes, interruption "consists in . . . a juxtaposition that is almost unintelligible between two incompatible figures of being."[46] The basic visual layout of *Footnotes* consists of a background that establishes a scene, which "bleeds" beyond the borders of the page, and multiple superimposed or inset panels. This structure has remained much the same since Sacco's early work. *Goražde*, however, indulged in gory depictions of violence, something much less common in *Footnotes*. Sacco's spatial positioning of inset panels has become more refined and violence has, in part at least, moved onto a formal level: what cuts open human bodies is no longer artillery shells, or a surgeon's medical saw, but the violent imposition of a panel onto its background: severing a woman's legs, blocking out her upper body, and juxtaposing

Figure 10.1. Joe Sacco, *Footnotes in Gaza* (New York: Metropolitan, 2009), 100.

the immediate aftermath of the massacre with her testimony in the present of narration. Such clashes between different time frames constitute the most frequent instance of interruption in the book. Repeatedly, Sacco destabilizes the chronology of past and present in visualizing the day of the massacre. Thus, a survivor looks at a stone wall on the town square of Khan Younis, and is next found staring at the wounded and dead in the same place forty-five years later. In Rafah, Sacco speaks to the school gardener Abdullah in one panel, and in the next Abdullah stands in front of Israeli soldiers aiming their rifles at cowering Palestinians, his face turned towards the reader (see Figure 10.1).

It is not enough to say that past and present invade each other in Sacco's *Footnotes*. Their sudden confrontation in this, his most accomplished and challenging work, unhinges their sequence and the supposed continuity of history. What is put into doubt is history's givenness, what is opened up to possibility is the future the past may yet become. In *Footnotes*, the present of Palestinian self-determination creates the history of the massacres, and it is in fidelity to the First Intifada that Sacco subtracts from knowledge to present his readers with the inconsistency of time. As Badiou has remarked, such faithful perseverance is not memory but "not-forgetting."[47] In his insistence on the presence of the past, Sacco's encounters in Palestine forge a new subject of militant art in the medium of comics.

NOTES

1. Tristram Walker, "Graphic Wounds: The Comics Journalism of Joe Sacco," *Journeys* 11.1 (2010), 69.

2. Johanna Drucker, "What Is Graphic About Graphic Novels?" *English Language Notes* 46.2 (2008), 40.

3. I offer a briefer interpretation of *Footnotes* in the context of post-9/11 trauma culture in: Alexander Dunst, "After Trauma: Time and Affect in American Culture *beyond* 9/11," *Parallax* 18.2 (2012): 56–71.

4. See the essays recently collected in Alain Badiou, *Cinema*, trans. Susan Spitzer (Cambridge: Polity 2013).

5. Andrew Gibson, *Beckett & Badiou: The Pathos of Intermittency* (New York: Oxford University Press, 2006); and Alex Ling, *Badiou and Film* (Edinburgh: Edinburgh University Press, 2011).

6. Gibson, *Beckett & Badiou*, 285; and see also Jacques Rancière, "Aesthetics, Inaesthetics, Anti-Aesthetics," in *Think Again: Alain Badiou and the Future of Philosophy*, ed. Peter Hallward (New York: Continuum, 2004), 218–31.

7. Alain Badiou, *Saint Paul: The Foundation of Universalism*, trans. Ray Brassier (Stanford: Stanford University Press, 2003), 12.

8. Alain Badiou, *Handbook of Inaesthetics*, trans. Alberto Toscano (Stanford: Stanford University Press, 2005), 83; and Alain Badiou, "Philosophy and Cinema," in *Infinite Thought: Truth and the Return to Philosophy*, trans. and eds. Oliver Feltham and Justin Clemens (New York: Continuum, 2004), 113.

9. Alain Badiou, "Fifteen Theses on Contemporary Art," *Lacanian Ink*, http://www.lacan.com/frameXXIII7.htm.

10. Alain Badiou, "Politics and Philosophy: An Interview with Alain Badiou," in *Ethics: An Essay on the Understanding of Evil*, trans. Peter Hallward (New York: Verso, 2001), 140.

11. Alain Badiou, "Does the Notion of Activist Art Still Have a Meaning?" *Lacanian Ink*, http://www.lacan.com/thesymptom/?page_id=1580.

12. Badiou, *Handbook of Inaesthetics*, 79.

13. Jean-Paul Gabilliet, *Of Comics And Men: A Cultural History of American Comic Books*, trans. Bart Beaty and Nick Nguyen (Jackson: University Press of Mississippi, 2010).

14. Thierry Groensteen, *The System of Comics*, trans. Bart Beaty and Nick Nguyen (Jackson: University Press of Mississippi, 2007), 17.

15. Badiou, *Handbook of Inaesthetics*, 78.

16. Groensteen, *The System of Comics*, 40.

17. Badiou, *Handbook of Inaesthetics*, 78.

18. Joe Sacco, *Footnotes in Gaza* (New York: Metropolitan, 2009), 262.

19. Badiou, *Handbook of Inaesthetics*, 81, 85–86.

20. Neil Cohn, "The Limits of Time and Transitions: Challenges to Theories of Sequential Image Comprehension," *Studies in Comics* 1.1 (2010), 136.

21. Alain Badiou, "The Philosophical Recourse to the Poem," *Conditions*, trans. S. Corcoran (New York: Continuum, 2008), 43.

22. Gibson, *Beckett & Badiou*, 20.

23. Hillary Chute, "Comics Form and Narrating Lives," *Profession* 11 (2011), 113.

24. Aryn Bartley, "The Hateful Self: Substitution and the Ethics of Representing War," *Modern Fiction Studies* 54.1 (2008), 51, 57.

25. Sacco, *Footnotes in Gaza*, 173.

26. Alain Badiou, *Ethics: An Essay on the Understanding of Evil*, trans. and intr. Peter Hallward (New York: Verso, 2001), 22.

27. Stef Craps, "Wor(l)ds of Grief: Traumatic Memory and Literary Witnessing in Cross-Cultural Perspective," *Textual Practice* 24.1 (2010), 56.

28. Joe Sacco, *Safe Area Goražde: The War in Eastern Bosnia, 1992–1995* (Seattle: Fantagraphics, 2000), 50–56, 192.

29. Badiou, *Ethics*, 35.

30. Sacco, *Safe Area Goražde*, 153.

31. Peter Hallward, "Translator's Introduction," in *Ethics*, xxxv–vi; and Alain Badiou, *Ethics*, 27.

32. Peter Gowan, "The NATO Powers and the Balkan Tragedy," *New Left Review* 234 (1999), 83; and see also Susan Woodward, *Balkan Tragedy: Chaos and Dissolution After the Cold War* (Washington, DC: Brookings Press, 1995). The dominant narrative of the Balkan wars in the West was and is a very different one, of course.

33. Gary Groth, "Joe Sacco, Frontline Journalist," *Comics Journal* Special Edition (Winter 2002), 61; cited in Walker, "Graphic Wounds," 80.

34. Sacco, *Safe Area Goražde*, 174.

35. Gibson, *Beckett & Badiou*, 194.

36. Joe Sacco, *Palestine* (Seattle: Fantagraphics, 2001), 191.

37. Alain Badiou, "Politics as Truth Procedure," in *Metapolitics*, trans. J. Barker (New York: Verso, 2005), 145.

38. See his collaboration with Chris Hedges, which includes illustrations and short comics by Sacco, as well as the features collected in *Journalism*: Chris Hedges and Joe Sacco, *Days of Destruction, Days of Revolt* (New York: Nation, 2012); and Joe Sacco, *Journalism* (New York: Metropolitan, 2012).

39. Alain Badiou, *Logics of Worlds: Being and Event*, 2, trans. A. Toscano (New York: Continuum, 2009), 65–66.

40. Badiou, *Being and Event*, 173-77.

41. Peter Hallward, "Order and Event: On Badiou's *Logic of Worlds*," *New Left Review* 53 (2008), 107.

42. Badiou, "Does the Notion of Activist Art Still Have a Meaning?"

43. Ibid.

44. Alain Badiou, "Mallarme's Method: Subtraction and Isolation," in *Conditions*, trans. S. Corcoran (New York: Continuum, 2008), 60.

45. Sacco, *Footnotes in Gaza*, 348–49.

46. Badiou, "The Philosophical Recourse to the Poem," 75.

47. Badiou, "Politics and Philosophy: An Interview with Alain Badiou," 52.

11. Joe Sacco's Comics of Performance

Rebecca Scherr

One of the signatures of Joe Sacco's comics is the presence of the artist as a character on the page. His cartoon avatar activates, contextualizes, and often ironizes the narrative within and across the panels. Simultaneously, although Sacco's primary intent is to represent the pain of others, Sacco-the-artist is also always present through the very line of his artistry. Every line is a kind of resonance, carrying a trace of the artist's hand, acting as a reminder of the labor involved in the creation of the work.[1] Jared Gardner claims that this reminder is unique to the comics form, and furthermore functions as a kind of performance; in comics, line can be thought of as a "voice-print," Gardner writes, likening this voice-print to the performance of the storyteller.[2] While I find Gardner's point about graphic line as a kind of narrative performance compelling, I would like to expand on it by claiming that performance functions on many more levels within the comics medium. Performativity can also be a useful lens through which to examine comics' transitive potential—that is, its ability to *do* things, to intervene in a reader's world through properties that go far beyond line drawing. Sacco's work presents an especially interesting case study for examining the potential of comics as a performative medium for two reasons: first, Sacco's work incorporates several aspects of performance in terms of both form and content; and second, performativity in Sacco's work highlights the ability of comics to intervene in specific ethical debates concerning the politics of representing pain and trauma.

Sacco includes layer upon performative layer in his comics, so much so that I would call Sacco's comics a comics of performance; a discourse of performance pervades just about every aspect of his art. Beyond the narrative performance embedded in line itself, performance is also very present in terms of the actual content framed within the panels. For example, Sacco not only represents himself as artist and journalist as he interacts with others (what I will refer to as his journalistic performance), but he continually restages his informants' past traumatic events, what Øyvind Vågnes calls Sacco's method of "comics reenactment."[3] In addition, Sacco often draws ritualized performances of mourning and grief, and his work represents the intricacies involved in the performance of giving and receiving testimony. Performance and performativity are thus palpably present dimensions of Sacco's work on the explicitly visible level of content, and on the resonant level of comics' particular affects and effects. The first two parts of this essay explore the various formal and affective dimensions of performance and performativity in Sacco's work, while the final part examines how Sacco's comics of performance stage highly constructed spectacles as a way to frame difficult questions regarding the politics of humanitarian witnessing.

The Performance of Pain

Kim Deitch's *The Boulevard of Broken Dreams* opens with a quick glance back at the early days of comics and animation: it is 1927, and the fictional Windsor Newton, "venerable cartoonist and animation pioneer, does the beloved act that thrilled audiences of 1910."[4] Newton, on stage interacting with his own animation creation—an elephant named Milton, projected onto a screen—references how early cartooning functioned quite explicitly as performance. Similar to J. Stuart Blackton's *The Enchanted Drawing* (1900) and the films of Winsor McCay, human, film, cartoon, and animation coalesce into a staged performance that foregrounds the creator's labor; the creator is as present as the creation.[5] As *Boulevard* goes on to point out, however, these performances rose to prominence and died out quickly; Newton in 1927 gives his performance in much reduced circumstances, the audience no longer thrilled but rather drunk and belligerent. The thrill of the stage performance, *Boulevard* goes on to argue, gave way to more factory-like processes of reproduction, the industry ultimately ruled not by the "enchantment" of performance but by market forces, the logic of capital, whereby the labor of the artist is no longer "part of the show," so to speak. Yet the performative dimension of comics and animation has not disappeared completely. Instead, it can be located in other and subtler aspects of the form where the artist's or creator's conscious act of creation becomes palpable, identifiable. Built into the form itself are specific sites where the artist can be seen, heard, and even felt in the reader's or viewer's encounter with the form, a kind of dim echo of the showmanship of the early work I mention above.

As Gardner argues, one of the most performative aspects of the comics form is found in line drawing itself, for it is the line that in a very physical sense calls attention to the labor or the "trace" of the artist's presence on the page:

> To read a story in a comic is to be reminded constantly that this is a story told *by* someone—and a storyteller who is necessarily and fundamentally bound to often brutal physical realities: the physically demanding and time-consuming work of composing, penciling, erasing, inking, coloring, lettering on one hand; *and* the physical constraints of a narrative form that demands

greater use of ellipses and compressions than novel or film to tell even the most basic stories. Too much time, too little time: with every graphic narrative we have an inevitable encounter with the laboring body of the graphiateur and the constrained body of the form itself.[6]

In such a formulation, the line in comics represents a specific kind of storyteller, one who is "bound to brutal realities," whose acts of creation constitute *difficult* labor, and it is this difficulty, according to Gardner, that emanates powerfully from the page and becomes one with the artist's "voice-print." Thus, the "voice-print" is associated with a kind of pain, emerging through bodily constraint and struggle. Certainly Deitch's *Boulevard* dramatizes this brutality as both physical and psychological. Yet I think that in general the drawn line is infused as much with *desire* as it is with constraint and struggle. Later in this essay, I will return to the importance of this idea in thinking about image production and performativity, and how this desire relates to Sacco's project.

What happens when the artist's performance of pain competes with the much more pressing pain of others, pain grounded in the trauma of displacement, death, incarceration, war, and torture? Any number of pages in Sacco's works present such a "competition," if we do indeed think of the artist's line as a product of pain and struggle. Sacco's comics trade in brutal realities on many levels, not just in the act of creation. Sacco's drawn worlds of people affected by war and human rights abuses are literally worlds of constraint: people are constrained through geography and architecture, imprisonment, and the rule of law and politics. While the brutality of the content in Sacco's work often overwhelms the sense of line as a product of struggle, and certainly these two kinds of pain communicate very different levels of intensity, the two also work in concert to underscore just how thoroughly Sacco's comics are shot through with a discourse of pain.

In fact, many of the most celebrated autobiographical comics, a body of works Gillian Whitlock calls "auto-graphics,"[7] such as Marjane Satrapi's *Persepolis*, Art Spiegelman's *Maus*, Alison Bechdel's *Fun Home*, and Sacco's works, are praised for the inventive ways that their authors use narrative and visual methods to represent pain, suffering, and the trauma of war and loss. All of these works question the boundaries of what constitutes private and public pain. Therefore, it seems that within the emerging canon of autobiographical graphic narratives, representations of pain itself are always in competition—and alignment—with the struggle inherent in the act of comics creation. The performative as it functions within *both* form and content in these works is inseparable from a discourse of pain.

Sacco's representations of pain, however, differ from the other autobiographical works I mention above since he neither has firsthand experience of the pain of displacement and war, nor does he possess a kind of kinship link to trauma, as does Spiegelman. Consequently, in Sacco's work there is always an added distance in his representations of pain, a gap he acknowledges and fills with a critique of what it means for him, a journalist, to be a tourist in the landscapes of pain. In other words, this gap is mediated by meta-commentary regarding the role of journalistic performance.

In *Palestine*, Sacco acknowledges these gaps several times, and this is made particularly manifest, I would suggest, whenever Sacco expresses his desire to witness other people's pain. Sacco, nearly always self-ironic, recognizes that such desire makes him a "vulture," but he rationalizes this desire via his journalistic skepticism: "I'm a skeptic. Journalistically speaking, you gotta be a Doubting Thomas; you gotta make sure. It's good to get your finger in the wound. Your whole head would be better."[8] Sacco does not refer to digging into his own wounds here, but to metaphorically sticking his fingers into the wounds of others. This is, in a sense, how he characterizes his entire Palestinian project: his role as journalist is not one of simply recording the pain of others, but he recognizes that in having his subjects retell their stories, that is, in initiating the performance of testimony and witnessing, his interventions bring pain back into being.[9] He provocatively suggests that such intervention can even make the initial wounds larger (putting "your whole head" in the wound "would be better"). He pokes the pain of others so that it comes to the surface again for him to collect and re-present. Thus, he is aligning the journalistic act with the forces of oppression, with forces that wound. He is suggesting that the work he performs participates not only in the reproduction of pain as it can be expressed in comics form, but also in the more immediate *production* of pain, even as he is offering these stories to the world in order to shed much needed light on pressing humanitarian crises.

This way of characterizing journalistic performance as a purveyor of pain is also found in many of Sacco's other works. In the short piece "Trauma on Loan," Sacco interviews two Iraqi men who are suing the US government for unlawful detention and torture, and they duly tell him the story of their captivity and the beatings and humiliations they were subject to, including sexual assault. At the end of their time together, Sacco thanks them, wishes them a good journey, and writes, "And, once again, they are released."[10] In this single, short comment, Sacco-the-journalist aligns his role with the US army's powers to detain and to inflict pain. In another poignant example, towards the end of *Footnotes in Gaza*, Sacco realizes that he and his collaborator Abed were "arguably ... the world's foremost experts" regarding two massacres of Palestinians by Israeli soldiers in 1956, a "footnote" of history only because official powers consider these atrocities insignificant.[11] In musing about this, and while depicting himself being driven along the very streets where one of the massacres took place, Sacco likens the process of bringing the past into the present to that of the actions of the Israeli soldiers: "How often we forced the old men of Rafah back down this road lined with soldiers and strewn with shoes.... How often we shoved the old men between the soldiers with sticks and through that gate. ... How often we made them sit with their heads down and piss on themselves. ... In the end, when we'd finished with them, we let them break down the wall and run home."[12]

These last two examples are also interesting in that within the panels Sacco as a *character* is as present as Sacco-the-artist and Sacco-the-narrator. This speaks to the fact that autobiographical comics extend the notion of "the laboring body of the graphiteur," for in these cases the laboring body materializes as an explicit representation *within* the comics panels, and provides metacommentary on the creative process itself. In auto-graphics, the presence of the artist is not just a resonant trace via line drawing, but is indexically woven into the discourse of the narrative. In this way, the presence of the artist as a character can be compared to Blackton's and McCay's interactions with their own animation creations, although in autobiographical comics this is complicated by the fact that most of the cartoonists' drawn figures—including of him or herself—have real-life counterparts. Charles Hatfield points out that self-representation in comics (what he calls "ironic authentication") almost always speaks to the making of the work itself,[13] thus allowing the *performance of work* to be made manifest within the graphic text. Sacco keeps his representations of work strictly focused on his journalistic performance, that is, the gathering of testimony through listening, writing, and taking photographs, and he also depicts some of the ethical dilemmas that arise in his trying to ascertain his informants' reliability. Unlike in *Maus*—or more recently in Bechdel's *Are You My Mother?*—Sacco rarely reflects on his *comics* creation as part of the narrative performance. Since the fact of Sacco as comics artist is a given in the presentation of the material, such a focus on journalistic performances gives this side of his work as much prominence as the performance of drawing. These two kinds of performance, the artist and the journalist, are inseparable.

When Sacco appears as a figure in "Trauma on Loan," for example, it is in dialogue with his informants, notebook, or camera in hand.[14] For most of this piece, the character we recognize as Sacco appears facing the reader, or at a slight angle, or drawn from the back but with enough of an angle to showcase the ubiquitous "blank" glasses that function as Sacco's trademark. In an interesting pictorial move, in the final panels of "Trauma" Sacco shifts the perspective so that instead of Sacco as an object of vision, readers are placed

Joe Sacco's Comics of Performance 189

Figure 11.1. Joe Sacco, "Trauma on Loan," in *Journalism* (New York: Metropolitan, 2012), 105.

in a position so as to align their gazes with Sacco's. This is signaled through hand imagery, for in these panels we don't view Sacco's face but we are aware of his presence through his hands, hands that furthermore are handling the tools of the journalist's trade: notebook, pen, tape recorder. In the next panel, we witness a handshake, again positioned as if we are looking through Sacco's eyes at the two Iraqi men. The sudden absence of a face, but with hands that are framed as our "guide's" hands, strengthens the imaginative connection between the reader and Sacco's avatar: he is no longer a figure simply to be observed, but by deliberately placing the face outside of and the hands inside of the frame, Sacco becomes an almost "absent" figure we are literally drawn into.

Similarly, in the driving sequence I mention in *Footnotes*, in three sequential panels we zoom in on Sacco's face, so that by the third panel we no longer view the full face but only a fragment, the eyes, cheek, and nose (see Figure 11.1): it is as if we are being asked to take on Sacco's own gaze, to see through his eyes (or through his glasses, as the case may be). The text in both of these examples, as I discuss above, centers on the link between journalistic performance and pain; and in both of these cases, Sacco-the-artist manipulates the drawings so that we as readers are brought up close to these musings on work and pain; he closes the distance between author, reader, and image/text in a moment of ironic authentication, and right at the site of a discourse on pain. In this way, calling attention to self-performance is also a kind of call out to the reader, a request to reflect on what it means to examine people's pain secondhand. Thus, in Sacco's work, ethics are embedded into self-performance, an ethics that turns on the question and representation of pain. Furthermore, by establishing a close connection and a kind of dialogue with readers in such instances, Sacco also turns performance back out, asking readers to become conscious of the difficulties of witnessing the pain of others. In other words, such instances frame humanitarian witnessing as a particularly fraught kind of performance.

Perhaps the most powerful example of performance and pain in all of Sacco's work occurs in the final sequence of *Footnotes*. As so often is the case in *Footnotes*, Sacco uses depictions of space and place to "move" the reader back and forth in time, using landmarks and drawings of time-specific vehicles and building structures to alert the reader to these time jumps. Here, we begin with a contemporary car; then a modern, bustling street; then the next panel's style alerts us to having traveled back in time, as we are now presented with the refugee camp as it appeared in the 1950s, with smaller, uniform buildings.[15] We are in a sense being told that we are traveling the same street in these panels; this is in fact an extension and pictorial literalization of the sequence I mention above, where Sacco is being driven down the street. Sacco's use of the cinematic technique of jump cuts also serves to carry us deeply into the frame in a very visceral way. As with the close-ups of Sacco's hands and face, we are being brought in close to the subject, in a sense being sucked back in time as much as we are being sucked into the frame itself. On the very next page, the fact that the panels' color scheme shifts from white to black connotes a significant reversal in focus. No longer are we simply looking in on others' pain as voyeurs, but the black background, in combination with the composition of the drawings, confronts us, the readers, quite directly; we are being told to follow a new direction of reading. In this reversal, "we" are being looked at by three others, as we are being visually positioned into the role of a potential victim. This is underscored in the following panels, all drawn from an eyewitness perspective: the hands (again), in particular, are drawn to be "our" hands, for they are placed in a way that interpellates us readers into the visual frame. In other words, we are being asked to inhabit an imagined Palestinian body that exists *within* the frame.

In the subsequent sequence and following the line of vision, "we" are forced by soldiers to join a queue of other men; it is impossible to see clearly what is up ahead, until we are confronted with a swinging bat and then blackness. Confusion, fear, pain, annihilation: this is the trajectory of our imagined movements. This functions as a pictorial form of empathetic, corporeal address, as we imaginatively become a victim of this violence. We are being asked to perform victim here, with no redemptive ending; this is no longer a kind of distanced reflection on pain, but a bodily, imaginative encounter with it. Sacco's deliberate use of framing shortens the distance between reader and the object of vision, and in narrowing this gap we are forcibly led into discovering what Judith Butler calls "shared precariousness," whereby we become aware of our connection to others based on the very human apprehension of the body's frailty, the potential for pain, instability, and loss that always exist as possibilities in this life.[16] In this instance, shared precariousness is experienced through the realization, or the potential, of feeling pain inflicted by a source outside our control. And this is precisely where Sacco decides to end the book.

I would argue that all of these performances that speak to and about pain are as resonant as the "voice-print" of line drawing. The presence of the artist in the process of work, in the laborious process of creation, also makes itself palpable through self-portraiture, framing, sequencing, and the careful juxtaposition of text and image. All of this comes together to perform a dialogue with the reader: it is in this dialogue that stretches from form to content to ethical contemplation that the work and presence of an activating authorial figure is powerfully manifest.

Performance, Pain, and "Drawing Desire"

What is interesting in Sacco's work is that this discourse of pain is also intimately tied to the workings of drives and *desire*: the desire to see, to make certain. Desire cannot be separated out from pain in Sacco's comics, and it is this juxtaposition that often infuses the comics with a deep sense of unease. Susan Sontag suggests that the desire to look at images of pain also touches upon deeper desires associated with the forbidden and taboo: "It seems the appetite for pictures showing bodies in pain is as keen, almost, as the desire for ones that show bodies naked."[17] In addition, she continues, this kind of scopophilia may also be linked to the bodily charge of provocation, that there just might be an element of pleasure in the sensation of flinching at the sight of suffering, at least as it is witnessed at a remove.[18] In arguing this, Sontag points to one of the more uncomfortable aspects of looking, via photographs and drawings, at the pain of others: the existence of an element of desire within all the outrage, compassion, discomfort, and full range of emotions that encompass humanitarian witnessing.

Furthermore, the fact that the comics medium is associated with reading pleasure often tied to adolescent nostalgia further complicates this knot of pain and desire.[19] Such habits of reading comics, then, mean that when engaging with Sacco's work, readers negotiate the general pleasure of reading sequential art with that of seeing and ethically contemplating other peoples' pain. That Sacco obliquely addresses this issue reveals his awareness of the connections between pleasure, pain, and desire: to read Sacco's comics about trauma and atrocity is to partake not only in the desire to look, but also in the desire to look away.

I also think the pleasure in reading comics can be located in a more basic pleasure, and here I want to return once again to Gardner's emphasis on line, and to the ways line drawing is linked to the performative. An examination of line does not only lead to thoughts on the way an comics artist manages to make him or herself "present" or "resonant" in the text. It can also speak to the performative quality of images themselves. To paraphrase W. J. T. Mitchell, a close look at line and performativity also leads to an examination of what a picture, or what an *image* wants.[20] This is a very different kind of framing of the performative in drawing, as such desire, Mitchell explains, can function independently of the intentions of the artist, and has little to do with the storytelling aspects of the voice-print.

The notion of "drawing desire," Mitchell writes, "is meant not just to suggest the depiction of a scene or figure that stands for desire, but also to indicate the way that drawing itself, the dragging or pulling of the drawing instrument, is the performance of desire. Drawing draws us on. Desire just *is*, quite literally, drawing, or *a* drawing—a pulling or attracting force, and the trace of this force in a picture."[21] Desire, in other words, is an inescapable dimension of the performance of drawing for *both* artist and viewer, although this manifests in different ways. In terms of the viewer, Mitchell is writing about a kind of desire that precedes the reader's formation of specific meanings, or rather is independent of predetermined meaning: "What pictures wants is not the same as the messages they communicate or the effect they produce; it's not even the same as what they say they want. Like people, pictures don't know what they want; they have to be helped to recollect it through a dialogue with others."[22] Line thus possesses a certain kind of desire that is seemingly contradictory in the sense that this desire is both autonomous from the intentions of the artist, *and* dependent on a viewer to help that desire come into being. What is key here is the importance of the notion of *dialogue* as a major component of the performance of desire via drawing.

Another way of framing the desiring dimension of the performative in drawing is a consideration of the *textural* qualities of lines on a page, for a focus on texture circles back to this notion of dialogue. Texture is that which initially calls out for attention, that which draws a person into the page. Sacco in particular is a master of the textural: in his work, line appears variously textured, from fine crosshatching to more expressionistic lines to lines so thin and ethereal they barely register; this is part of what constitutes the voice-print Gardner theorizes. Eve Kosofsky Sedgwick explores the links between the perception of the textural and performativity, arguing that the perception of texture—whether that perception is primarily visual, tactile, or even auditory—activates the observer in ways that speak to a work's power to move or touch a viewer both emotionally and intellectually. Sedgwick suggests that the perception of texture raises questions that span the historical, the affective, and the transitive: "To perceive texture is never only to ask or know What is it like? . . . Textural perception always explores two other questions as well: How did it get that way? and What could I do with it?"[23] As with "drawing desire," texture functions as a kind of calling out, a visual embodiment of the desire to be looked at, and the image's desire to detain a viewer. But the textural also speaks to what Sedgwick characterizes as texture's activating—and thus performative—principles: its ability to get us to ask questions, to search for what to *do* with texture, and this resonates powerfully with Mitchell's ideas on the dialogic desire of drawing.

What a picture desires—through its very existence, and through its textural qualities—is to open a dialogue with the reader, and in the case of Sacco's work, after we are drawn in to look we are also confronted with the desire to look away: in Sedgwick's formulation, what do we *do* with such overwhelming displays of pain? Again, it is this notion of dialogue that points powerfully to performance, to the transitive potential of the drawn image, for dialogue is a kind of speech act: in such an act, new forms and ideas are created and put into the world, opening for the potential for deep change.

The image desires a *witness*, and following Mitchell's argument, *that* is its most basic desire. Thus, the performance inherent in drawing, and in the textural quality of line, is akin to the performance of *testimony*, even when testimony as it is generally understood is not being explicitly sought by the image. The fact that testimonial rhetorics *are* a part of Sacco's project—testimony is quite literally a major part of the overall picture—means that the aspects of desire and drawing lead directly to the difficulties of humanitarian witnessing, for it is within that kind of witnessing that the pain/desire/performance connections take on their most confounding and pressing forms in Sacco's work.

Performativity and the Problematics of Humanitarian Witnessing

Two of Sacco's most well-known works already mentioned—*Palestine* and *Footnotes in Gaza*—can for the moment serve as bookends for Sacco's career, for *Palestine* was his first collected work, and *Footnotes* a later long-form work. Comparing these two works, it is possible to trace the development of Sacco's style, his attitude towards his subjects, and his own increasing professionalization as both artist and journalist. But there is an even more important thread running through these two works: though more than twenty years have elapsed since the start of Sacco's Palestinian projects, his work indicates there is not only no improvement in the quality of life for Palestinians living under occupation, but one could also see their situation as represented in the narrative present of *Footnotes* as far worse than that in *Palestine*. As Sacco reiterates in *Footnotes*, one of the most heartbreaking and disturbing developments happening now is the systematic destruction of Palestinian homes: a family's entire home—all their possessions, their shelter, their family unit, their already precarious sense of safety (if they have any at all)—can be bulldozed into ruins at a moment's notice. Because of this very present and acute situation, throughout Sacco's time investigating the 1956 massacres in *Footnotes*, he encounters bewilderment as to his interest in this particular historical atrocity: "What good would tending to history do [for Palestinians] when they were under attack and their homes were being demolished *now?*"[24]

This focus on continuous and worsening conditions creates a tension in Sacco's work, a tension that I want to discuss using the language of performance theory and performativity. I want to shift focus for a moment to examine how performativity can function not only via the coexistence of pain and desire as it manifests as part of the author's performative strategies, but also how Sacco's representations of pain and atrocity contest some of the critical theory that positions performativity as an emancipatory discourse.

Most literary and visual culture scholars who use performance theory do so in the service of discussing the emancipatory potential of various aesthetic or social forms. Judith Butler's pioneering work, which draws on Austinian speech act theory, shows that all language—even language in its bodily, gestural form—is performative, and in learning to *see* this, in recognizing our words and actions as performance (and therefore not as essence, not as natural), we can begin the process of performing new identities, breaking the patterns of old social codes.[25] Performativity, in this context, is productive: it does things, produces reality, and can be harnessed, according to Butler, to produce forms and conceptions that are freeing and democratic. While performance in Butler's work initially referred to the ways in which our words and actions have solidified over time to cement certain realities and construe them as natural, most scholars have seized upon the emancipatory dimension of her theories, looking for the ways that performance can point to routes out of sedimented ways of thinking, acting, and seeing. As Sedgwick sees it, theories of performativity as they function in literary and cultural criticism perform "the bossy gesture of 'calling for' an imminently perfected critical or revolutionary practice that one can oneself only adumbrate."[26] In our eagerness to side with what we see as the possibilities for change for the better, we call for revolutionary practices via the power of performativity, and in doing so we often ignore those works that centralize the performative *and* focus on a *lack* of emancipatory potential.

One of the deep tensions in Sacco's work is that while his style and methods revolve around the performative, the emancipatory potential of the performative in his work is reserved for the *readers*: his work gives readers new vistas, new ways of thinking about and framing suffering, new ways of connecting and seeing a shared vulnerability across differences. All the while, the objects of the readers' vision—the drawn images of Palestinians suffering under occupation, that is, the sites of vision that Sacco draws so as to lead us to these new ways of conceptualizing the pain of others—are locked within the frames of suffering. What we see is that the Palestinians' everyday lives are seemingly hopeless, the possibility of emancipation nearly impossible to conceive of within the current social and political situation. It is here that the notion of constraint comes across in an overwhelming manner, thus producing as powerful an affect as the constraint of the comics form itself. What does it mean that the performativity of Sacco's work speaks to a reader's sense of ethics and freedom, while the images of Palestinians are depicted as locked into cycles of violence and degradation? How do the notions of pain and desire also contextualize this dynamic?

The readers' desires—to see and make certain, for establishing a dialogue with the text and images, and to shift our conscious and unconscious attitudes towards shared precariousness—are activated through witnessing the pain of others, and this pain is emphasized through observing the others' forced stasis. Sacco focuses on this dynamic again and again throughout his Palestinian works. In other words, "drawing desire" is associated with movement, the force of attraction inherent in the presentation of the image and its effects and affects; pain, in this context, is associated with stasis, with the images of people in pain who are framed as having nowhere to go.

In fact, it is in the very act of comics framing where this kind of double dynamic becomes most apparent, for the frame itself functions as a visual literalization of constraint. In general, in the comics medium, readers move through the texts and images, yet panel borders, while directing the movement of reading, also denote the fact that the panels are pinned down. Our engagement on both physical and emotional levels as readers of comics is based on the images staying in their places as much as it is on the movement of our eyes and minds. Furthermore, comics artists play with frames—and the absence of frames—to connote the shrinkage and expansion of space.

A specific panel from *Footnotes* can illustrate the power of the frame to produce a simultaneous sense of movement and stasis, and this panel also speaks to how such a dynamic points towards the problematics of humanitarian witnessing. In this panel, a woman's face is framed and surrounded by a larger frame; the inside frame connotes that the woman, named Ra'esa Salim Hassan Kaloob, is giving testimony, and the surrounding frame is where Sacco imagines and reconstructs a moment from that testimony.[27] This kind of framing—a kind of talking head framed tightly and surrounded by an image that depicts one piece of the testimony—occurs at various junctures throughout *Footnotes*, and in almost all of these double-framed panels, we see that in striking contrast to the mostly expressionless faces giving the testimony, the moments Sacco chooses to draw are ones that express the informants' experiences of intense pain, fear, and acts of mourning. In this panel, we have a scene of mourning that is marked as ritualistic, and is therefore presented as a kind of performance, albeit one in which performance functions as a means of gesture and language in the face of pain and grief so intense that language's expressive power does not suffice.

This kind of double framing offers the face as an initial point of spectator identification, a kind of ground for recognition: the face, as Levinas reminds us, stands as the very site of ethical understanding, where we move beyond narcissistic identification and into a space where acknowledgment of the other leads to a sense of responsibility for that other.[28] Butler, drawing on Levinas, writes,

"To respond to the face, to understand its meaning, means to be awake to what is precarious in another life or, rather, to the precariousness of life itself."[29] In this panel, the inside face opens a palpable space between reader and image; this is a kind of movement, a drawing forth, in other words, a performance of desire both in Mitchell's sense, and beyond that into the realm of ethical contemplation. A kind of dialogue is established in this meeting, which continues as we move outwards into the larger frame. It is in the outer frame, I would contend, where the personal identification with a particular face is transferred into a more generalized identification with grief, with precariousness itself, as Butler puts it. And yet, with all this visual, emotional, and intellectual movement happening for the reader, the double framing simultaneously emphasizes a forcible circumscription; in a single panel, the woman represented is pinned down twice.

The cumulative effect of such a framing choice is that we as readers—and particularly as Western readers who might have been trained to view Palestinians as terrorists, as a people unworthy of human sympathy—are being asked again and again to rethink our notions of Palestinian pain and grief, to shift our conscious and unconscious attitudes and engage viscerally with the pain of others. Sacco's comics ask us to emancipate ourselves from ignorance, through performing various identificatory processes with both comics form and content. Obviously, this kind of work is necessary, and Sacco shows the profound ways that comics can participate in this politically significant emotional work; his comics perform or enact the ethical work of rendering particular bodies as grievable, bodies that much of American culture attempts to frame as ungrievable.[30] Yet again, this sort of emancipatory movement is framed as a kind of "revelation" for the readers: it is us who must be shocked and moved out of our complacency and ignorance, while Kaloob is presented quite literally as locked within these moments.

The effect of this, in Sacco's work at least, is that such a dynamic evokes "the ethically disturbing image of the Western witness able to leave, to go home, even to forget . . . while those she has come to witness remain stuck in the geographic and psychological danger zones."[31] In other words, reading Sacco's comics mimics this kind of spectatorial situation, a situation that has become a staple of Western visual culture, as images of human rights have become so ubiquitous that they now *form* a part of modern visual culture.[32] Yet in revealing this kind of dynamic—and making it even more visceral at the very end of *Footnotes*, with the sequence I described earlier, when readers are forcibly interpellated into performing the role of victim with no redemptive ending— Sacco's work circles back on itself, offering no answers as to how to negotiate the very problem of humanitarian witnessing he so carefully incorporates into the form and content of his comics. All of these performances and performative strategies, which speak mainly to a lack of emancipatory potential for Palestinians, emphasize the seriousness of the situation, all the while edging any reader's sense of revelation with deep unease. In *not* providing any relief to this unease or any clear answers as to how to think or feel about this spectatorial situation, Sacco's comics also mimic the affect of precariousness that is key in directing the pain and desire we feel when engaging with such images into the realm of ethics.

Overall, Sacco's use of performativity to highlight comics' transitive potential, and his use of it in making apparent all the ways in which the artist is "directing the show," so to speak, coalesce to create a much bigger picture: Sacco is creating a *spectacle* out of the various testimonies and experiences of people in crisis, and I don't mean this in a pejorative way. Especially in his Palestinian works, Sacco is consciously making a spectacle of subjects who are generally not given the space to do so, at least not in the way Sacco is allowing the stories to be told and to unfold. He uses the performative to actively create a spectacle—a spectacle out of himself as artist and journalist, out of his informants, and out of the comics form itself—in order to reinforce the fact that when it comes to the lives of everyday Palestinians under occupation, the world *lacks* spectacles that reflect the reality of the situation; he is making the "hidden archives" of peoples' experiences visible. "Spectacle," Wendy Hesford writes, "is a function of politics, it is highly rhetorical—that is, situational and performative."[33] Applying such a formulation to Sacco's work, I would say that he uses the performative to create a *comics* spectacle, a spectacle that resituates particular lives and bodies into new rhetorics and discourses that challenge mainstream notions of Palestinian lives. Yet a kind of purposeful failure is built into this spectacle, which also becomes a dimension of the politics of Sacco's work. Sacco's comics of performance do not allow for a reader or critic to call for some kind of perfected critical practice with fully emancipatory or revolutionary potential; his emphasis on pain, claustrophobia, and worsening conditions blocks this move. "Failure" to find redemption in this case can be read as a comment on the politics of humanitarian witnessing, for redemptive moves allow for readers to feel a kind of triumph or possibility for change, and thus ironically close down avenues for thinking and rethinking the pain of others. In this way, the comics form—with the various formal strategies the artist uses to both literally and affectively *move* the reader into circles of revelation and blockage—can perhaps most closely mimic for readers the reality of the situation at hand.

NOTES

1. For further discussion on this idea, see Jared Gardner, "Storylines," *SubStance* 40.1 (2011): 53–69; and Rebecca Scherr, "Shaking Hands with Other People's Pain: Joe Sacco's *Palestine*," *Mosaic* 46.1 (2013): 19–36.
2. Gardner, "Storylines," 66.
3. Øyvind Vågnes, "Comics Re-enactment: Joe Sacco's *Footnotes in Gaza*," unpublished paper.
4. Kim Deitch, *The Boulevard of Broken Dreams* (New York: Pantheon, 2002), 12.
5. For more discussion on these kinds of performances, see Scott Bukatman, *The Poetics of Slumberland* (Berkeley: University of California Press, 2012).
6. Gardner, "Storylines," 66.
7. See Gillian Whitlock, "Autographics: The Seeing 'I' of Comics," *Modern Fiction Studies* 52.4 (2006): 965–79.
8. Joe Sacco, *Palestine* (Seattle: Fantagraphics Books, 2001), 71–77.
9. It is important to note that this is always contextualized by the ongoing pain of Palestinians under occupation, an issue explored in Joe Sacco, *Footnotes in Gaza* (New York: Metropolitan, 2009).
10. Joe Sacco, *Journalism* (New York: Metropolitan, 2012), 105.
11. Sacco, *Footnotes in Gaza*, 383.
12. Ibid., 383.
13. Charles Hatfield, *Alternative Comics* (Jackson: University Press of Mississippi, 2005), 131.
14. "Trauma on Loan" originally appeared in the *Guardian Weekend* (21 January 2006), and it is collected in Sacco, *Journalism*, 98–105.
15. Sacco, *Footnotes*, 285.
16. See Judith Butler, *Precarious Life: The Powers of Mourning and Violence* (New York: Verso, 2006).
17. Susan Sontag, *Regarding the Pain of Others* (New York: Farrar, Straus and Giroux, 2003), 41.
18. Ibid.
19. Gillian Whitlock, *Soft Weapons: Autobiography in Transit* (Chicago: University of Chicago Press, 2007), 196.
20. See W. J. T. Mitchell, "What Do Pictures 'Really' Want?" *October* 77 (Summer 1996): 71–82; and his longer book on the subject, W. J. T. Mitchell, *What Do Pictures Want?: The Lives and Loves of Images* (Chicago: University of Chicago Press, 2005).
21. Mitchell, *What Do Pictures Want?* 59.
22. Mitchell, "What Do Pictures 'Really' Want?" 81.
23. Eve Kosofsky Sedgwick, *Touching Feeling: Affect, Pedagogy, Performativity* (Durham: Duke University Press, 2003), 13.
24. Sacco, *Footnotes*, xi.
25. Here, I am referring to the theories of performativity first articulated in Judith Butler, *Gender Trouble: Feminism and the Subversion of Identity* (New York: Routledge, 1990).
26. Sedgwick, *Touching Feeling*, 8.

27. Sacco, *Footnotes*, 317.

28. See Emmanuel Levinas, *Ethics and Infinity: Conversations with Philippe Nemo*, trans. Richard A. Cohen (Pittsburgh: Duquesne University Press, 1985).

29. Butler, *Precarious*, 134.

30. This notion of grievable lives is taken from Judith Butler, *Frames of War: When is Life Grievable?* (New York: Verso, 2010).

31. Elizabeth Swanson Goldberg and Alexandra Schultheis Moore, "Old Questions in New Boxes: Mia Kirshner's *I Live Here* and the Problematics of Transnational Witnessing," *Humanity* 2.2 (Summer 2011), 236.

32. For a longer discussion on this topic, see Sophie A. McClellan and Joseph R. Slaughter, "Introducing Human Rights and Literary Forms," *Comparative Literature Studies* 46.1 (2009): 1–19.

33. Wendy Hesford, *Spectacular Rhetorics: Human Rights Visions, Recognitions, Feminisms* (Durham: Duke University Press, 2011), 64.

Section IV
Drawing History, Visualizing World Politics

12. Overtaken by Further Developments: The Form of History in *Footnotes in Gaza*

Ben Owen

A journalist asked Joe Sacco why his book *Footnotes in Gaza*, ostensibly about two massacres that took place in 1956, gave so much space to accounts of housing demolitions in the Gazan city of Rafah in 2003. Sacco replied that he thought the 2003 events were worth recording in their own right, but also said that he wanted to show how, for Palestinians in Gaza, "events are continuous."[1] By this he meant that people whose experiences since 1948 consist primarily of violent deferrals and defeats "can never look back at 1948 and just think about that. There is no closure."[2] *Footnotes in Gaza* is Sacco's attempt to convey the Palestinian experience of resolution's absence, of each new injury immediately recalling numerous other injuries. In doing so, *Footnotes* recreates a sense of time unfamiliar to many of his European and North American readers, in which events are not given a strict linear sequence because their importance seems continuously present.

As several critics have observed, Sacco's work amounts to a kind of ethical witnessing, in which he draws the suffering of people in terrible situations, but also tries to think through the trickiness of his own role as a journalist, a cartoonist, and a Westerner potentially implicated in that suffering.[3] I argue that Sacco's emphasis on different ways of experiencing time, and on the related conflicts between different ways of describing history, is a major part of his work as a witness. The idea that the choices we make about how to narrate history can have profound ethical effects is certainly not new. But it is also an idea that can seem abstract. Part of the value of Sacco's work is that it provides a detailed and particular account of the human cost of describing history in one narrative mode versus another. Whose history to draw, and how to draw it, are live questions throughout the book, and are plainly visible when a Palestinian father, angry that Sacco insists on asking about 1956 when there are fresh Israeli bullets in his wall, yells, "Every day here is '56!"[4]

In the first part of this essay, I show how *Footnotes* presents several different modes of narrating history, focusing on the conflict between two different modes, the progressive and the cyclical. Sacco offers a pointed critique of progressive, linear history throughout the book, showing both how it fails as a way to describe Palestinian history, and how it is implicated in the relegation of that history to "footnotes." Instead, his book attempts to depict Palestinian ways of telling history, which are necessarily less cleanly linear, and it is here that Sacco's use of the comics medium is of particular importance. As Hillary Chute writes, "comics can address itself powerfully to historical and life narrative," in part because of its "ability to use the space of the page to interlace or overlay different temporalities, to place pressure on linearity and conventional notions of sequence, causality, and progression."[5] Sacco uses this ability of comics in a particularly pointed way, continually using the page to make different historical moments butt up against one another, showing the resonances between them.

But although Sacco presents the nonlinear view of history as truer to the lived experiences of at least some Palestinians, he does not make them fully his own. While Sacco represents the stories of Palestinians who see history as essentially cyclical—a series of inevitable defeats—his own project resists that premise by its insistence on the specificity of 1956 and of 2003. The past is fundamentally *not* an interchangeable series of catastrophes, even if those catastrophes do echo one another. In asserting this, Sacco tries to maintain openness to different ways of narrating events. This openness is most apparent in the ambiguous interlude to *Footnotes*, "Feast," which juxtaposes a time of Palestinian ritual—the feast of Eid Al-Adha—with the lead-up to the American invasion of Iraq.

The value of *Footnotes*'s specific historical project—to provide a fuller account of the Khan Younis and Rafah massacres—is substantial in itself. But the value of Sacco's work beyond Palestinian history is, in part, as a model for a kind of popular history that can accommodate itself to telling the stories of places where the dominant modes of history—of progress, of decline—are not adequate to the task. In the second part of my argument, I consider Sacco's method of juxtaposing conflicting ways of telling history as characteristic of the current trend in comics, particularly in book-length comics, towards difficult, contested, and forgotten history.

Beginning with Joseph Witek's seminal *Comic Books as History*, critics have tended to view the suitability of comics for historical subjects as a formal property of the medium.[6] So, for example, comics are good at doing history because of their arrangement of different chronologies on the page, either in separate panels or through the combination of retrospective verbal narration and "present-tense" pictures. While this medium-specific approach has led to a great deal of useful work, critics have paid much less attention to the ways in which changes within the way comics are created, sold, and read—particularly the shift towards the book-length comic as a standard form—have shaped how comics address historical subjects. My interest in the specificity not just of comics as a medium, but in the distinctions among different kinds of comics traditions, aligns my work with the scholarship of critics such as Bart Beaty, Rebecca Wanzo, and Henry Jenkins in making the history of particular cartoonists and comics more central to thinking about what does and does not define comics as a medium.[7] Some of the most significant criticism on the profound differences between book-length comics, comic strips, and comic books has tended to come from cartoonists themselves. To take perhaps the most well-known example, it is easy to see much of Chris Ware's work as an extended meditation on the relationship between comics' different historical forms and other kinds of history—among them, personal, architectural, and metropolitan. This kind of work ought to serve as a guide to comics scholars and critics.

My general claim is that the book-length comic (whether or not "graphic novel" is a suitable name for it) ought to be understood as a more particular object of study, distinct from other kinds of comics. My specific argument is that the sophistication with which book-length comics show stories about contested or contradictory histories is partly the result of the fact that the artists who create them are conflicted about the recent history of comics. *Footnotes in Gaza* is a good example of this because it is not explicitly about comics at all, and yet its most conspicuous formal experiment—the three-and-half-page wordless coda—relies on a discrepancy between the kind of self-contained short story typical of the pamphlet-format comic book anthologies Sacco worked on for most of his early career, and the meticulous long-form narrative of the rest of the book. I do not mean to suggest that *Footnotes* is secretly about comics history, but rather that it uses the tension between different forms of comics as a structuring metaphor for the difficulty of drawing a story based on eyewitness testimony that is both an accurate account of what happened and a faithful record of the emotional experience of those witnesses.

Historical Time and *Footnotes in Gaza*

Footnotes in Gaza mocks the idea of historical progress. It does this in a number of ways, but perhaps the most striking is Sacco's juxtaposition of two pictures of Khan Younis refugee camp in Gaza, past and present. The pair of full-bleed splashes in Figure 12.1 show the same view of the camp at two different times: the first in the mid 1950s, and the second in the early 2000s. They conclude an account of the flight of Palestinian refugees to Gaza in 1948, which Sacco draws based on the testimonies of elderly Palestinians whose families fled the fighting

Figure 12.1. Joe Sacco, *Footnotes in Gaza* (New York: Metropolitan, 2009), 27.

between Israelis and the Arab armies, or who were expelled from their homes by Israeli forces. Narration in captions explains the comparison between the two pictures of the camp. In the upper left corner of the first page in Figure 12.1 are the words: "And so we have taken ourselves from 1948 to the middle of the

The Form of History in *Footnotes in Gaza* 207

Figure 12.2. Joe Sacco, *Footnotes in Gaza* (New York: Metropolitan, 2009), 29.

1950s—when the camps looked like this." And on the final page in Figure 12.2, in the upper right corner: "And now they look like this." In the first picture, we see regular blocks of identical single-story brick houses (the preceding pages have explained that these brick houses replaced the clay houses that preceded them; which, in turn, replaced UNWRA and Quaker-supplied tents; which replaced the shelters of branches, dugout pits, and blankets that the refugees first constructed in 1948). In the second picture, we see a dense sprawl of three- and four-story buildings, their top floors generally unfinished.

What is arresting about the two pictures (and Sacco's other diptych showing the scene of the Khan Younis massacre on the day of its occurrence in 1956, and again in late 2002) is that their angles of view are identical, though temporally separated by almost half a century.[8] Because the buildings have changed so much, the use of identical perspective and framing encourages the reader to see similarities that might otherwise escape attention. It is perhaps a small shock to realize, gradually, that this is the same corner of the same street. The sense of similarity is reinforced by the fact that the identically framed images in Figures 12.1 and 12.2 are both on the right-hand page, meaning that the drawing of the mid-50s scene physically overlays the drawing of the early 2000s.

The identical perspective and the meticulous detail parody the form of an architect's "before and after" drawing, particularly those in which a semi-transparent sheet can be laid over the "before" image to show what will happen "after." Sacco's images challenge the architect's presentation of progress through construction. The story of steady improvement, which functions as one of the default modes for structuring history in Europe and America, does not apply to Gaza. At the most simple level, we see this argument in the fact that it is very difficult to read the state of the camp in the 2000s as an obvious improvement. The unpaved streets of the 1950s are still unpaved. Many of the kids in the later picture do not have shoes, just like their parents and grandparents in the earlier picture. The material accumulation depicted in the later picture—additional floors to the buildings, telephone wires, water heaters, and satellite dishes—may be interpreted as progress, but might also appear as part of the increase of flotsam and junk, kin to the bricks and old tires laid down on corrugated iron roofs to prevent them blowing away. Indeed, the inspiration for these pages could come from either Walter Benjamin or R. Crumb.

Benjamin's figure of the angel of history from his cryptic late work "Theses on the Concept of History" is useful for understanding this scene because it is attuned to the idea of history as a perpetual disaster that Sacco finds in Gaza: "Where a chain of events appears before us, he [the angel] sees one single catastrophe, which keeps piling wreckage upon wreckage and hurls it at his feet."[9] In Sacco's image of Khan Younis, the piling of the wreckage is rendered literal. Events do not move on in a linear chain, but rather accumulate. Where in other places refugees might have moved on, allowing for the maintenance of an idea of progress, "Khan Younis camp has had nowhere to build but into the streets and up."[10] The pages also appear to consciously echo that of his most direct influence as a cartoonist, Crumb, particularly the 1979 comic strip "A Short History of America," in which overhead wires, concrete, and what Crumb regards as the crap of modernity consume the beauty of nature in a scene viewed from the same perspective for twelve successive panels, representing perhaps 150 years.[11] Even the layout of Sacco's pages reinforces the sense of an untidy sprawl, since the first picture takes up only the right-hand page, whereas the second picture covers the entirety of both the left- and right-hand pages.

The possibility that this is a narrative of decline or disaster, as in Crumb and Benjamin, is fully present, but it might also be read as a kind of stasis, or perhaps as a version of history in which these evaluative terms do not make sense. The structure of the diptych certainly seems open to different kinds of narrative. The hidden similarities between the two pages encourage the reader to flip back and forth, playing an inverted game of spot-the-difference, and thereby pausing the forward motion of the narrative, at least for a moment. This exaggerates the general effect of a splash page, which tends to arrest the reader's forward movement through a comic and allow either for the cessation of narrative, or for the interpretation of narrative in a less ordered sequence via various points distributed across the page.

A non-progressive connection between historical moments is truer to Palestinians' understanding of their own national history, at least as Sacco represents it. His account of the story of the fedayee—one of the guerilla fighters who fought the Israelis in the years immediately following 1948—is divided between his rendering of the fedayee's account of those years, and an account of Sacco's own struggle with the fedayee to get him to stay on the topic of the early 1950s, without mixing it with accounts of other fighting from later years.[12] Though quite different in intent from the angry father's assertion that "every day here is '56!" the fedayee's lack of interest in strict chronology shares with it a sense that the date of any given moment of violence matters less than the way in which it expresses an unchanging injustice: Palestinian exile and Israeli occupation. One way to interpret this vision of history would be as something akin to Benjamin's concept of "eternal return," an idea he adapted from Nietzsche, and saw as a kind of negative version of progress. Benjamin argued that where those who believe in progress under capitalism always celebrate the new and the better, those who are disillusioned with progress view novelty as an endless circular parade of the same old stuff—an eternal return, or "time in hell," where no action results in a change.[13]

The articulation of this strongly negative sense of Palestinian history as a cycle falls to Khaled, the fighter whom Sacco describes as the old fedayee's contemporary successor.[14] Khaled is "mutarad," wanted by the Israelis, and is one of the central figures in *Footnotes*. Showing Khaled in his multiple roles—political tactician, killer, father, friend, wanted man—allows Sacco to get at some of the strangest contradictions of modern Palestinian life. At one point, late in the book, Sacco recounts events from around the end of March 2003. Gazans succumb to a rare moment of communal cheer, celebrating the early victories of the Iraqis against the Americans reported via the Abu Dhabi and Al-Jazeera satellite channels. It seems that this may represent a glimpse of progress, a long-delayed fulfillment of some of the promises of Arab nationalism, delivered by one of its last unrepentant champions, Saddam Hussein. Superimposed over a collage of triumphal images beaming out of Iraq, Sacco's friend and guide Hani proclaims, smiling, "Saddam will be victorious. The entire Arab world and the whole world in general will change owing to the American defeat."[15] It is a grand narrative indeed, and understandable, even if Sacco balks at the footage of dead American soldiers on TV. Sacco knows that for the Palestinians an "American victory would assure Israel of its never-ending supremacy.... But not everyone is so caught up in the cheap propaganda and the minor American setbacks to expect Iraq to prevail. Khaled's view is the most philosophical. It is stripped of illusion and seems somehow self-reflective. 'It's not a matter of victory. It's a matter of resisting till the end.'"[16] Khaled speaks these last two lines slumped in a plastic chair. In contrast to the three panels above, a panel border does not frame his picture, suggesting that he himself is aloof from the story going on around him.

In those upper panels, Sacco and his Palestinian fixer Abed hear pro-Iraqi sentiments from Gazans on the street on three occasions, in different settings but almost identical frames. The optimism the speakers express has, in Sacco's rendering, a whiff of cyclical recurrence, and Khaled's exemption from the frame confirms this. He floats free at the bottom of the page, over a roughly defined circle of black ink, which peters out to hatching at its edges. It is the period at the end of the page, its darkness drawing and arresting the viewer's eye, emphasizing the repetition of the previous panels by its exemption from their pattern. It is a portrait of a man resigned to a version of fate that necessarily excludes the possibility of victory—the black circle is quite plainly his abyss.

It would be wrong to say that Sacco directly opposes this cyclical account of history. His purpose, after all, is to show stories generally missing from the mainstream American and European account of life in Palestine, and much of that means giving voice to Palestinian ideas without prior judgment. Moreover, there is little in the book to suggest that Sacco's interpretation of the political situation is substantially less despairing than Khaled's. But Sacco's account of cyclical history is not purely one of defeatism or despair; the sense of time he finds among Gazans is more contradictory, weirder, and potentially more hopeful than that. "Feast," the short section of *Footnotes* sandwiched between

Figure 12.3. Joe Sacco, *Footnotes in Gaza* (New York: Metropolitan, 2009), 139.

the two longer sections "Khan Younis" and "Rafah," resists easy interpretation, and it seems like this may be part of its point. The complexity of its symbolism also suggests the complexity of its representation of time.

The title chapter of "Feast" depicts the slaughter of a bull for the feast of

Eid Al-Adha, the Islamic religious holiday celebrating Abraham's willingness to sacrifice Ishmael.[17] *Footnotes* depicts the killing of the bull as richly and ambiguously symbolic. While waiting for the butcher to arrive, Abed explains Sacco's 1956 project to a relative, Abu Hamed. Abu Hamed was six in 1956, but he remembers running from an Israeli air attack in the market before the Israelis entered Khan Younis. The present moment seems "just as bleak" to him, and he states that "we make a sacrifice of the bulls, and [Israeli Prime Minister Ariel] Sharon makes a sacrifice of us."[18]

Sacco's composition of the page highlights Abu Hamed's dark parallel (see Figure 12.3). The center panel of the middle tier is a flashback to Abu Hamed's memory of 1956, placed between two panels of Abu Hamed chatting with Sacco and Abed. The panel shows Abu Hamed as a small boy running barefoot, looking up at two jets in the sky through a scene of the market in panicked disarray. It is placed just beneath the single panel bleed that takes up the top tier, showing the present day street scene of children making handprints on the walls with the blood of a bull slaughtered just down the street. The main figure in the foreground of the picture is a young boy joyfully holding up the palms of his hands dark with bull's blood, looking very much like the picture of the six-year-old Abu Hamed in the flashback panel directly below his right hand. The image of the children resonates further because it recalls at least two other scenes from Sacco's depiction of the Khan Younis massacre of November 3, 1956.

First, it suggests the most shocking image from Sacco's drawings of that day, a row of more than a hundred bodies of Palestinian men gunned down by Israeli soldiers against the wall of the Mamluk castle, which Sacco takes from the eyewitness account of Faris Barbakh.[19] The stream of blood from the sacrificed bull recalls the pools of blood Sacco draws beneath the bodies of the men. Second, the marking of the wall with bloody handprints recalls the actions of Omm Nafez, who darkened the walls of her house with handprints of ash in mourning for her husband and his two brothers shot by the Israelis on the day of the massacre.[20]

Abu Hamed's reading places the weight of its emphasis on the human side of the bull/Palestinian analogy, using the bull as a figure for Palestinian suffering. And yet Sacco unsettles this use of the bull as just a symbol. He ends the chapter with Abed's joke that Sacco "ought to interview bulls about *their* massacre."[21] It is a joke, and Sacco does not suddenly transform his story into a protest against animal cruelty, but his detailed focus on the mechanics of its slaughter, from beginning to end, and his account in the subsequent chapter that Hani could neither kill the bull nor eat the meat, suggest that the suffering of the bull does not function purely as a metaphor.

Complicating matters even further, the question of who is butcher and who sacrifice, and what each role might mean, has both religious and larger geopolitical resonance. The story of Abraham and Ishmael is, after all, one of species substitution, ram for human boy, and the Koranic telling of the story emphasizes Ishmael's willingness to be sacrificed for God. Likewise, Hani's disagreement with his friend, the teacher Abu Mohammed, over how to interpret the history and current state of the Arabs involves the question of whether Muslims were ever occupiers. Hani believes the Moors' takeover of southern Spain was not an occupation because "they brought enlightenment," while his friend believes it was because "we came with the sword."[22] The contemporary connotations of "occupation" are doubled, indicating the Israeli occupation, and—in early 2003—the threatened American invasion of Iraq. The range of possible allegorical or symbolic interpretations is large and contradictory. As in Mikhail Bakhtin's account of the carnival, Sacco's rendering of the holiday of Eid Al-Adha seems to open up the possibility of a suspension of rigid hierarchies for thinking about the world.[23] The positioning of the short "Feast" section between the two longer, more emphatically historical sections of the book reinforces this sense of "Feast" as a moment when things are in suspension.

The multiplicity of interpretations offers a useful analogy for how "Feast" might also provide multiple ways for thinking about different senses of time. The yearly recurrence of Eid Al-Adha is fully cyclical, like the conception of Palestinian national history as one of recurrent defeat, and yet understood in the context of religious ritual time, the cycle becomes a way to think about resilience and the continuity of regular life. One of the great strengths of *Footnotes* resides in the fact that Sacco does not decide in favor of one of these cycles, but rather lets them play out in the contradictory interpretations of the different Palestinians he draws. The implicit argument is not in favor of this or that solution to the occupation, but rather for an understanding of history as contingent upon a debate about how to interpret events, and so for an understanding of Palestinian history to involve a debate among Palestinians, rather than any single determined narrative.

The Comic, the Book, and the Coda

As I have argued, Sacco's work depicts a tension between different understandings of the basic narrative structure of history. Although Sacco's work is one of the most sophisticated examples of comics as means to express this tension, it is far from the only one. The interest in difficult, contested history is one of most prominent characteristics of the current generation of book-length graphic narratives. A list of the more commercially and critically successful examples within the United States might include Sacco, Alison Bechdel, Chris Ware, Carol Tyler, and Gene Luen Yang, though it would be easy to construct a considerably longer list. Art Spiegelman's *Maus* set a precedent for this success, and to some extent a standard for the evaluation of these works.

There are various ways to interpret the success of these works, and their tendency in certain situations—the college classroom, the public library, the independent bookstore, the newspaper "top ten" list—to stand in for what is best about comics as a whole. One would be to say that the world is an increasingly visual place, with the burden of semantic meaning increasingly placed on graphics, and comics, with their long history of working out complex meaning through pictures, are a natural place to turn for ways to think about the world. The corollary to this might be to say that as comics become a more recognized form of objectified cultural capital, indicating sophistication on the part of the reader, they require weightier and more serious subjects in order to separate them, slightly, from their associations with children and the illiterate.

I do not dispute the broad terms of this explanation, but I approach the question of the fit between book-length comics and contested history from a somewhat different angle. Essentially, my argument is that the ambivalence comics creators express about the recent history of the comics form—particularly the dominance of the book-length comic over other forms, such as the pamphlet comic book or newspaper comic strip—makes the book-length comic an extremely good place to articulate other kinds of contested history. When Art Spiegelman delivers one of his great epigrams, "They say I'm the father of the graphic novel, but I'm disputing paternity," he is not just arguing the semantics of the term "graphic novel," which so many cartoonists and scholars find objectionable.[24] Rather, he is to some extent voicing a concern about the gentrification of comics, and the collapsing of various messy, discontinuous comics forms into the polished shape of the book. An examination of what is lost and gained in the change in the forms of comics, and also in the places in which they may be bought and read, is one of the major themes of some of the most well-known cartoonists working in the North American "alternative" comics tradition. My claim is that an ambivalent feeling about what is lost and gained in the book-length comic also informs the work of other cartoonists of the same generation whose work is not overtly concerned with the history of comics itself. The form of *Footnotes in Gaza*, particularly the relationship between its wordless coda and the rest of the book, can be read in this light. The short, formally experimental coda resembles the kind of short strips Sacco produced for magazines and anthologies prior to his first long work of comics journalism, *Palestine*, and is visually and narratively distinct from the rest of the book.[25]

Recent examples of work that wrestles with the history of comics form might include Daniel Clowes's *Wilson* and Adrian Tomine's "A Brief History of Hortisculpture" from *Optic Nerve* #12.[26] Each uses the formal conventions of the newspaper comic strip to tell its story, though *Wilson* is a graphic novel and *Optic Nerve* a comic book. *Wilson* is Clowes's first book-length work not to appear first in serialized form, and so there is a deliberate irony in the fact that its form—which switches cartoon style each page—forces the question of the degree to which the main character's identity may be discerned in spite of (or perhaps because of) discontinuity. "A Brief History of Hortisculpture" uses its newspaper-strip form to tell the story of an artist who creates an ungainly hybrid medium—sculpture and horticulture—only to see it misunderstood by his friends and family. The main character appears as both intellectually innovative and an arrogant jerk, and there is a clear sense that the failure of his hybrid art to find respect as fine art is meant to parallel the hybrid word-and-picture art of the newspaper cartoonist. Tomine's short autobiographical strips in the front and back of issues #12 and #13 of *Optic Nerve* heighten the parallel, presenting a narrative commentary on the cartoonist's concerns and frustrations about publishing a comic book in the era of the graphic novel and the Web comic.

Clowes's and Tomine's work typifies an obsession with comics history among a generation of cartoonists who started producing "alternative" comics during the 1980s and 1990s. Their careers have spanned a profound change in the comics marketplace, from a period when most comics work was published in pamphlet-format comic books and sold primarily in direct-market comic book stores, to a period in which much comics work is published in book format and sold in a variety of places, including direct-market comic book stores, but also in book stores and via online retailers. Many of the comics by these creators evince a powerful nostalgia for the past, and this of course includes a tendency to see both the form of the book-length comic, and its odd labeling as the "graphic novel" in ambivalent terms. On the one hand, the book form presents new artistic and economic possibilities, allowing a much larger space in which to craft narratives and new audiences ready to buy those narratives. On the other hand, the very accessibility of the book-length comic flattens the careful curation and labor of the collector, who assembles the collection over years via diligent searching through comic book stores, flea markets, and careful trading with other collectors.

The book-length comics by these creators (the most well-known of which might include Tomine, Clowes, Ware, Spiegelman, Ben Katchor, Seth, Joe Matt, and Kim Deitch) become, in part, a place to deliberate on the form's history. In one sense, they may simply mourn and memorialize older comics

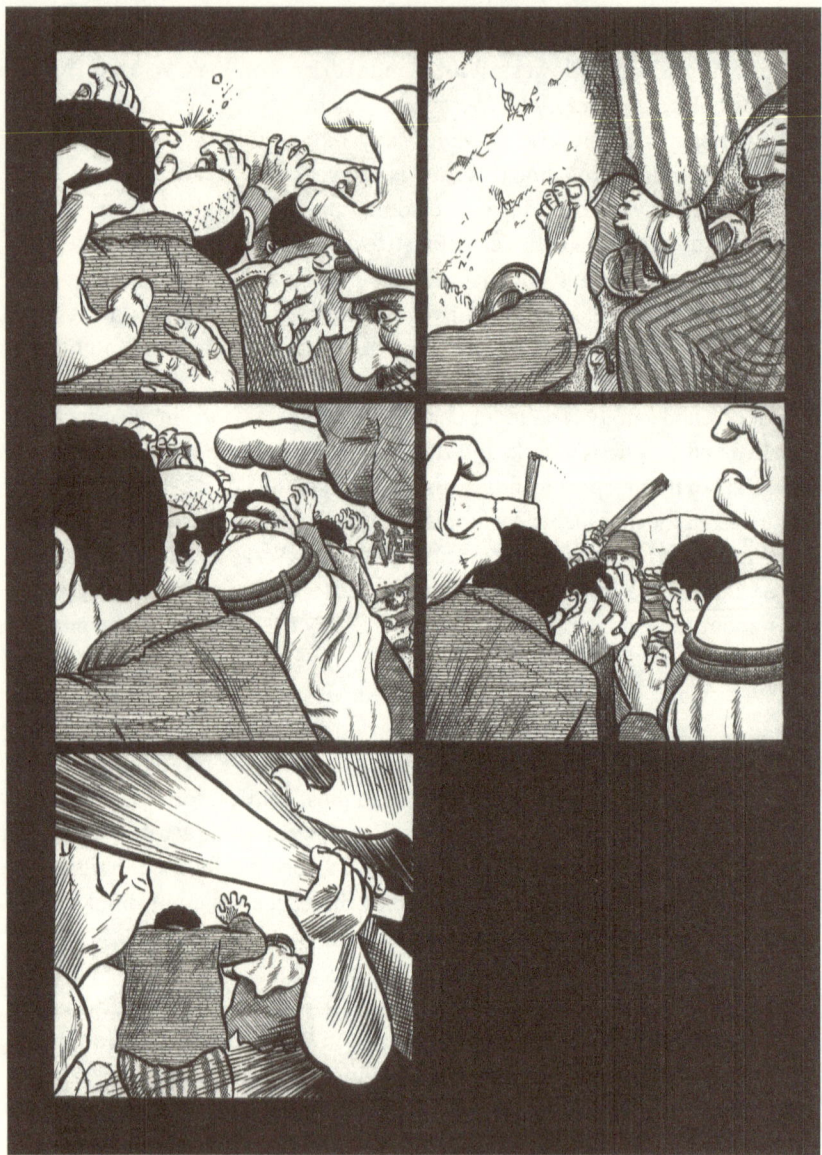

Figure 12.4. Joe Sacco, *Footnotes in Gaza* (New York: Metropolitan, 2009), 388.

forms. But the mania these books exhibit for the ordering of the ephemeral may also provide what Jared Gardner calls "a way of experimenting with new modes of telling stories about time that allow for the past and present, the monumental and the ephemeral, to speak to each other across seemingly irrevocable divides."[27] That is, focusing carefully on bits and pieces of short-lived culture from the previous century may not only provide flesh and texture to the history we already know, but also require an adjustment to the way we think about time.

As I have argued, *Footnotes in Gaza* provides an excellent example of an experiment "with new modes of telling stories about time." Its obsession with brief sections of decades-old United Nations reports and the stories of elderly Palestinians (both are the "footnotes" of the title) is fully in keeping with the preoccupations of Sacco's cartoonist peers. Moreover, I think it is useful for critics to think of *Footnotes* as expressing different ways of telling stories about time through a play on older comics forms. The coda to the book exemplifies this play on forms. It is a wordless three-and-a-half-page summary, marked off by black pages, of Sacco's longer account of the 1956 Rafah massacre, which takes up the last third of the book. The longer account is drawn as an overlapping series of eyewitness testimonies, including inset portraits of the interviewees and drawings of their memories. In contrast, the coda is a single, short narrative, apparently drawn from the point of view of a Palestinian man caught in the events (see Figure 12.4). Read in isolation from the rest of the book, the coda could be taken as the view of one person. But because it comes at the end, the reader understands that it combines repeated points of agreement among dozens of oral histories; it is a representation of the consensus among Sacco's Palestinian interviewees.

Formally, the coda mimics the kind of short comics Sacco spent much of his early career producing for anthologies, as well as for his own multi-story comic book, *Yahoo*. The brevity of its narrative demonstrates a command of compression, a quality that Spiegelman describes as defining what is interesting about comics, at least in the American cartoon tradition. He argues that the "cartoon is a drawing that gets to essences. And narratively, comics are an essentialized form of diagramming a narrative movement through time. For me, it's an art of compression that breaks narrative events down to their most necessary moments."[28] More than just using compression effectively, the coda actually demonstrates the process of compression for the reader by distilling events that took dozens of pages and thousands of words to narrate down to three-and-a-half pages of pictures.[29]

In doing so, it also highlights some of the differences between the comics short story as the typical narrative form of the alternative comic book and the much longer form of the book-length comic. We might read these differences as a vehicle for Sacco's larger point about the ethical difficulties of the kind of history he is producing. He is concerned that his own journalistic process of trying to establish the bare facts of the situation may, in fact, have underplayed the suffering of the men and women he draws, and thereby repeated the process of marginalizing their stories that he intended his project to counteract. The rise of the book-length comic, collecting and tidying the scattered narratives of the alternative comic book, presents a suggestive (and less ethically fraught) analogy for the situation.

Sacco includes the coda because he is concerned that in researching his story he may have lost sight of the emotional truth of the Rafah massacre—the "fear" that Abu Juhish, one of Sacco's final interviewees, recalls as the worst thing from that day.[30] Sacco worries that he has put his interviewees through the pain of remembrance simply to establish a factual narrative for his own satisfaction as a privileged outside observer.[31] Seeing the sequence from the point of view of a Palestinian caught up in the events allows the reader some glimpse of Abu Juhish's fear. But that emotional truth is not an expressionistic speculation. Each panel of the coda is also the nodal point of agreement among cross-referenced testimony; together, the panels combine to make the coda the hard kernel of established facts about the massacre. The reader can take a single image from a panel in the coda, and then refer back to a section from the earlier pages and see which of Sacco's witnesses talked about it, and how their versions compare. Indeed, the book prompts the reader to do so, since the grid layout of the coda visually recalls the chart Sacco shows himself and Abed using to cross-reference testimony. Just as Sacco draws himself using the chart to triangulate historical truth via the cross-comparison of testimonial evidence, so we as readers mimic his efforts.[32]

In effect, the main body of the book becomes a footnote by which we may interpret the coda. By contrasting hundreds of pages of main text with a compressed three-and-a-half-page section, *Footnotes in Gaza* insists that the history of the event can only appear as a dialectic—the emotional truth and the factual truth cannot coexist as a single, seamless narrative, but must instead serve as discontinuous indexes of one another, their discontinuity prompting the reader to further investigation. The book cannot simply overcome the politically loaded difficulties of its telling any more than Sacco can abandon his privileged status as an outsider to Gaza. But by requiring the reader to reconstruct the factual truth of what happened from a physically separate set of words and pictures, *Footnotes in Gaza* at least asks its reader to consider questions of hierarchy and subordination on both a textual and an ethical-historical level. The coda is an encapsulation of the tension around the notion of the "footnote" emphasized by the book's title. Sacco wants the reader to understand the unequal dynamics of political and economic power that make one historical event into a footnote, while another a part of history's main text.

The argument of this chapter has pursued two interrelated tracks, showing how Sacco finds means to express conflicting senses of history, and how the current form of the book-length graphic novel provides a strong setting for expressing those conflicts. The analytical assumption in each track has been that not only the content of history, but even its guiding narrative assumptions, look different from different specific vantage points. This is as true for the history of the Gaza Strip as it is for the history of the book-length comic.

My discussion has focused on the North American "alternative" comics tradition of the 1980s and 1990s. It would be worth seeing whether or how ambivalence about the politics of the book-length comic plays out in the work of a cartoonist not directly associated with that tradition, such as Alison Bechdel. Bechdel's career, as a creator of a weekly comic strip whose success with a book-length work profoundly changed her relationship to that strip, is in some ways quite similar to Sacco's. But because Bechdel worked on a different kind of narrative (the newspaper comic strip rather than the alternative comic book), with a distinct audience (particularly a queer audience, and one not necessarily invested in comics per se so much as queer storytelling in a variety of media), her career is also markedly different. Bechdel's work seems particularly worth reading in terms of the nexus between form and politics, since her second graphic memoir—*Are You My Mother?*—deals so clearly with the ambivalence of mainstream success, where success must be read both in terms of the recognition of her first memoir (*Fun Home*) as part of the graphic novel canon, and in terms of the problematic status of normalization within queer politics.[33] Bechdel's problem with mainstream success parallels Sacco's problem in *Footnotes*: that he wants to make the Gazan experience of 1956 visible to a non-Palestinian audience, but he does not want to make it a fully assimilated part of a European or American history of the Middle East. For Bechdel, one of the questions is: if the disreputable hybridity of an alternative newspaper comic strip comes to symbolize the hybridity of a queer community creating modes of expression in spite of the hostility of large parts of society, then what does it mean to draw a book about how you came to create that strip after you have stopped making it? Thinking through the complicated ethics of graphic narrative in Sacco's work offers us a way to start answering such questions.

NOTES

1. Leila El-Haddad, "Interview: Joe Sacco," *Al-Jazeera*, January 18, 2010, http://www.aljazeera.com/focus/2010/01/201011783113578937.html.

2. Ibid.

3. See, for example, Aryn Bartley, "The Hateful Self: Substitution and the Ethics of Representing War," *Modern Fiction Studies* 54.1 (2008): 50–71; and Rebecca Scherr, "Shaking Hands with Other People's Pain: Joe Sacco's *Palestine*," *Mosaic* 46.1 (2013): 19–36.

4. Joe Sacco, *Footnotes in Gaza* (New York: Metropolitan, 2009), 253.

5. Hillary Chute, "Comics Form and Narrating Lives," *Profession* (2011), 112.

6. Witek writes that comics is well suited to historical subjects because of its nonlinearity, particularly in the combination of words and pictures: "In sequential art, the visuals give an immediate representation of a present-tense moment in time, while the narration can range over time, choosing the information which will establish the historical situation without overshadowing the event at hand." Joseph Witek, *Comic Books as History: The Narrative Art of Jack Johnson, Art Spiegelman, and Harvey Pekar* (Jackson: University Press of Mississippi, 1989), 65.

7. Beaty's *Comics Versus Art* considers the mechanisms by which comics get recognized by the fine art world, including the impact of different physical forms of comics on that recognition. Wanzo and Jenkins delivered talks at the 2013 Festival of Cartoon Art at Ohio State University. Wanzo's talk, "Rethinking Sequential Aesthetics: Comics, Cartooning, and Definitions," emphasized the need for comics studies to understand how looking at comics from the standpoint of a specific body necessarily alters the way we understand formal categories. Her example was of an African-American comics tradition, which might need to emphasize a genealogy of caricature in order to make sense, and might downplay definitions of comics based on sequentiality. Jenkins's keynote address, "Comics . . . and Stuff," also sought to reconsider sequentiality as the definition of comics, using single-panel comics from *Hogan's Alley* to emphasize a kind of narrative storytelling not based on multiple panels and the gutter. See Bart Beaty, *Comics Versus Art* (Toronto: University of Toronto Press, 2012).

8. Sacco, *Footnotes in Gaza*, 98–99.

9. Walter Benjamin, "On the Concept of History," trans. Harry Zohn, in *Selected Writings, Vol. 4, 1938–1940*, ed. Howard Eiland and Michael Jennings, trans. Edmund Jephcott et al. (Cambridge: Harvard University Press, 2003), 392.

10. Sacco, *Footnotes*, 30.

11. R. Crumb, "A Short History of America," *CoEvolution Quarterly* 25 (Fall 1979), 21–24. A scan of the magazine is available online at http://www.wholeearth.com/issue/2023/.

12. Sacco, *Footnotes*, 42–50.

13. Benjamin touched on this idea in several of his works, both published and unpublished, but for a condensed introduction, see the fragment from the Arcades Project on Louis-Auguste Blanqui in Walter Benjamin, "Blanqui," trans. Edmund Jephcott, in *Selected Writings, Vol. 4, 1938–1940*, ed. Howard Eiland and Michael Jennings, trans. Edmund Jephcott et al. (Cambridge: Harvard University Press, 2003), 93–94.

14. Sacco, *Footnotes*, 50.

15. Ibid., 369.

16. Ibid., 370–71.

17. The typical Islamic version of this story differs from the typical Christian and Jewish versions. In Christian and Jewish versions, God asks Abraham to sacrifice his son, Isaac. In most Islamic accounts, God asks Abraham to sacrifice his first son, Ishmael. See Koran 37:102–12 and Gen. 22:1–13.

18. Sacco, *Footnotes*, 139.

19. Ibid., 98.

20. Ibid., 111.

21. Ibid., 145. Underlining in original.

22. Ibid., 149.

23. In *Rabelais and His World*, Bakhtin argues that during the Middle Ages and the Renaissance, carnivals temporarily reversed social hierarchies, prioritizing the lower functions of the body and profaning sacred ritual. See Mikhail Bakhtin, *Rabelais and His World*, trans. Hélène Iswolsky (Bloomington: Indiana University Press, 1984).

24. Artist's talk at the Wexner Center for the Arts, Columbus, Ohio, October 17, 2010.

25. The six-issue comic book series *Yahoo* (Seattle: Fantagraphics, 1988–92) was an anthology of Sacco's short-form work, and he contributed strips to many other magazines and anthologies. Much of his output from this period is collected in *Notes from a Defeatist* (Seattle: Fantagraphics, 2003).

26. Daniel Clowes, *Wilson* (Montreal: Drawn & Quarterly, 2010); Adrian Tomine, *Optic Nerve* 12 (Montreal: Drawn & Quarterly, 2011).

27. Jared Gardner, *Projections: Comics and the History of Twenty-First-Century Storytelling* (Stanford: Stanford University Press, 2012), 165.

28. Art Spiegelman and Hillary Chute, "What Art Spiegelman Drew Before He Made *Maus*," *Slate*, October 5, 2011, http://www.slate.com/blogs/browbeat/2011/10/05/art_spiegelman_before_maus.html.

29. *The Great War* (New York: W. W. Norton and Company, 2013) shows Sacco continuing to experiment with the dynamics of compression. In stark contrast to the short, titled chapters of his journalistic work from *Palestine* through *Footnotes*, *The Great War* presents the first day of the Battle of the Somme via a single, twenty-four-foot-long wordless tableaux. As my student Andrew Carringer argued, the overwhelming detail of *The Great War* makes the experience of "reading" it—of following the battle chronologically from left to right of the scroll—something like the experience of creating history from the jumble of events. Depending on what you notice, or choose to interpret as significant, the story you construct will be different.

30. Sacco, *Footnotes*, 384.

31. Sacco satirizes his own callousness towards the painful memories of elderly Palestinians throughout the book, perhaps most pointedly in the chapter "Time Management." The chapter ironically plays up the commonness of Palestinian trauma by emphasizing how routine it is. It describes how Sacco and Abed develop a screening method so they know that an old man's story is relevant to the 1956 project "before someone puts the kettle on and we're trapped for another half hour" (*Footnotes*, 201). The end of the book—the interview with Abu Juhish and the coda—places emphasis on the moment where that functional callousness breaks down.

32. Sacco, *Footnotes*, 203.

33. See Alison Bechdel, *Are You My Mother?: A Comic Drama* (New York: Mariner, 2012) and *Fun Home: A Family Tragicomic* (New York: Mariner, 2006).

13. Graphic Representations of Language, Translation, and Culture in Joe Sacco's Comics Journalism

Brigid Maher

Journalists and foreign correspondents often work in a multilingual environment, dealing on a daily basis with problems of translation and cultural difference. Yet accounts of these challenges reach consumers of news and reportage only rarely, as there is often a preference for a finished product that presents information and analysis exclusively in the target language, meaning the role of translation goes unnoticed. In this respect, Joe Sacco's comics journalism is quite unique. Rather than glossing over the input of translators, interpreters, and other mediators in the creation of a journalistic product, he often puts them center stage. His work on Palestine and Bosnia shows, both linguistically and visually, the involvement and intervention of translators, interpreters, and fixers, as well as a network of more informal contacts. Cultural translation is always a strong presence, too, as Sacco depicts his struggles as a cultural outsider seeking to investigate complex, sensitive, and divisive issues.

Comics journalism provides a flexibility not always present in more traditional forms of journalism; the multimodal nature of comics makes available a range of interesting semiotic and narrative techniques for the depiction of acts of linguistic and cultural mediation. Multiple voices and perspectives can be conveyed in such a way as to present some of the complexities of working in a multilingual environment. The medium also lends itself to irony, which can be created by the contrast between different textual and/or graphic interpretations and representations of a given scene. Comics also allow a visual juxtaposition of objectivity, on the one hand, and the journalist's inner state, particularly his doubts and fears, on the other. All these carefully deployed features allow Sacco to take readers beyond the illusion of unmediated research and reporting towards a more nuanced depiction of the involvement of different stakeholders in newsgathering. In this essay, I will trace Sacco's representation of newsgathering and translation in three of his best-known book-length comics: *Palestine*, recounting his visits to a number of different parts of Palestine and Israel; *Safe Area Goražde*, about the war and its aftermath in the United Nations' so-called "safe area" of Goražde in Eastern Bosnia; and *The Fixer*, also focusing on the war in Bosnia, and on the figure of Neven, who worked for Sacco as an interpreter, guide, and all-around fixer during his visits to Sarajevo in the mid-1990s, and whom he meets again in 2001.

In interviews about his work, Sacco has explained that he sees himself as telling stories he feels usually do not get told or do not get enough attention, particularly in the United States.[1] He tends to stay longer in a place than many journalists would, and his interviewees are not generally prominent decision-makers, military men, politicians, and bureaucrats, but ordinary people trying to survive in a conflict situation. Indeed, as Sacco has pointed out, "The powerful are excellently served by the mainstream media or propaganda organs"; his goal is to focus instead on "those who seldom get a hearing."[2] In both Palestine and Bosnia, Sacco uses local contacts to find his subjects, and he frequently employs translators, interpreters, and fixers to overcome linguistic and logistical barriers. These people are among those who "get a hearing" in his work.

Making the News: The Role of Translation

Sacco's attention to translation and interpreting is not just illuminating but also unusual in light of what is generally seen as a widespread preference for "invisible" translators across a range of text types. For example, in the domain of literary translation, it has been observed that publishers (in the English-speaking world in particular) often favor translation strategies and packaging that draw as little attention as possible to the fact that a text has been translated. There tends to be a preference for a style that is "fluent" or "smooth," the translator's name is generally relegated to the title page rather than being displayed on the front cover, and translators' notes are usually welcome only in canonical texts and classics.[3]

In news texts, too, traces of translation are rarely to be found, even though international newsgathering often involves negotiating a mix of languages and cultural identities. The speed imperative is pressing, and relates both to the speed with which translations are completed, and the speed with which news reports are consumed.[4] Thus, a newspaper article, for example, could have involved an interpreter during face-to-face interviews in the field, or in-house translation of press releases, background material, or whole articles, yet this largely takes place behind the scenes and readers are likely to remain entirely unaware of it.[5] Television news sometimes makes translation visible through subtitling or voice-over of interviews, but in written journalistic texts, translation and interpreting tend to be relegated to the background.

In general, there is the perception that audiences prefer not to have to think about the multiple agents behind a news story; the focus is rather on getting the news across in the most succinct, effective, and speedy way practicable. Indeed, in an interview, the academic and former journalist Barbie Zelizer says:

> It's not in journalism's best interest for the public to realize how dependent the story is on an interpreter.... It's kind of like the maid. You want your house to be clean; you want it to look like it always looks clean. But you don't want anybody seeing the maid coming in and that you're paying dirt-cheap wages.[6]

Bielsa and Bassnett point out the gulf between the prestige and glamour attached to the globetrotting foreign correspondent, and the low status (not to mention poor pay and conditions) afforded their local interpreters,[7] and this low status is reflected in Zelizer's ironic comparison with maids.

In conflict zones where there is strong international media interest, translators and interpreters can be in high demand. Journalists do not necessarily have the luxury of drawing on the skills of a trained and experienced professional; sometimes they may simply have to make do with someone who has reasonable aptitude in the target language and hope for the best. Generally, "translation" refers to work with the written word, and "interpreting" to spoken language, but in urgent news translation practitioners are often required to carry out both. Indeed, the skills required of translators and interpreters in conflict situations often go well beyond the task of transfer between two languages, as they may be required not only to provide linguistic and cultural expertise, but also to find interviewees, organize transport, make bookings, check facts, and much more.[8] In other words, the kinds of qualities that are most sought after are not only translation and interpreting skills but also journalistic and networking skills.[9] Yet in cases where a translator has provided input for a news item, the extent of their contribution to the finished product often goes unrecognized, although there are exceptions, as some print outlets are now beginning to acknowledge in the byline the role of local contributors in the production of news stories.[10]

The blurring of the roles of journalist, interviewee, local expert, and translator/interpreter means, inevitably, that ethical complications sometimes emerge. Given their varied backgrounds and the stressful conditions in which they work, translators, interpreters, and fixers in a conflict zone are not always entirely impartial, a point Sacco himself makes in *The Fixer*, while also conceding that "journalists are dependent on these people, for good or bad."[11] Interpreters and translators generally live in the community to which they belong, but their employment by an outsider sets them apart somewhat. Thus, local native-speaker interpreters may have divided loyalties; indeed a study by Catherine Baker documents concerns about this with interpreters in Bosnia.[12]

In short, it is not difficult to see why, in situations that already involve significant conflict and time pressure, the complexities of translation and linguistic difference are often glossed over. The widespread assumption articulated by Zelizer is that just as we would not be interested in hearing how our friends' floors got so shiny, we would not care to know how an interviewee was found, how their eyewitness account got put into English, what risks a translator takes by working for a journalist, or other such details of the cultural and linguistic exchanges that lie at the heart of much international news.[13] Sacco's work, because of its different medium, mode of production, and audience, provides a corrective to this. He draws attention to the presence of local interpreters and fixers in his interactions, acknowledging and elucidating their crucial role, and thus reminding readers of the mediated nature of much journalism and the ethical implications of this.

The Semiotics of Visible Translation

Compared to someone seeking to publish in the traditional news media, Sacco, as a freelance practitioner of the innovative subgenre of comics journalism, has a greater degree of independence and different demands to meet. He uses many of the newsgathering methods of traditional journalism, such as eyewitness input, research, and careful fact checking, but the very different way in which he presents his reportage allows him the space and time to shed light on aspects that more conventional journalistic texts often have to elide or ignore.

He is under less time pressure during research and writing,[14] and his works have a longer life than regular journalism, especially now that they have appeared in bound collections. This distinguishes his works from more transient forms of news production, such as reports in daily newspapers or in television bulletins. Furthermore, the level of energy and concentration put in by readers is likely to be considerable, because while the word count may be low, close attention is required in processing the semiotically complex messages of these comics, particularly the drawings, characterized by painstaking scenic detail.[15] For these reasons, as well as the fact that he does not rely on the patronage of a major news outlet, Sacco's journalism can be more personal and can include a range of perspectives and considerations, including questions of linguistic and cultural difference.

Part of Sacco's creative and research process includes seeking input from friends and acquaintances, who act as his guides, interpreters, and translators. In addition, these linguistic mediators render day-to-day life in Bosnia or Palestine comprehensible and livable for Sacco, by offering him the kind of cultural information and friendly human contact an outsider needs to understand and move comfortably in an unfamiliar environment. He, in turn, includes some of their stories, comments, and experiences in his comics. By allowing these traditionally "invisible" interpreters to be both seen and heard, Sacco dispels any illusion that he might be working single-handedly.

In one scene in *Palestine*, for example, he meets and interviews Ammar; his friend Larry, an American expatriate, interprets for them, and this mediating role is depicted quite clearly. By including Larry in the picture, Sacco draws the reader's attention to the fact that this is translated discourse with a third figure present who enables the interaction to occur. This is further underscored by Larry's repeated use of "he says . . ." The norm in professional interpreting is to use the first person ("I haven't worked in two years," etc.), which here could create the illusion that the translation was simply a straightforward substitute for the original utterance. However, the constant "he says . . ." explicitly requires readers to bear in mind that Ammar's remarks were in Arabic and reached Sacco through an interpreter's mediation. It should also be observed that a further "translation" from oral to written discourse has taken place here, as the original conversation is "reshaped" to fit into the spatial and rhythmic constraints of the word balloon. It is easy to forget that dialogue presented in comics journalism—as in travel writing or reportage—is not necessarily reported verbatim, and even when it is, the author has performed a process of selection and presentation.

Indeed, the word balloon itself is a tool whereby Sacco is able to make translation visible. Even without using any foreign-language dialogue, he ingeniously depicts the double-voiced nature of translation by varying the placement of the word balloon, showing that both the interviewee and the interpreter are speaking in a given interaction, building the final meaning between the two of them. Escorted by Sameh, a resident who acts as his interpreter and guide, Sacco visits an elderly woman in Jabalia refugee camp; in one scene of the interview, the word balloon comes from the woman's mouth, but Sameh is also pictured and appears to be speaking.[16] Several pages later, the woman finishes her tragic story as follows: "Seven months after Ahmed died, my husband died. . . . He had a heart problem. . . . They didn't give him permission to go to Egypt to be treated until the end. . . . He died on the road. . . ."[17] In the final panel of the sequence, the word balloon containing this last utterance—"He died on the road"—is attached to Sameh instead of the interviewee (see Figure 13.1). This depiction of one story coming from two speakers gives a sense of the way both contribute to its enunciation. Sameh's facial expression at this dramatic

Figure 13.1. Detail of Joe Sacco, *Palestine* (Seattle: Fantagraphics, 2001), 158.

moment reflects his emotional pain as he translates the woman's trauma. He has, in a sense, taken on her story as his own, hence his appropriation of a word balloon that had previously been hers.

Rendering translation visible in this way, Sacco also shows the traumatic effect the translation of conflict can have on the individuals involved. Because of the visual nature of his medium and his desire as a journalist to represent his interviewees' experiences faithfully, Sacco requires a great deal of detail and "vivid descriptions," routed through his translators and interpreters.[18] Reflecting on Sameh's role as mediator, Sacco writes,

> How many soldiers? *How* did they beat you? *Then* what happened? He helps me wring it out of the people I interview. . . . And he's heard every blow and humiliation described twice, once by the person telling me, and again when it's come out of *his* mouth in translation . . .'[19]

The translation theorist Mona Baker makes a similar point about the traumatic effect of interpreting in child abuse cases or in the Truth and Reconciliation trials in South Africa. She suggests that "ontological narratives"—which she defines as "personal stories that we tell ourselves about our place in the world and our own personal history"—may be the most difficult to translate or interpret as they require the translator to take on another person's story, and in conflict situations this is all too often a painful story.[20] Sacco's panels certainly seem to corroborate this, as he depicts the personal toll the translation of trauma can take. Speaking another's story, as Sameh does in the example discussed above, means living that story, at least for a time. The shifting word balloon expresses this shared identity in a visual way, reminding readers that the interpreter does not simply parrot or ventriloquize but is actually part of the collective narrative into which each interviewee's individual narrative fits.

At the end of their conversation, the woman interviewed in Jabalia expresses her cynicism about journalists, questioning what can really be achieved by yet another one observing and commenting upon her people's misery. As Sacco prepares to leave, she fires a barrage of questions at him, through his interpreter:

> She asks, what good is it to talk to you? . . . She wants to know how talking to you is going to help her . . . Aren't we people too? She says [people in Germany support us] with words only. . . . She says she wants to see action.[21]

Sacco makes some attempts to justify his presence and convey the West's goodwill, but the woman is unmoved. We share his discomfort as ultimately he seems to concede he has no answer to her question: "Well . . . Tell her I don't know what to say to her. Where's my shoes?" Relayed through Sameh, the woman's speech becomes more powerful because we get a sense of *two* voices relentlessly asking these questions on behalf of a whole community. The faces crowded into some of the panels further add to this impression of a collective challenge issued in two languages, even though the text on the page is all in English. The depiction of Sameh's active participation in the exchange makes clear that he is both a member of the community affected, and an element of the complex machinery bringing us the story.

Intercultural Exchange

The very fact that they often eliminate or move beyond language is one of the reasons why multimodal texts like comics can provide a refreshing perspective on language.[22] One extreme example of the replacement of words with meaningful images is Shaun Tan's picture book *The Arrival*, which tells a story of migration and exile without using any written language at all. Instead, Tan completely defamiliarizes all language and communication, using bewildering symbols and bizarre urban settings to convey his protagonists' sense of isolation and incomprehension, thus focusing his readers' response on the story's emotional content rather than on details of time or place.[23]

It appears that, at a basic level, Sacco's work can also transcend language barriers. In an interview, he has commented on the identification that his work generates:

> My guide had a copy of *Palestine* on my last trip to Gaza. He'd bring it out and show people what I was trying to do. That usually went over pretty well

... they were able to look at it and say, "Oh, this is me, this is much like the refugee camp I'm living in."[24]

By showing people the kind of work he does, Sacco can win trust and encourage collaboration even without a shared language. While images are by no means culturally neutral, and are no less at risk of manipulation than words, a recognizable drawing can be an important reassurance for people who might otherwise feel somewhat uneasy about foreign languages and the prospect of being translated. Translation and translators sometimes inspire distrust because the nature of their intervention is by definition opaque to those engaged in an interaction, so being able to see the finished product in pictures allows participants an element of recognition and involvement. This can create a sense of trust among groups that feel vulnerable, victimized, misrepresented, or misunderstood.[25]

Many aspects of day-to-day life appear in Sacco's accounts of Bosnia and Palestine. For example, he often shows the way he is welcomed into the homes of his interviewees, and presents his particular variety of journalism as involving not only investigative work and factual documentation, but also interpersonal and intercultural engagement. Culture and experience are transmitted, stories are shared, and relationships and trust are fostered through the journalist's investment of time and effort into social activities centered on meals, tea drinking, and parties.

This interpersonal aspect means that Sacco's work has some overlaps with travel writing, but at the same time his journalistic training and methods show through, and his comics offer revealing insights into the human side of the news-gathering process. He highlights the journalist's reliance on people's generosity with their stories, homes, and often-scarce food. In the unequal power dynamic between foreign journalist and local victims of conflict, hospitality and a sense of home are the gifts people are most able to offer Sacco, and in numerous scenes he depicts himself as a rather greedy recipient of this warmth and generosity: "I eat like a king in refugee camps," he writes; one family's "chicken fried crispy in a sort of lemon sauce" is "finger-lickin' good!"[26] Ironically citing the slogan of a fast-food multinational among people living such a deprived and precarious existence underscores the gap between their world and his.

If locals provide enormous emotional, material, and logistical support to Sacco, we also see that he and his fellow journalists bring something highly valued to the conflict zones they visit: the capacity to transmit people's stories to an international public, as well as a much-needed breath of fresh air in a stifling atmosphere of conflict and frustration. For example, in the isolated "safe area" of Goražde, the arrival of the press is greeted with excitement by people who have felt neglected because of all the attention focused on "media darling Sarajevo," and Sacco's mobility, his freedom to come and go with UN convoys, is envied.[27] It becomes clear from Sacco's work that media interest can result in opportunities for cultural exchange that local residents sometimes delight in. In Bosnia, his English-speaking friends love his idiomatic expressions—*figure out, nothing to write home about,* and *you're full of shit*—and use them at every opportunity.[28] There is also a shared familiarity with American popular music and cinema that brings Sacco and his new friends together. He writes out the lyrics to American pop songs for his friend Riki, and he and his Goražde friends watch Hollywood action movies on video—"'American Ninja II' or whatever other video [Edin's] brother had dug up"—as long as the homemade generator on the river Drina holds out.[29] Neven describes a highly dramatic moment in his colorful (and possibly partly apocryphal) career as a soldier as being "like in the Doc Holiday [*sic*] movies."[30]

Films are central in shaping Sacco's Bosnian friends' perceptions of the US, and it is interesting to note the way Neven uses the familiar genre of the Western to "translate" his own wartime experience for Sacco and his readers. However, Hollywood Westerns, for all their dramatic shootouts, cannot be as graphic and gruesome as the actual experience of war. Sacco himself knows this from more than once being invited to sit through a very different kind of film, one he calls "Goražde's own Most Horrifying Home Videos"—grisly amateur footage of wartime attacks, injuries, and surgery.[31] The shared global heritage of the Hollywood movie serves as a way of bringing to life the tension and excitement of war, yet at the same time, for the reader safely ensconced in a peaceful country, this scene underscores just how difficult it is for most people to comprehend the unsanitized, unglamorous violence of real-life war. As Sacco's work shows, war does not take a conventional narrative shape with a beginning, middle, and foreseeable end, and it comprises not only moments of adrenaline-fueled action, but also a punishing daily grind to survive.

Negotiating Conflicts of Interest

Personal relationships with fixers and interpreters are by no means portrayed as unproblematic, however, and the journalist's debt of gratitude can cause discomfort. In Sarajevo, the charismatic Neven, protagonist of *The Fixer*, serves as a kind of protector and guide, but naturally needs to profit from the relationship too. And as an impecunious freelancer, Sacco feels alarmed at how, when Neven is around, "my wallet . . . eases out of my trousers and starts spewing money!"[32] His account of his relationship with Neven constantly reminds us of the power of money in a conflict zone. In her short piece "10 Things Journalists Should Know About Fixers," Kathlyn Clore includes as number two on the list: "The motivations of a good fixer should be transparent. Is he in it for love or for money?" And she seems to prefer the idea that a fixer will be "passionate" about their work.[33] However, it seems rather naïve and even unfair to hope that in a conflict zone a fixer would not be motivated at least partly by the prospect of earning some money; certainly, Neven wants to exploit his skills in any way possible to get ahead during a time of hardship, when people have little to live off apart from their own initiative and imagination. And at the same time, Sacco reminds us that a journalist has quite a bit in common with their interpreter—both make a living out of conflict and pain and, in a sense, the greater the pain, the better the living to be made: "'When massacres happened,' Neven [tells him], 'those were the best times. Journalists from all over the world were coming here.'"[34] While, for Sacco, "let's face it, my comics blockbuster depends on conflict; peace won't pay the rent."[35]

As Francis Jones has observed, literary translators—but it applies to all translators and interpreters—are "individuals with relationships, loyalties and political/social ideologies of their own,"[36] and in a conflict situation, such as Bosnia or Palestine in the 1990s, they cannot possibly be expected to pretend otherwise. Sacco is initially rather naïve and wide-eyed when it comes to Neven's transition from fixer to interviewee. However, he comes to learn that while Neven may be a well-connected fixer and genial companion, he is not always a reliable informant, and is wont to exaggerate his own heroic participation in the war.[37] Yet in a sense, this is just a more extreme manifestation of the ambiguity that can stem from the complex combination of agents involved in all newsgathering. As John Milton and Paul Bandia note, while translators are crucial in enabling intercultural exchange and shaping our knowledge of the other, we should not fall into the trap of assuming that all translators are benevolent and trustworthy.[38] Through the directions in which they guide the journalists for whom they work, translators, interpreters, and fixers play a key role in shaping international news reports, even when not relating their personal stories for their overseas charges.[39] Sacco's work brings this complexity to the forefront by depicting his reliance on such people, who contribute to his knowledge about their country and its conflict, and indirectly help him put together his story.

The Author's Position

Of course, it is not only his interpreters who Sacco puts into his comics; the author, too, is always a presence. For Sacco, journalists are not "flies on the wall," they do not deal in "cold science," and his self-depiction is a way of drawing attention to the inevitable subjectivity of his work.⁴⁰ This subjective element is further emphasized through the pervasive use of irony in Sacco's comics journalism. D. C. Muecke defines contemporary uses of irony in literature by their capacity to activate a range of interpretations on the part of readers: "The old definition of irony—saying one thing and giving to understand the contrary—is superseded; irony is saying something in a way that activates not one but an endless series of subversive interpretations."⁴¹ In comics, ironic potential is increased because the superimposition of modes can be exploited in triggering such contrasting interpretations.⁴² For example, in *Fun Home: A Family Tragicomic*, Alison Bechdel at times uses captions as an expression of inner voices and feelings, creating a stark ironic contrast between the wry commentary of the first-person narrator and the way her autobiographical self is depicted as a scene unfolds.⁴³

Sacco, too, exploits the interplay between words and images, and in this way he achieves ironic distance from traumatic or frightening situations and is able to reflect in critical and humorously self-deprecating ways on his own role as journalist. So while he gives a sense of the potential for translation—and journalism—to create a space for cultural exchange and understanding, he also displays a cautious irony towards his own desire to find voices of harmony or optimism.⁴⁴ Expressing both hope in humanity and awareness of the complications of long-term conflict, his ironic and self-deprecating tone echoes that found often in contemporary travel writing which, in a globalized and postcolonial era, begins to turn to irony and irreverence to express the decentered position of the present-day traveler and international commentator.⁴⁵

One key feature of Sacco's self-depiction is its cartoon-like quality: unusually small and weedy with exaggerated facial features, he hardly strikes the pose of fearless and intrepid reporter, and there is none of that "streak of machismo" that Ulf Hannerz finds in the autobiographical writings of many foreign correspondents.⁴⁶ This self-deprecating image results in the kind of self-irony that Muecke has characterized as a form of self-protection from outside attack.⁴⁷ One might think of it as a kind of preemptive strike against those who would point out Sacco's relatively privileged position in these interactions. Sacco's self-mockery is evident when he first arrives in Palestine. He declares: "I will alert the world to your suffering! Watch your local comic book store . . ."⁴⁸ In ironic contrast to his hopes of achieving great things through his journalistic intervention, the cartoon Sacco reminds us of his—and our own—sense of powerlessness in the face of war. Likewise, while many of Goražde's residents get excited about the presence of an American journalist in their midst, "One old man took one look at me and abandoned all hope that the U.S. military *could* rescue Bosnia. 'Americans are short and wearing glasses,' he noted to Edin [the translator]."⁴⁹

Self-directed irony has been said to contribute to a sense of community between an author and readers.⁵⁰ Moreover, cartoon-like figures, as opposed to more detailed, realistic depictions, are generally believed to facilitate reader involvement and be easier for readers to identify with.⁵¹ Thus, Sacco's multimodal depiction of his own moments of apparent self-importance in ironic contrast with a decidedly unprepossessing cartoon image of himself as bespectacled and at times befuddled, enables us to put ourselves in his shoes as cultural outsiders trying to make sense of complicated conflicts.

The frequent deployment of irony emphasizes Sacco's occasional discomfort with his role, as well as the unequal power dynamic in which the foreign journalist functions. Sacco is totally dependent on his local contacts, but he also knows he can leave at any time and return to the comforts of home. I discussed above the distressing effect on Sameh of having to translate accounts of personal trauma in Palestine. In another moment in *Palestine*, Sacco learns that Sameh's job is at risk and he might be demoted, possibly because he has been working for Sacco. He writes: "It's an office politics thing . . . But my presence has been the catalyst . . . Well think about how *I* feel . . ."⁵² The pair of them walk despondently through the squalor of Jabalia, but in the first panel of the next page, we see that Sacco's inner journalist never rests: "That'd make a good picture . . ." is his thought as they pass by some goats nosing around in the rubbish.⁵³ Here, the irony comes from the juxtaposition of Sacco's empathy for Sameh with his greedy desire for evocative images of Palestinian misery. Sacco uses irony as a way of distancing himself from certain aspects of his work as a journalist, including the potentially exploitative elements, and the tendency to be always on the lookout for a good story or image, even as someone else's life might be falling apart.⁵⁴ So while he gives readers what they want (realistic, heartrending depictions of suffering), his self-referential irony draws attention to his own intervention as mediator and interpreter of this environment.

The fact that we never see the cartoon Sacco's eyes behind his glasses has often been commented upon. Obradović posits that it might be seen as representing either the purity of his gaze, or the blindness of an outsider, whereas for Walker it serves as a "screen" for the projection of the interviewees' trauma.⁵⁵ It also means that Sacco often comes across as rather naïve and lost, and he is certainly very open about the fear he feels at times in the conflict zones he visits, especially in Palestine.⁵⁶ Sacco himself has suggested that this feature of his self-depiction might be a way of protecting himself and concealing his own emotional response to his interviewees' trauma.⁵⁷ He has spoken movingly about the effects this kind of work has on him, explaining that while he is able to remain detached and "clinical" when interviewing his subjects about the violence and hardship they have suffered, the subsequent drawing process can be quite traumatic:

> When you're drawing it's hard to be distanced. In fact you have to inhabit what you're drawing—the person you're shooting and the person falling to the ground. You have to feel how their hands would be placed and so on. You find yourself almost doing this reflexively with your own body, to find out how you would draw those muscles. Is it depressing? If you see enough of the world it's depressing. Drawing it is like taking a concentrated dose of it.[58]

Sacco's glasses, then, function as an indicator of both absorption and distance, emphasizing, once again, the personal side to the reporting of war and conflict.

The different stages of mediation from interview to published comic are made visible through Sacco's deployment of a range of semiotic, stylistic, and narrative techniques unique to comics. He uses space and framing, word balloons, and ironic self-reflexivity in order to depict cultural and linguistic exchange, as well as his own artistic mediation, as he takes the content of his interviews and his own experiences and research, and reformulates them as comics. Through this interaction between medium and method, the journalistic and the sociocultural, Sacco's work sheds light on the complex role foreign journalists have in a community in conflict: they bring outside influences, power, wealth, and status, but also compassion, ironic detachment, and a sense of humor. At the same time, Sacco depicts the problematic aspects of this relationship, exploring his own vulnerability and naïveté as he weighs up the obligations of friendship against the demands of his profession. His work gives a hearing not only to the unheard voices of war, but also to those unheard agents helping to bring us news of war, including those people who, whether by circumstance or by vocation, find themselves interpreting for foreign correspondents, often assisting not only in conveying but also shaping news content. Because international conflict is a site of cultural exchange in which the role of language, translation, and interpreting is often ignored, Sacco's comics provide an interesting contrast to more conventional forms of news reporting. Thanks to this willingness to engage—often through the prism of irony—with the complexity of both his own task and that of the interpreter, Sacco is able to introduce readers to the positive exchanges enabled by translation and intercultural communication, as well as to the ethical challenges and ambiguities that can be associated with the translation of conflict, including the personal sacrifice or inconvenience it may entail for the interpreter. This sensitivity to questions of language and culture mirrors Sacco's emphasis on the effects of conflict on people's daily lives and on their sense of identity. As mediation becomes personalized, we see that translation and interpreting are not purely instrumental modes of facilitating communication; they also shape relationships and narratives.

NOTES

1. Alex Burrows, "The Myth of Objective Journalism—Joe Sacco Interviewed," *Quietus*, December 9, 2012, http://thequietus.com/articles/10916-joe-sacco-journalism-interview; Desiree Cooper and Angela Kim, "Joe Sacco's 'Palestine,'" *American Public Media*, December 15, 2007, http://weekendamerica.publicradio.org/display/web/2007/12/12/sacco/); Christopher Farah, "Safe Area America," *Salon*, December 5, 2003, http://www.salon.com/2003/12/05/sacco/; Omar Khalifa, "Joe Sacco on Palestine," *Al Jazeera*, July 19, 2008, http://english.aljazeera.net/news/middleast/2007/11/2008525185042679346.html.

2. Joe Sacco, *Journalism* (New York: Metropolitan, 2012), xiv.

3. Lawrence Venuti, *The Translator's Invisibility: A History of Translation* (London: Routledge, 1995).

4. Sara Bani, "An Analysis of Press Translation Process," in *Translation in Global News: Proceedings of the Conference Held at the University of Warwick 23 June 2006*, eds. Kyle Conway and Susan Bassnett (Coventry: University of Warwick Centre for Translation and Comparative Cultural Studies, 2006), 37.

5. Bani, "An Analysis of Press Translation Process," 35; Esperança Bielsa and Susan Bassnett, *Translation in Global News* (London: Routledge, 2009).

6. Eric Goldscheider, "Found in Translation," *Boston Globe Magazine*, October 24, 2004, http://www.eric-goldscheider.com/id20.html.

7. Bielsa and Bassnett, *Translation in Global News*, 60.

8. Elisabeth Witchel, "The Fixers," *Committee to Protect Journalists*, October 13, 2004, http://cpj.org/reports/2004/10/fixers.php; Russell Working, "Speaking in Tongues: You're Only as Good as Your Translator," *Columbia Journalism Review* (January/February 2004), 12.

9. Goldscheider, "Found in Translation."

10. Goldscheider, "Found in Translation"; Witchel, "The Fixers."

11. Kristine McKenna, "Brueghel in Bosnia," *L.A. Weekly*, January 1, 2004, http://www.laweekly.com/2004-01-01/news/brueghel-in-bosnia/.

12. Catherine Baker, "The Care and Feeding of Linguists: The Working Environment of Interpreters, Translators, and Linguists During Peacekeeping in Bosnia-Herzegovina," *War & Society* 29.2 (2010), 166.

13. It is worth pointing out that in situations of violent conflict, translators, interpreters, and other go-betweens are sometimes directly targeted because of the work they do. In 2010, as more and more instances of such attacks hit the news, the organization Red T was set up to increase

awareness of this issue and to advocate for the rights and protection of translators and interpreters (see http://red-t.org/).

14. This can be observed, for example, in the comparison of his method to that of the journalists who come in and out of Goražde in a day, seeking nothing more than quick sound bites and a couple of iconic images. See Aryn Bartley, "The Hateful Self: Substitution and the Ethics of Reporting War," *Modern Fiction Studies* 54.1 (2008), 54.

15. Chute has commented on the "labor-intensive 'decoding'" that Sacco's work demands. Hillary Chute, "Comics as Literature? Reading Graphic Narrative," *PMLA* 123.2 (March 2008), 460.

16. Joe Sacco, *Palestine* (Seattle: Fantagraphics, 2001), 235.

17. Ibid., 241.

18. Ibid., 219. In prefaces and interviews, Sacco has explained that he asks his interviewees for detailed visual descriptions, and in some cases even sketches, to aid in his depiction of flashback scenes. See, for example, Sacco, *Palestine*, xxii–xxiii; Gary Groth, "Joe Sacco, Frontline Journalist: Why Sacco Went to Goražde," *Comics Journal* (Winter 2002), 61–63.

19. Sacco, *Palestine*, 219 (original emphasis).

20. Mona Baker, *Translation and Conflict: A Narrative Account* (London: Routledge, 2006), 32, 28.

21. Sacco, *Palestine*, 242–43.

22. Indeed, comics have proved a very translatable and transnational medium over the course of the twentieth century and beyond. Extensive translation among a wide range of languages and cultures has ensured global diffusion of the medium as well as the development of significant culture-specific differences in form and the range of subject matter, readerships, and so on. See, for example, Federico Zanettin, ed., *Comics in Translation* (Manchester: St. Jerome, 2008).

23. Shaun Tan, *The Arrival* (Sydney: Lothian, 2006).

24. Dave Gilson, "The Art of War," *Mother Jones*, July/August 2005, http://www.motherjones.com/media/2005/07/joe-sacco-interview-art-war.

25. Further to this, Banita points out the narrative and ethical importance of "silent panels," those with neither word balloons nor captions, in Sacco's work. Georgiana Banita, "Cosmopolitan Suspicion: Comics Journalism and Graphic Silence," in *Transnational Perspectives on Graphic Narratives: Comics at the Crossroads*, eds. Shane Denson, Christina Meyer, and Daniel Stein (New York: Bloomsbury, 2013).

26. Sacco, *Palestine*, 43, 164. On pages 75 and 174 of *Palestine*, and page 35 of *Safe Area Goražde*, too, Sacco depicts himself eagerly indulging in the repasts prepared for him.

27. Sacco, *Safe Area Goražde: The War in Eastern Bosnia 1992–1995* (Seattle: Fantagraphics, 2000), 6, 65.

28. Ibid., 101.

29. Ibid., 151, 49.

30. Sacco, *The Fixer: A Story from Sarajevo* (Montreal: Drawn and Quarterly, 2003), 43.

31. Sacco, *Safe Area Goražde*, 120.

32. Sacco, *The Fixer*, 59.

33. Kathlyn Clore, "10 Things Journalists Should Know About Fixers: Covering Minorities," *European Journalism Centre*, February 4, 2009, http://ejc.net/magazine/article/10-things-journalists-should-know-about-fixers-covering-minorities#.Uix5q7xPpmk.

34. Sacco, *The Fixer*, 49.

35. Sacco, *Palestine*, 76.

36. Francis R. Jones, "Ethics, Aesthetics and Décision: Literary Translating in the Wars of the Yugoslav Succession," *Meta* 49.4 (2004), 712.

37. Sacco, *The Fixer*, 61.

38. John Milton and Paul Bandia, "Introduction: Agents of Translation and Translation Studies," in *Agents of Translation*, eds. John Milton and Paul Bandia (Amsterdam: John Benjamins, 2009), 14–16.

39. McKenna, "Brueghel in Bosnia."

40. Sacco, *Journalism*, xiii–xiv.

41. D. C. Muecke, *Irony and the Ironic* (London: Methuen, 1982), 31.

42. Chute picks up on the "double (but nonsynthesized) narratives of words and images" that comprise comics: "In one frame of comics, the images and the words may mean differently, and thus the work sends out double-coded narratives or semantics." Chute, "Comics as Literature?" 459.

43. Alison Bechdel, *Fun Home: A Family Tragicomic* (Boston: Mariner, 2006).

44. See, for example, Sacco, *Palestine*, 76, 131.

45. Loredana Polezzi, "Translation, Travel, Migration," *Translator* 12.2 (2006), 180–81. The affinity between Sacco's work and travel writing has been noted by Tristram Walker, "Graphic Wounds: The Comics Journalism of Joe Sacco," *Journeys* 11.1 (2010): 69-88.

46. Ulf Hannerz, *Transnational Connections: Culture, People, Places* (New York: Routledge, 1996), 123.

47. Muecke, *Irony and the Ironic*, 26.

48. Sacco, *Palestine*, 27.

49. Sacco, *Safe Area Goražde*, 190 (original emphasis).

50. Marina Mizzau, *L'ironia: la contraddizione consentita* (Milan: Feltrinelli, 1989), 105–106.

51. Scott McCloud, *Understanding Comics: The Invisible Art* (New York: HarperPerennial, 1993), 27–59, 204; Groth, "Joe Sacco, Frontline Journalist," 61.

52. Sacco, *Palestine*, 220 (original emphasis).

53. Ibid., 221.

54. One is reminded here of the title of Edward Behr's book on his career as a foreign correspondent, *Anyone Here Been Raped and Speaks English?* (London: New English Library, 1982), another blackly ironic assessment of the journalist's craft. Behr overheard a British television reporter asking this question of refugees from the former Belgian Congo.

55. Dragana Obradović, "The Aesthetics of Documentary War Reportage: Joe Sacco's *Safe Area*

Goražde," in *Nation in Formation: Inclusion and Exclusion in Central and Eastern Europe*, ed. Catherine Baker et al. (London: School of Slavonic and East European Studies, University College London, 2007), 101; Walker, "Graphic Wounds," 76.

56. See, for example, the scene on page 118 of *Palestine* in which Sacco hears percussion grenades for the first time and overreacts, mistaking them for explosions. His sweat beads and arm-waving, along with the chaotic crowding of the panels and captions on the page, convey the panic of a novice war correspondent.

57. Cooper and Kim, "Joe Sacco's 'Palestine.'"

58. Burrows, "The Myth of Objective Journalism."

14. What Washes Up onto the Shore: Contamination and Containment in "The Unwanted"

Maureen Shay

In the winter of 2011, shortly after the Jasmine Revolution and its incitement of the Arab Spring, I found myself walking along the Tunisian coastline. The day was chilly, the skies were darkening, and the wind was kicking up. Gazing out over the tempestuous Mediterranean Sea, I tried to imagine looking hard enough to spot, somewhere out there, the islands I knew were in that empty expanse of space—Lampedusa, 70 miles away, and beyond it, Malta, another 100 miles after that. I tried to reconcile in my mind the boat journeys of Tunisian and Libyan migrants occurring that very moment across that sea with the sheer size of its waves and the ominous dull horizon of gray stretched out in front of me. It seemed unlikely that any boat could ever move through that treacherous space and survive intact to reach solid ground. And yet the numbers indicate that vessels do, in fact, reach a destination out there. As regimes across North Africa collapsed, the United Nations High Commissioner for Refugees (UNHCR) cited that an estimated 58,000 migrants traversed the Mediterranean Sea in 2011 and arrived onto European land; 28,000 of these were Tunisian. Another 2,000 individuals drowned or went missing that same year.[1]

A year before the Arab Spring, comics journalist Joe Sacco published a two-part graphic narrative in the *Virginia Quarterly Review* entitled "The Unwanted," in which he considers the fate of those thousands of boat migrants once they reach land. Opening with a single word—"Globalization!"—his piece explores the ways in which trafficked migrants are perceived as an undesired aspect of more seemingly productive globalized industries, and reduced to the status of ecological waste that must be contained but ultimately cannot be assimilated. Unlike Sacco's more popular work on conflicts in Palestine and Eastern Europe, "The Unwanted" is among his more autobiographical work to date. Here, he examines the plight of sub-Saharan African migrants and asylum seekers in detention on the island of Malta, Sacco's own birthplace. In *Journalism*, Sacco observes that in returning to Malta he felt that he would finally be able to journalistically maneuver with the ease of a local, rather than having to negotiate his subject through his typical iconic, bespectacled outsider status. He writes, "I thought there was no better place to report the issue of African migration to Europe than my own birthplace, Malta.... As a Maltese I figured local people would be less reticent with me about their feelings towards the Africans who had landed on the island."[2]

While the project permits Sacco easier access to his subject—due to his familiarity with language, the island's relatively small geography, and an ability to readily approach migrants in open camps—it also becomes a reflective lens for Sacco. What he swiftly discovers in the course of the project is that in returning to Malta to cover immigrant populations, Sacco must consider his family's own emigration from the island to Australia. In Figure 14.1, Sacco juxtaposes two different forms of mobility in order to underscore the discrepancy between his own experience leaving Malta years ago, and the migrants' experience of arrival to that same place. In the top panel, the text reads: "Time for me to come clean: I was born in Malta. My family immigrated to Australia when I was a baby ... and the Australian government, eager to populate its large continent with white-faced Europeans, paid most of our passage."[3] The panel features an impressively large boat sailing into the Australian harbor as waving (and racially uniform) hands in the foreground enthusiastically beckon. The image suggests openness: from the expansive sky to the spread hands, the journey appears effortless and its reception hospitable. In contrast, the caption below it maintains,

> But no one sent the Africans—the vast majority of whom are single Muslim men—an invitation to Malta, a Catholic and, until recently, homogenous country. When African immigrants arrive here, they are welcomed by detention for up to a year and a half ... before being released to open centers, where they can come and go as they please.[4]

The spaciousness of the top panel is made more obvious by the bottom panel's attention to constriction. With only a small portion of the sky visible in the top left corner, the rest of the image offers a suffocating scene of fracture. With the reader's lowered perspective, the four men in the foreground appear to be overshadowed by the massive angular lines of a concrete building that looms dizzyingly above. Their bodies are under the gaze of other migrants' scrutiny as laundry lines, like corrals, form a horizontal visual border that pens them in. The image is crowded, with even the rectangular caption on the left appearing squashed into the panel in order to press down upon the back of the tallest man, who slumps under its implied weight. Here, African migrants hoping to reach Italy's shores (and thus access mainland Europe) discover only their

Contamination and Containment in "The Unwanted"   241

Figure 14.1. Parallel migrations. Joe Sacco, "The Unwanted," in *Journalism* (New York: Metropolitan, 2012), 113.

disappointment. They have landed instead on Malta and receive no gracious welcome.

Indeed, one of the most compelling aspects of "The Unwanted" is that the piece is inflected with this discrepancy of twinned migration journeys and its fundamental sense of irony. As such, Sacco's sympathies towards the African migrant communities in Malta are twofold; they emerge from his political position on the contentious issue of irregular immigration (referring to border crossings conducted without legal consent from the destination nation) to Europe, but they also come from a more personal sense of the fickleness of hospitality. For certain communities, bright new opportunities await after a long sea crossing, while others are condemned to systemic containment within the infrastructure of detention centers and halfway homes, left to subsist on minimal monetary handouts and food stamps. Sacco's act of "coming clean" is an admission of the privilege implicit in his family's access to a particular kind of transnational global mobility, so different from the forced migration and restricted mobility of the world's most vulnerable populations that flee conflict, poverty, and violence.

When Sacco heads to his homeland to investigate African migration, he is not simply a neutral observer, but rather an insider of sorts who is continually asked to articulate his identity and recognize his own problematic implication within the tense situation that surrounds him. Several instances within "The Unwanted" depict his uncomfortable insider-outsider position. Sacco is asked repeatedly by detained women to help them out in their asylum rejection appeals, and elsewhere, city mayor Francis Debono approaches a group of locals, explaining to them in Maltese that Sacco is investigating popular opinion on the issue of African immigration. One resident replies in Maltese—"What should we say? That we're for them or against them?"—before realizing that Sacco understands the language.[5] Although Sacco is Maltese by birth, he does not fit into the binary that the narrative broadly presents: native, white Catholic Maltese versus foreign, predominantly Muslim black African men and women. This is a binary succinctly offered by resident Romina in her assertion, "This country is ours, not theirs."[6] When he later engages a group of Nigerian men, Sacco is first asked, "Are you Maltese? We don't like Maltese,"[7] because the men's trust in Sacco's journalism—and its perceived neutrality—is premised on Sacco's outsider status. Sacco, in response, is very obviously uncomfortable and silent, his face partially hidden under a panama hat and his mouth grimacing. The only other figure in the narrative who complicates this binary is Ahmed Bugri, a black resident originally from Ghana who has integrated into Maltese society and now works as the manager of one of Malta's open centers (tent villages that function as halfway homes following release from detention facilities). While the figure of Bugri suggests a potential progress model for successful assimilation within Maltese society, he, too, gestures towards reifying black migrants as fearful agents of rupture: "They bring their anger back to the center," he warns. "You think there is peace, but underneath it's simmering. That's why Maltese don't feel secure, and I don't blame them."[8]

The piece sustains this native/foreign dichotomy in order to highlight the polarity of the immigration and hospitality debate, while also critiquing the general lack of information available that would rework the binary. Sacco does, however, locate counterdiscursive subject positions in his interviews. There is the aforementioned Ahmed Bugri, who has integrated within Maltese life; humanist mayor Debono, who ultimately supports the establishment of better infrastructure to meet the migrants' long-term needs; and Maltese Jesuit services that provide outreach and advocacy for refugees. To a certain degree, this is what Sacco's trademark journalism performs: a steady reworking of perceived binaries in order to reveal the shifting grounds of a far more complex subject matter. The piece is structured around interviews with Maltese fishermen, local residents, politicians, bus drivers, café owners, and even the infamous cultural icon Norman Lowell: a white power fanatic whose dangerous rhetoric advocates the use of torture and brutality as government approaches to the crisis of displaced refugees. Some interviewed residents are cautious, others concerned, and a few outright furious about the changing demographics of their island.

Sections devoted to exploring local Maltese sentiment employ a particular visual gaze that objectifies migrants and exposes their fixedness and containment. Sacco uses this visual technique (mimicking the biased perspective of local residents) in order to reveal the limits of representation and the loaded consequences of image circulation. In this case, this visual point of view recalls for us transnational media's images of vulnerable migrant and refugee communities that perpetuate the very disenfranchisement they take as their subject. Anthropologist Liisa Malkki terms this nuanced visual discourse "regimes of representation" that promote speechlessness and "depoliticize the refugee category . . . to construct in that depoliticized space an ahistorical, universal humanitarian subject."[9] Malkki's concern is that without the precise historical, socioeconomic context in which to situate the refugee, we see only a nonpolitical subjectivity. As we sympathize with the represented desperate masses, we take an image's fixedness for discursive silence, a silence that inevitably works like a regime of oppression.

"The Unwanted" stages this collective depoliticization in images representing African migrants as locals view them. Close-ups of black faces behind vertical bars suggest the criminality of migrant bodies, while elsewhere the read-

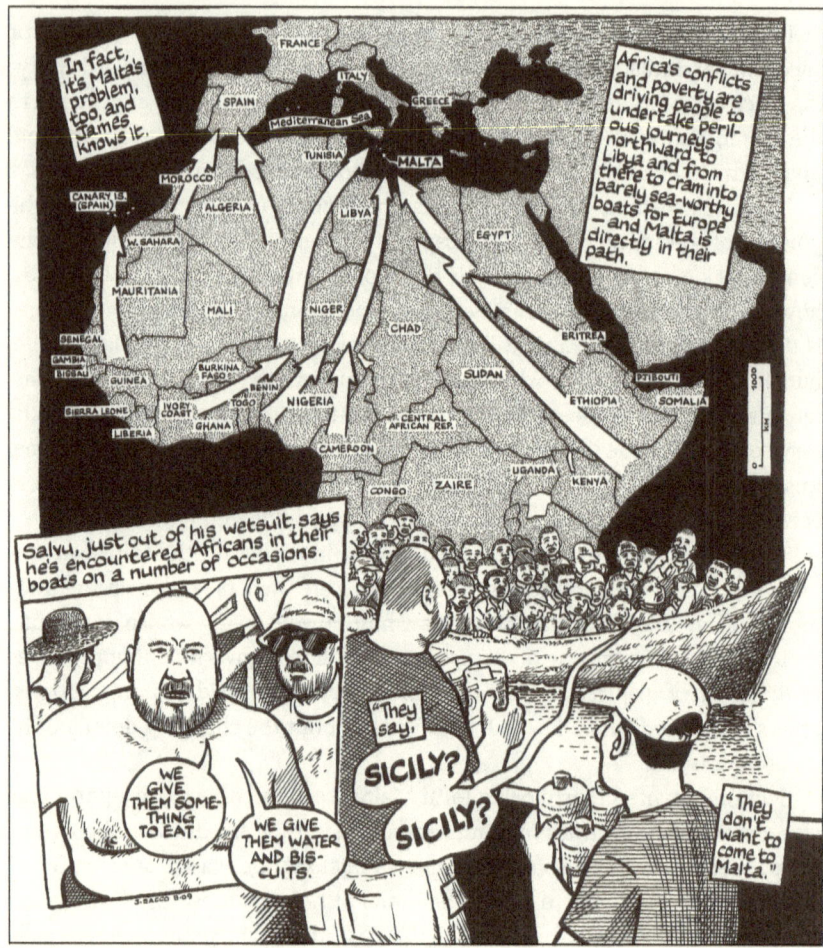

Figure 14.2. Reworking depoliticized subject positions. Detail of Joe Sacco, "The Unwanted," in *Journalism* (New York: Metropolitan, 2012), 110.

er's visual perspective lies directly behind the shoulders of white guards as they fearfully look out on a mass of angry, rioting men, each indistinguishable from the next because they are not allotted speech and individual subjectivity[10]. Similarly, an early panel positions the reader behind the contours of Maltese fishermen (thereby signaling that we assume the same directional gaze) and depicts in front of the fishermen an impossibly crowded fishing vessel full of desperate, terrified, beseeching migrants (see Figure 14.2). The migrants appear consistently alike in their discomfort, and only one is permitted language with his inquiry "SICILY? SICILY?" though even those words are mitigated through the fisherman's interlocution (it is the fisherman who repeats a story of what he heard the migrant asking)."¹¹ Figure 14.2's background, however, demonstrates the piece's investment in undermining generalized representations of depoliticized migrant subjectivities. Behind the group of boat migrants, we can see an enormous map of the African continent with broad, sweeping arrows tracing diverse transnational migration patterns. While most of the arrow paths seem to end in Libya (headed towards Malta and the European continent) or Morocco (headed towards Spain), they reveal contrasting points of origin: Ivory Coast, Cameroon, Somalia, Eritrea, Algeria, Mali. The regional and national specificity of those arrows, insisting on a more nuanced, precise context for migration and trafficking, becomes an implied imperative towards revisionist representation—a revision that considers the plurality and heterogeneity of migrants' identities.

We see this significant shift elsewhere, particularly within the second part of "The Unwanted" which explores more thoroughly migrants' back stories leading up to the moment of migration. In one panel, the reader assumes the perspective of a detainee gazing through chain-link fencing to observe three intimidating Maltese soldiers in uniform staring back at him.¹² Our view now has shifted to the migrant's, whose vision is disrupted and compromised by the barrier of fence. The upper left corner caption emotionally attests to the image's—and the migrant's—brokenness with "[we] are people who are in need of help."¹³ While the text's use of a collective "we" lacks the precise specificity that would enable us to think beyond Malkki's "universalized humanitarian subject," it is nonetheless clear that Sacco engages in a perspective-shifting technique, wherein we move between the Maltese gaze and the migrants' experience.

Consider, then, an instance where this shift is made most obvious: towards the end of this second part, two panels depict a simultaneous moment in time from opposing angles, each aligned with a different population. The top panel of Figure 14.3 clearly delineates the point of view of the white Maltese couple who look over their shoulders at a group of black migrants seated at a table, drinking and laughing. Below this is a reflection of the couple in migrant African faces. The top suggests the common perception of locals towards refugees; they are lazy and take advantage of the system, occupying valuable space on the tiny island. The bottom image, by contrast, depicts what it means to be objectified by suspicious locals who have no interest in extending hospitality towards unwelcome guests. Sacco links the two images together with a caption, located directly in the center of the pair, that cuts across the literal gutter (and its figurative divide). Figure 14.3's text illuminates a central irony of the two seemingly polarized groups: "'The Maltese are scared having black people populate this place. . . . [They] want the migrants out.' And the Africans want

Figure 14.3. Inside and outside, the politics of hospitality. Detail of Joe Sacco, "The Unwanted," in *Journalism* (New York: Metropolitan, 2012), 154.

exactly the same thing: to get off this small island, to reach the European mainland."[14] While the pair of panels stages societal friction, the text suggests an unlikely similar interest shared by both groups.

"The Unwanted" spends a considerable amount of time exploring what it means to be an unwitting guest in Malta. "John the Eritrean" offers his harrowing testimony of human trafficking and border crossing that subverts the objectification and silencing of migrants previously discussed in this chapter. While his plight might be a common one in Malta, Sacco's attention to the historical specificity of his narrative provides John with an active rather than static subjectivity. John's story begins in Eritrea, where he is the victim of governmental oppression and flees a forced labor sentence in a work camp. From there, he takes a bus through twenty-two checkpoints en route to Sudan and pays smugglers to run him across desolate land into a United Nations refugee camp. He leaves the camp for Khartoum, and from that city is trafficked between Sudanese, Libyan, and Ethiopian hands, each time making multiple-day Saharan crossings and each time handing over hundreds of Euros to different human smugglers, who then rob him of his remaining money. He is shoved into the backs of buses and jeeps, hidden in dilapidated buildings, arrested, and detained. Finally, he pays an Eritrean to put him into contact with Libyans who, for another 800 Euros, offer him a place on a shoddy wooden boat leaving from Tripoli and bound for a Mediterranean crossing. At sea, surrounded by emptiness in all directions, he recounts, "[The Libyans] gave us wrong information. They told us, 'After eight hours you will find Malta . . . and then . . . turn one degree and you will be there in Sicily.' And we traveled eight hours and we saw nothing."[15] After two days of traveling at sea with a desperate and disoriented group, John spots land. He maintains, "[Some] thought this must be Sicily [because] we traveled so long. But we all agreed that it was not a matter of choice: we saw a land mass and we had to land."[16] When he jumps out of the boat and, waist-high in water, asks a tourist where he is, John reaches the end of a five-year journey.

Most of the African migrants in "The Unwanted" express a frustrated desire to leave Malta, and John's Mediterranean crossing highlights the cruel absurdity of that one-degree directional shift at sea which constitutes the difference between reaching Sicily and Malta. Malta—a tiny but significant geographical obstruction—lies between these migrants and their ultimate dream: Sicilian shores, and with them, easy access to European mobility via Sicily's proximity to the Italian mainland (at their closest point, the ferry journey from the Sicilian city of Messina to Villa San Giovanni in Reggio Calabria takes a mere twenty minutes). Although surrounded by miles of ocean in every direction and at once completely accessible and vulnerable to immigrant overcrowding, for the migrants who unintentionally land there Malta is an impermeable border between Africa and Europe. Once there, migrants will be processed through the Maltese system and contained; Malta, for them, is a dead end. For this reason, John's discovery that his boat has not reached Sicily but Malta instead is a tragic moment, tantamount to a sense of absolute failure.

John's journey ends on the beach surrounded by exhausted and confused African diasporic migrants, as bikini-clad tourists with beach balls and sunglasses look on in utter astonishment. That image, which concludes the first part of "The Unwanted," is curiously paralleled in the final image of the second part of "The Unwanted." In the first part of "The Unwanted," John is washed up onto the shore and awaits Malta police. In the background, a single swimmer offers a fellow migrant some water while John stands, stupefied. Behind him his boat is intact, resting on an empty ocean under an empty sky. Historically idiosyncratic in its seemingly random insertion within the narrative, the conclusion of the second part "The Unwanted" presents a fascinating foil to John's beach landing: St. Paul's shipwreck on Maltese shores in the year 60 AD. En route from Crete to Rome to appeal a trial for his political rebellion, St. Paul's boat was thrown off course, violently struck a sandbar, and began disintegrating while its panicked crew ("two hundred threescore and sixteen souls"[17]) was flung onto Maltese shores. The Acts of the Apostles describes the arbitrariness of that landing:

> And when it was day, they knew not the land . . . And falling into a place where two seas met, they ran the ship aground; and the forepart stuck fast, and remained unmoveable, but the hinder part was broken with the violence of the waves . . . they which could swim should cast themselves first into the sea, and get to land: And the rest, some on boards, and some on broken pieces of the ship. And so it came to pass, that they escaped all safe to land. And when they were escaped, then they knew that the island was called Melita.[18]

St. Paul's three-month sojourn on Malta is one of the most significant events in its history, for it marks the spread of Christianity on the island. It also represents the original narrative of Maltese hospitality. As Sacco observes in the panel's left caption, "The Maltese, who play host to hundreds of thousands of European tourists every year, have long taken pride in their reputation for hospitality . . . natives showed [St. Paul] and the other survivors 'unusual kindness.'"[19]

The image of a disoriented man staring absently at the reader, and surrounded by other trembling lost bodies, is eerily familiar. John's and St. Paul's arrivals are of course parallels of each other, with each staging a dislocated landing onto unknown shores. Their differences are crucial, however. The depiction of St. Paul's shipwreck is an image of communal empathy as a young girl offers a jug of water while locals wrap him in a warm cloak, holding him in their arms, and offering compassionate, searching faces. Behind St. Paul, sailors are fighting powerful waves, the huge ship begins to sink into water (its masts torn), and the sky is an expanse of rolling, ominous shapes. This distinction is critical: unlike the emptiness that marks John's landing, St. Paul's background evinces a previous life on the ship and a story of a tempestuous sky full of movement. In contrast, John's image—a mere glimpse of a boat, a blank sky, only a contour line of a horizon—suggests that the migrant is not allotted the same sense of history and narrativized past. It is as though the migrant is an empty vessel, washed mysteriously ashore on Malta, bearing no story and accessing no compassion: a tabula rasa awaiting inscription.

When Sacco asks his relatives about St. Paul's earlier historical moment vis-à-vis the experience of contemporary African migration, he writes that they "would have none of it. 'But St. Paul was here for a while and left,'" they tell him.[20] Although Sacco excavates a longer history of global migration and Maltese hospitality in the example of St. Paul's journey, his relatives' response clarifies that hospitality in this space is *temporary*, rather than permanent, a qualification that concludes the "The Unwanted" and reveals how impoverished Maltese hospitality truly is. And if, as Sacco indicates, Maltese take pride in their "reputation for hospitality," then the ironic pairing of these two images challenges that communal identity and historical memory.

But this is also a commentary on the perceived menace of global transnationalism for Malta. By Sacco's relatives' logic, St. Paul was an acceptable guest to host because he only stayed for a short time before departing for another destination, a place to which he may have, or should have, belonged. In contrast, John the Eritrean is terrifying and does not merit the accommodation of hospitality precisely because he belongs in the nowhere of multiple nations—a homelessness rendered even more debilitating through the specific racial and class-based persecutions that inform John's subjectivity in Malta. He has fled his country of origin, does not yet belong to another, *and has no other place to go*. He is particularly troubling because one cannot imagine where a transnational migrant should return to, and in this way he complicates the cohesion of Malta as a sovereign national social space (that is racially and economically homogenous), revealing it instead to be a porous intersection within a transnational crossroads.

Indeed, with that compelling opening ("Globalization!"), "The Unwanted" introduces us to a local fishing industry that remarkably links, through globalized networks, Maltese fishermen and their catch with Tokyo's restaurants. When Sacco mentions "a darker feather in globalization's cap, the 12,500 mostly sub-Saharan Africans desperate to reach Europe who have washed up on the island's shore," he writes that "fishermen want to know what Malta has got to do with Africans."[21] During this conversation, images depict fish being strung up, dripping and gutted, with bloodied decapitated heads thrown into a bin piled up with waste. In this way, "The Unwanted" begins with a consideration of dual facets of globalization: the expansive globalized fishing networks (connecting Malta, Italy, France, and Japan) that enable Maltese fishermen to earn their living, alongside the aborted mobility of migrants, washed ashore like fish. And like fish, John the Eritrean's exhaustive journey between various transnational smuggling operators would suggest that migrants are a global commodity, traded and bartered for as they are shuttled across national borders. Without actually conflating migrants with fish, I would argue that "The Unwanted" is actively invested in demonstrating the ways in which boat migrants have come to be envisioned as a kind of expendable ecological waste—the byproduct of globalization—within the normative Maltese popular imaginary. The space where this transformation first occurs—of migrants to waste—is on the seashore.

In both John the Eritrean and St. Paul the Apostle's landings, the beach becomes the uneasy and fluid boundary between sea and land, the space where lost, uprooted objects appear out of the broad nothingness of the ocean. In her essay "Danger Happens at the Border," Emma Haddad considers the symbolic threat of that space:

> The border is discursively identified as a site of danger . . . the border is the boundary between inside and outside: the inside is safe, outside there is danger. . . . Where inside and outside merge, there is a danger of pollution. Pollution is a type of danger likely to occur wherever there are clear lines and boundaries.[22]

Haddad is interested in considering how the twin discourses of environmental pollutant and refugee pollutant coalesce in articulating the crisis of human migration. "Neither inside nor outside," she writes, "the refugee moves across borders as an inherently polluting person who defies the order that the border would like to dictate."[23] The border "would like to dictate" its clear demarcation because the sovereign state is predicated on the assumed autonomy of its territory. But Haddad's usage of the conditional phrase "would like to" indicates the discrepancy between some imagined notion of national borders as fixed, absolute delineations and the global realities that demonstrate their permeability. As "neither inside nor outside," John the Eritrean's boat emerges seemingly out of nowhere and the bodies washed ashore appear not to belong to this space. They are the debris of globalization, crudely thrown up onto the shore and resisting elimination. If we think about the pairing Sacco establishes—of fish and migrants—then unlike fish, migrants here are figured as the sea's unassimilable elements that do not productively integrate within a globalized network.

When, after days at sea, John the Eritrean's migrant boat finally approaches a landmass ahead, we see from its perspective the surreal Maltese cityscape that expands across the watery horizon. In the following panel, the reader's point of view shifts to that of a white beachgoer who swims nonchalantly along the shore's waves and spots, far into the placid horizon, the same tiny approaching boat. John recalls in this moment, "'There were people swimming. I jumped out of the boat and asked a guy. And he told me I am in Malta.'"[24] The moment of contact is eerie, for its juxtaposition of desperate, half-starved human bodies crammed into a fragile boat with a relaxing idyllic tourist scene suggests a kind of bizarre perversity. The setting functions as an example of ecocritic

Lawrence Buell's toxic discourse, which stages "narratives of rude awakening from simple pastoral to complex" and that focuses on "traumas of pastoral disruption."²⁵ Buell notes that even urban landscapes like the one presented to us in the image, of a modern, developed Malta, can be marked by qualities of the pastoral: "safe and clean communities, ample residential and public spaces . . . apartment windowboxes."²⁶ The scene therefore evokes a kind of pre-contact, prelapsarian Malta—where I read the *lapse* or fall as the moment when the island's insularity towards the broader global world is broken. This pastoral urbanity is disrupted by John's landing on the beach, where black migrant (foreign) bodies scatter across a group of white beachgoing (native) bodies—and in this formulation even the bodies of tourists transform into that which can be read as "native" given their racial and economic privilege to inhabit Malta's landscape. Here, in conceptualizing *foreign* and *native* bodies, I employ a language of pathogen to consider the image's engagement with Buell's observations on toxic discourse: "Disenchantment from the illusion of the green oasis is accompanied or precipitated by totalizing images of a world without refuge from toxic penetration."²⁷ In "The Unwanted," this penetrating toxicity arrives in the messy spread of human trafficking (in the form of migrant boats). Maltese fear associated with this "penetrating pathogen" is both racial (black bodies invade and contaminate an almost exclusively white social space) and nationalist (stateless bodies washed ashore through global networks belie the sanctity of sovereign borders and boundaries).

Local Maltese express Buell's "disenchantment from the illusion of the green oasis" in statements wherein their terror of penetration constructs the refugee as ecological waste and pollutant body. At various points throughout both parts of "The Unwanted," interviewees discuss irregular African migration to the island through language marked with allusions to dirt, filth, and contagions that have perversely washed up onto Maltese land. Benny, a middle-aged man, complains, "Maybe they're bringing diseases with them," while the fascist Lowell warns, "They are breeding furiously in our midst."²⁸ Not only are migrants viewed as pollutants, but they are also cast as contagions, "breeding furiously" and spreading illness. A panel representing Malta's refugee facilities depicts the body of a migrant, from the torso down, standing at a sink.²⁹ Surrounding him are cans, crumpled trash, an overflowing bin. The tile walls, sink, and pipes of this space appear filthy and soiled with stains. The caption reads, "As to the charges of degraded facilities, [Lt. Col.] Gatt says, 'West Africans take pride in keeping their areas clean [but] East Africans don't give a damn. . . . The majority are Muslim, they are Arab-oriented, and living in squalor . . . for them is no problem.'"³⁰ The image then is Gatt's projection of the (in this case Muslim Arab) migrant as a body submerged within an environment of waste and dirt, both the source of that filth and its object. What is most striking about the image is not its scene of dirt but its sense of *disorder*; it is not the migrant body's perceived inherent filth that disturbs Gatt, but its potential for spreading chaos (similar to Lowell's fear of "breeding") within what he views as a pristine, unsoiled, and ordered Malta.

Haddad remarks that "dirt is a by-product of the creation of order, just as the refugee is a by-product of the creation of separate sovereign states and thus a source of disorder and instability."[31] In fleeing one nation and inserting himself uninvited within another, the transnational refugee no longer observes the rules of sovereign citizenship that dictate an adherence to life lived within distinct national boundaries. For this reason, he disrupts the social order. In order to counter this potential for chaos and disruption, the migrant body must be contained, detained, isolated. Haddad comments: "To remove the risk of pollution, the potential transgression must be separated, purified, demarcated, or punished."[32]

In a pair of parallel images, Sacco illustrates both the manner in which the Maltese popular imaginary views the migrant body as trash, and systemically contains it in order to halt its toxic potential for reproduction. In the first part of the story, Sacco's small figure is poised beside Mayor Debono as the two look down on an entropic pile of leaking garbage. The image is careful to situate the reader's perspective (and correspondingly aligned sympathy) from below, penned inside the rubbish receptacle and gazing acutely up at the two who stand on the other side of the chain-link fencing, physically separate from it. The text tells us that we are amidst the "empty beer cans and other litter [Debono] says the immigrants leave behind."[33] In the second part of the story, despondent migrant bodies drawn within a similar concrete structure surrounded by barbed wire fencing have quite literally replaced the trash in the first part of the story.[34] Considered together, the panels stage a connection between the debris of global capitalist consumption—aluminum cans and plastic wrappers—and the human byproducts of that global economy who have been rendered useless excess.

The irony of place in "The Unwanted" is that Malta wishes to gain significance as a nation engaged within globalization's commodity production and consumerist networks. And yet it refuses to acknowledge the stresses those demands place on the environment, and to assume responsibility for other forms of global movement, such as migrating bodies. Its aim is to partake in the free global flow of goods and capital, but not to respond with hospitality to the disorderly flow of global peoples. More broadly, "The Unwanted" provocatively suggests a similarity in African migrants' complaints of being stranded on the island of Malta by a disinterested Europe and local Maltese sentiment.

After all, despite the European Union's 2004 creation of the FRONTEX security agency (a coinage collapsing the French words *frontières* and *extérieures*, or "external borders"), tasked with monitoring and protecting Europe's borders from perceived undesirable elements, various locals in Sacco's piece express anxiety at Malta's being left behind by Europe in the asylum debate to fend for itself against migrant populations. "They abandon us here," one Nigerian complains to Sacco of the Maltese, while a Maltese government worker remarks that "Italy can absorb the numbers; we just can't" and Sacco notes of Minister Mifsud Bonnici that "his job is to get the rest of Europe to acknowledge [Malta's stepping stone nature] and take Africans with humanitarian status off Malta's hands."[35] And in considering the irony of place, I argue that the island of Malta becomes its own vestigial debris—a geographical speck constantly struggling towards attaining European recognition and always marking the liminal space between mainland Europe and North Africa.

This point exemplifies Sacco at his best: his comics journalism is a study in empathy, regardless of his specific social and political views. In *Journalism*, he writes,

> Though obviously my sympathies are with the migrants, who had endured tremendous hardships to reach such an unwelcoming place . . . I thought it was incumbent on me to treat the fears and apprehensions of the Maltese people seriously. Few peoples, I'm afraid, are up to the challenge of absorbing large and sudden influxes of outsiders, especially those of a different color. My own people are no better than anyone else.[36]

The admission that his "own people" are just as prone to fearing the unfamiliar, and to perpetuating systems of subjugation and alienation as most other communities, demonstrates a problematic that is greater than a strictly Maltese problem. In approaching the journalistic subject with a sensibility for such complexity, Sacco demands of his readers that they develop a sense of their own ethical globalism. The very fact that Sacco refuses to eliminate any viewpoint affirms his desire not to reduce any individual subjectivity to the waste or debris that so haunts the panels of "The Unwanted." It is as though in collecting many different voices, Sacco indicates that no single voice can be contained, separated, trashed.

This ethical globalism seems more pertinent than ever before. Unrest in Syria means that Syrian populations have now replaced Tunisians fleeing the Jasmine Revolution, though these newer groups depart from the same Libyan zones, destined for the same tumultuous waters. As I write this, Europe has just seen its worst trafficking drowning disasters in history with over 360 migrants dying after a fire engulfed their sinking boat a mere quarter-mile off Lampedusa's coast—within view of the shore.[37] A week later within Malta's territorial waters thirty-four more migrants drowned in the ocean, and Malta's prime minister, Joseph Muscat, declared "as things stand we are just building a cemetery within our Mediterranean Sea."[38] Over 50,000 migrants crossed the Mediterranean and arrived in Italy during the first six months of 2014, and the *Guardian* newspaper cites over 600,000 more people "estimated to be waiting in Libya for an opportunity to make the treacherous sea crossing, prompting warnings by European authorities of an impending humanitarian crisis."[39] The EU has called for opening "humanitarian corridors" to protect migrant boats traversing the space between North Africa and Lampedusa, Malta, and Sicily—but there is, as yet, no sense of how this strategy would operate, nor which nations would be responsible for hosting the unwelcome guests of global upheaval.

From the Tunisian coastline, as I saw it that day, the vast and structureless Mediterranean seemed an impossible—and impossibly hopeful—transit route. Out there along the grey horizon are uprooted bodies traversing the seascape in precarious, insufficient boats. They are directed only by the force of their perseverance and the hope that, for the few who make it to a landmass, they may be recognized and claimed not as expendable flotsam to be discarded but as an integral, vital presence within the global human ecology.

NOTES

1. The numbers are taken from UNHCR, *Briefing Notes*, January 31, 2012, http://www.unhcr.org/4f27e01f9.html. The report summarizes a speech made by spokesperson Sybella Wilkes, delivered at a press briefing at the Palais des Nations in Geneva, Switzerland. The Mediterranean sea drownings figure is taken from Owen Bowcott, "4,000 refugees believed drowned at sea every year," *Guardian*, October 8, 2004, http://www.theguardian.com/world/2004/oct/09/immigration.uk, in which Bowcott contests that another 2,000 asylum seekers drown in Pacific and Atlantic crossings.

2. Joe Sacco, "The Unwanted," *Journalism* (New York: Metropolitan Books, 2012), 157.

3. Ibid., 113.

4. Ibid.

5. Ibid., 115.

6. Ibid., 153.

7. Ibid., 148.

8. Ibid., 147.

9. Liisa Malkki, "Speechless Emissaries: Refugees, Humanitarianism, and Dehistoricization," *Cultural Anthropology* 11.3 (1996), 378.

10. Sacco, "The Unwanted," 140.
11. Ibid., 110.
12. Ibid., 133.
13. Ibid.
14. Ibid., 154.
15. Ibid., 131.
16. Ibid., 132.
17. *Acts of the Apostles*, 27:37 "And we were in all in the ship two hundred threescore and sixteen souls." King James Version.
18. Acts 27:39–28:1 AV.
19. Sacco, "The Unwanted," 156.
20. Ibid.
21. Ibid., 109.
22. Emma Haddad, "Danger Happens At the Border," in *Borderscapes: Hidden Geographies and Politics at Territory's Edge*, ed. Prem Kumar and Carl Grundy-Warr (Minneapolis: University of Minnesota Press, 2007), 119–20.
23. Ibid., 119.
24. Sacco, "The Unwanted," 132.
25. Lawrence Buell, "Toxic Discourse," *Critical Inquiry* 24.3 (1998), 647.
26. Ibid.
27. Ibid., 648.
28. Sacco, "The Unwanted," 112, 120.
29. Ibid., 139.
30. Ibid.
31. Haddad, "Danger Happens At the Border," 124.
32. Ibid., 126.
33. Sacco, "The Unwanted," 114.
34. Ibid., 138.
35. Ibid., 149, 112, 154.
36. Ibid., 157.
37. "Lampedusa Boat Tragedy: Migrants 'Raped and Tortured,'" *BBC News*, November 8, 2013, http://www.bbc.co.uk/news/world-europe-24866338.
38. "Mediterranean 'a Cemetery'—Maltese PM Muscat," *BBC News*, October 12, 2013, http://www.bbc.co.uk/news/world-europe-24502279.
39. "Migrants crossing the Mediterranean: key numbers," *Guardian*, June 10, 2014, http://www.theguardian.com/news/datablog/2014/jun/10/migrants-crossing-the-mediterranean-key-numbers-libya-european.

15. Teaching World Politics with Joe Sacco: *Safe Area Goražde* in the Classroom

Kevin C. Dunn

For over a decade, I have regularly taught an introductory course on International Relations (IR) at a small, liberal arts college in western New York state. The course, POL 180: Introduction to International Relations, is designed to introduce students to broad themes of world politics. Recently, I began employing Joe Sacco's *Safe Area Goražde* as the first book of the semester. I have found that Sacco's explicitly outsider perspective, both in the narrative itself and with respect to the field of IR, usefully disrupts and displaces received ideas about the study of world politics. Doing so opens up a range of opportunities to challenge students' preconceptions, but also to engage those who might not normally find the field of IR particularly interesting. This essay examines the pedagogical issues associated with using that text to teach world politics, paying particular attention to its strengths and weaknesses.

Perhaps the most important pedagogical value of Sacco's text derives from its form: the graphic portrayal of violence and human suffering often evokes a visceral response in the reader that is usually lacking in sterile academic writing. Indeed, I have found that students tend to respond deeply—both on an emotional and intellectual level—to Sacco's finely detailed drawing style. Students have mentioned that they find Sacco's intricate photorealistic drawings more engaging than, say, Art Spiegelman's more stylized *Maus*. Because most academic writings tend to "bleach out" the blood and tears that typify much of human suffering experienced in contemporary world politics (from conflict and violence to disease and starvation), there is great pedagogical value in employing a provocative work like *Safe Area Goražde*. Moreover, using Sacco's text provides an excellent entrée for discussing a wide range of topics within IR. These include, but are not limited to, ethnic and religious conflict, nationalism, sovereignty, humanitarian intervention, international organizations, peacekeeping, rape as a weapon of war, genocide, international law, diplomacy, and the anarchical international system. *Safe Area Goražde* is the very first book I assign my students in the course, and for the rest of the semester it serves as a touchstone for these inquiries. Yet there are significant pedagogical challenges in using Sacco's text. While some students express resistance to taking "comic books seriously," others point out problems with the tension between Sacco's authoritative voice and his subjective and highly partial viewpoint throughout the text. In this essay, I discuss those challenges and how I have addressed them. The essay is divided into four sections. First, I briefly discuss how I incorporate *Safe Area Goražde* into the course and the assignments associated with it. The second section explores the "work" Sacco's text does in that course, specifically the themes and concepts about world politics that come to the forefront through my students' engagement with the text. The third section examines how my students have reacted to the text, both positively and negatively. The final section offers a broader discussion of the pedagogical challenges associated with employing Sacco's work in a college classroom like mine.

Safe Area Goražde in Introduction to International Relations

Safe Area Goražde is the result of Sacco's four trips to Goražde in 1995–96. Goražde was an UN-designated safe area during the Bosnian War. With a majority Muslim population, it was located in the eastern part of Bosnia, surrounded by hostile Bosnian Serb forces who repeatedly shelled the city and launched several assaults to capture it. As the rest of eastern Bosnia was ethnically "cleansed," including other UN-designated safe areas such as Srebrenica, the people of Goražde struggled to survive through years of warfare and siege. Sacco's journeys into the brutalized and besieged city took place towards the end of the Bosnian War, as people were just slowly allowing themselves to believe that the conflict was coming to an end. Sacco interweaves autobiographic tales of his travels with interviews conducted with many of the residents of Goražde, while also providing the larger historical context of the conflict and contemporaneous events. His four visits provide the loose narrative structure, but most of the graphic narrative is told in flashbacks from his interview subjects, interspersed with brief notes on the history of religious divisions, the creation and collapse of Yugoslavia, unfolding events in the region, and the international community's responses and non-responses to the conflict.

Safe Area Goražde is the first reading for my Introduction to IR course, a course that serves both the political science department and the International Relations program at my institution. The curriculum of our political science department is divided up into four subfields—American Politics, Comparative Politics, International Relations, and Political Theory—which is typical for most American Political Science departments. We offer an introductory course for each four subfields, as well as more thematically focused upper-level courses and a series of advanced seminars. Students majoring in Political Science are required to take at least one course in each of the subfields and many do that by taking a variety of the introduction courses. My institution also has an interdisciplinary International Relations program that students can major or minor in. This program draws heavily from Political Science, Economics, History, Anthropology, Sociology, Religious Studies, and other traditional disciplines. The program's curriculum reflects an interdisciplinary nature, requiring students to take a wide range of courses, but using POL 180: Introduction to International Relations as one of the required core courses. Thus, the thirty or more students who enroll in Introduction to International Relations tend to be students (usually first-years and sophomores, with a handful of juniors and seniors) who are either Political Science majors, IR majors or minors, or students who have an interest in those areas.

I tend to teach the course as a broad introduction to the study of world politics. As I tell my students multiple times throughout the semester, the course is a mile wide and an inch deep. It is designed to give students a brief introduction to the various and interdisciplinary subfields that make up the academic discipline of International Relations. Thus, the course is divided into the following sections: a historical overview of international society, theories of IR, international political economy, international law, international institutions and organizations, and international security. The course seeks to provide students with an understanding and appreciation of the core concepts, issues, concerns, and debates within each section. The expectation is that interested students would then enroll in more advanced courses within each of those areas (such as Globalization, Human Rights, Terrorism, and so forth).

I use a textbook for the course, *The Globalization of World Politics*, edited by Steven Smith, John Baylis, and Patricia Owens.[1] It is somewhat unusual in that it is more of an edited volume, with each chapter written by an individual expert on a given subject, as opposed to most textbooks which are written wholly by the author(s). In the section of the course that covers the evolution of the international society, I also use Sven Lindqvist's *Exterminate All the Brutes*, a concise but powerful examination of the forces that drove European colonization, conquest, and genocide.[2] I also include a handful of academic and journalistic articles that address contemporary issues.

Since incorporating *Safe Area Goražde*, I dedicate the second week of the course to an engagement with the graphic narrative. The course typically meets twice a week for eighty-five minutes each. The first two days of the course are reserved for a general introduction. The first day involves going over the syllabus and articulating my expectations of the students. The rest of that day and most of the second day involve going over some core concepts, such as the difference between a state and a nation, and the meaning of anarchy in world politics (lack of a central authority, not the absence of order). I then inform the students that we are reading *Safe Area Goražde* in order to introduce them to a range of ideas, concepts, and issues that will inform our discussions for the rest of the semester. We divide the book into two sections, reading the first half for one day and the second half for the next class period. On the first day, I have them identify what they thought was the most surprising page of the first half of the book and then spend 5–10 minutes writing down their thoughts about that page. I then have them get into small groups (3–4 students) to discuss those insights amongst themselves for about ten minutes. I then open it up to the whole class for a larger discussion of the issues they focused on in each group. For the second day, we have a more open, freewheeling conversation about the various themes they are drawing out of Sacco's work.

After they read Lindqvist's *Exterminate All the Brutes* a few weeks later, I have the students write a 2–3 page paper addressing the following prompt: "Discuss and analyze three similarities you see in the themes and issues discussed by both Joe Sacco in *Safe Area Goražde* and Sven Lindqvist's *Exterminate All the Brutes.*" The goal of this assignment is for them to both reflect on the IR concepts found within *Safe Area Goražde* and, by connecting them to similar concepts and themes in another historical context (e.g., African colonization by Europeans), to reflect on how these issues are central to a larger examination of world politics. Throughout the semester, we return to Sacco's work whenever we see connections between it and the material we are covering. During the sections that deal with international organizations and international law, students will frequently refer back to the events in *Safe Area Goražde* to illustrate their arguments. When I used the book for the first time, at the end of the semester I gave the students an evaluation of the book and its relationship to the course. I will discuss their responses later in this essay.

World Politics in *Safe Area Goražde*

I had multiple goals for using *Safe Area Goražde* in my Introduction to International Relations course. Perhaps the central goal was to make the reality of world politics more visceral for the students. All too often, I find academic prose to be too sterile when discussing issues of life and death. Part of this is the result of social science norms, in which we are trained to be dispassionate and removed from our objects of inquiry. To be clear, I believe that intellectual objectivity is impossible to achieve (a stance that Sacco eloquently conveys in many of his works). I believe that we try to obscure our subjectivity in part through the ways we chose to write, constructing the impression in the minds of our readers that we as scholars and our scholarship is somehow separate from and above reality. This is especially true in textbooks, where the authors often have to convey a substantial amount of information in a very limited space. I find that the sterile character of academic writing leads to quite stagnant and sanitized conversations in the classroom. Mimicking the aloofness of academic prose, students will often discuss issues of war, death, and human suffering in a dispassionate and disconnected manner, even when they clearly have strong and passionate opinions about the issues. I was hoping that assigning *Safe Area Goražde* would provide a much-needed reminder of the pain and suffering that often takes place in world politics.

In addition to my desire to make a presentation of world politics less sterile and more visceral, I also chose *Safe Area Goražde* because I believed it incorporated a number of the themes and concepts of the course. I believed using the book would be a useful way of introducing these themes and concepts at the outset, by bringing them to the forefront of our conversations. In the end-of-the-semester evaluation I gave my students, I asked them to list the concepts they thought *Safe Area Goražde* successfully introduced. The list they generated was very similar to one that I had constructed myself as I prepared for the course. I provide a brief discussion of many (but certainly not all) of the concepts identified by the students.

Conflict

At its core, *Safe Area Goražde* is about conflict. But much of the scholarship on conflict in International Relations actually concerns security and strategy. A discussion of the manifestations of conflict on people's everyday lives tends to be missing from these conversations. Moreover, in conversations about security, what is assumed to be secured are the institutions of state power. Issues of "human security" remain marginalized within the field of IR.[3] In contrast to these traditional ways of treating conflict, *Safe Area Goražde*'s multiple points of view approach allowed the students to understand how conflict is experienced on a very personal level, whether describing the experiences of soldiers like Edin—from the confusion of a fire-fight to the boredom of frontline inaction—or civilians fleeing a military advance or scrambling before an artillery barrage. Moreover, students tended to find the visual representation of conflict—from drawings of bullets piercing flesh to the rotting corpses of the dead—to be powerfully evocative and disturbing, challenging the traditional way in which conflict has been treated in IR and providing multiple access points for their own personal engagement.

Nationalism/Ethnicity

In the post-Cold War era, much scholarship on world politics noted the rise of nationalism and the increased saliency of ethnicity. Much of this literature has sought to explain why these forms of identity have become politicized and why they are such powerful motivators for political organization and action. There are two elements that I believe are particularly noteworthy: the constructedness of political identities and the role that political entrepreneurs play in activating such sentiments. In the first case, it has become accepted that national and ethnic identification are not natural, inherent facts. Rather, they are socially constructed. The idea of nationalism is rooted in what Benedict Anderson calls an "imagined community."[4] The process of "imagining" one's identification – both at the national and ethnic level—involves narrating history and memories to construct a sense of belonging and group coherence. This process is addressed by Sacco in *Safe Area Goražde* when he recounts how national identification was exacerbated during the breakup of the former Yugoslavia in the remembrances of historical events, particularly with regards to memories of victimhood committed at the hands of various ethnic "others" (whether they are identified as Croats, Serbs, or Bosnians).[5] A similar process was taking place at the same time in Rwanda, as "Hutu Power" worked very hard to construct fear amongst the Hutu majority about the intent and moral inferiority of the Tutsi population.[6] Regardless of the context, what is central to the process of constructing and politicizing these narratives of victimization and group identity are political entrepreneurs, who choose to focus on the construction of these group political identities for their own advancement. Sacco captures this process quite well in his representation of Milosevic and other Serbian nationalists.[7]

Religious Conflict

Related to this examination of national and ethnic identity is an exploration of the religious roots of contemporary conflict. The war in eastern Bosnia was frequently framed, both by participants and observers, in terms of a Christian-versus-Muslim conflict. But, as history attests, there is no inherent reason why religious differences necessarily lead to armed conflict. Again, religious affiliation is often used as a political mobilizer within a conflict, rather than being the source of the conflict itself. In religious conflicts, group solidarity is constructed through a particular articulation of a historical narrative that sometimes relies on portraying a rival religious "other." When memories of victimization are embedded in this narrative—as was the case with the massacres committed by the Ustasha (Croatian fascists) during World War II[8]—the possibility of religious conflict arises. Sacco's presentation draws the reader's attention to both the historical roots of religious conflict and the ways in which that history is politicized in the present context. The repeated refrain throughout *Safe Area Goražde* about how the Bosnian Christians and Muslims had very recently lived side by side opens fruitful avenues for reflection on the ways religious difference is politicized.

Genocide/War Crimes

Recent years have seen catastrophic killings in Rwanda and Darfur labeled by some observers as genocide. The term is powerfully evocative, in no small part because of its scale and its criminality. Yet there are a number of debates about what qualifies as genocide, what can be done to stop one, and what is the moral and legal obligation of outside powers in the face of genocide. Sacco's work raises these and other questions related to mass violence and genocide. Particularly evocative is his discussion of the events that took place in Srebrenica in July 1995.[9] While traditionally marginalized in the study of genocide, I find many students are increasingly aware and concerned about the use of rape as a weapon of war. Sacco's portrayal of the plight of Munira and other Muslim female hospital patients captured in the town of Foca provides a brief but disturbing point of reference for those conversations.[10]

International Law

The complexities of the conflict in the former Yugoslavia, as elucidated in Sacco's book, provide a backdrop for understanding the problems with interpreting and enforcing international law. Offering his own candid reflections as an American who can come and go from the conflict zone, Sacco embodies the voice of privilege as one can choose to ignore the human sufferings of others—a fact that underpins the inconsistent application and enforcement of international laws. Certainly, war crimes were being committed during the war in eastern Bosnia. But how does one actually hold the culprits accountable? Indeed, one of the themes of *Safe Area Goražde* that I identify is the challenge of recognizing the gulf between ethical intentions (as embodied by the existence of international laws) and practical actions. In semesters prior to using this book, students tended to hold strong convictions about international law on both ends of the spectrum: either placing their faith in international law for curbing unethical behavior or actively dismissing international law as meaningless in the face of raw power. Sacco's presentation, I believe, actually draws students into a more nuanced appreciation of the uneven, but still relevant, role of international law in world politics.

Humanitarian Intervention

This more nuanced understanding of international law largely stems from Sacco's excellent examination of the challenges, dangers, obstacles, and successes related to humanitarian intervention in Bosnia. His use of multiple points of view provides the reader with an understanding that external intervention is not a simple solution or an easy option, even when it would undoubtedly end human suffering and the carrying out of war crimes. When speaking in the first person, Sacco is highly critical of Western leaders, such as American president Bill Clinton, for their foot-dragging and inaction.[11] But, at the same time, he shows the difficulties of intervening and, perhaps more pertinent to my student readers, expresses his own confusion about the issues and his desire to physically leave. That is, the ambiguity of intervention and engagement is played out within Sacco's own relationship with the people of Bosnia.

In the literature on humanitarian interventions, there is as much debate over *how* one can effectively intervene as there is on *whether* or not to intervene. Sacco's *Safe Area Goražde* provides insights on a wide range of possible forms of intervention—from limited air strikes, to peace observers with no mandate to engage in hostilities, to a more activist form of military engagement.[12] These examples, spread throughout the book, offer useful points to enter debates around the ways in which certain types of interventions might be more effective in specific contexts, without ascribing simplistic answers to what are clearly complex challenges.

Refugees

Conversations about refugees can easily move into the realm of abstraction. For most commentators, especially in the West, refugees can be treated as faceless, distant numbers. In the classroom, I have often encountered the challenge of making students treat refugees as possessing both humanity and agency. On the one hand, there is a frequent move to just speak about refugees through numbers. How many internally displaced persons are there? How many refugees have taken refuge across international borders? In many ways, they become data points to be folded into abstract conversations along with the death tolls. On the other hand, there is also a patronizing move to portray these people as victims without agency of their own. Because so many of Sacco's interview subjects are, in fact, refugees, they become fully formed individuals in ways that textbooks often fail to achieve. Interestingly, my students often do not readily see them as refugees exactly because they are portrayed as real people with agency. While *Safe Area Goražde* certainly does important work in portraying the real-life challenges of being internally displaced, perhaps even more useful for my students is its ability to trouble their preconceptions about "refugees."

United Nations

Many observers' frustration with inconsistencies and/or inactions from the international community with regards to stopping war and its attendant humanitarian costs are usually aimed at the UN. The UN, after all, is *the* international organization tasked with maintaining world peace. In the language of International Relations, it is a "collective security organization"—a collection of states dedicated to maintaining security and cohesion within the group. If a member state violates the rules of the collective, the group can (but does not always) sanction the violator. In the case of the former Yugoslavia, member states were violating the accepted rules regarding the conduct of warfare, to say nothing of the aggression the Serbian state was engaged in towards Bosnia. The major complication that emerges regarding the effectiveness of the UN in realizing its goal as a collective security organization relates to its institutional structure. The Secretary-General is largely a powerless office. The General Assembly, in which every member state has equal representation, can pass resolutions but has no enforcement mechanism. The real power resides at the level of the Security Council, which is made up of fifteen members, ten of which rotate, and five of which are permanent seats held by the US, Russia, China, UK, and France. Each of those five has veto power, thereby allowing each to effectively block any resolution under consideration.

The Security Council had effectively been at loggerheads for decades because of the superpower rivalry between the US and the Soviet Union. By the mid-1990s, there emerged a new spirit of cooperation between the US and Russia, as well as a sense that the UN would play a far greater role in the post-Cold War era than it had previously. The case of the Bosnian war is an interesting one for the UN, as it was transitioning out of the Cold War context. Given Serbia's historic ties to Russia, the fragmentation of the former Yugoslavia greatly complicated these developments. Sacco's narrative captures some of the dynamics at work during this time, as well as underscoring many of the diplomatic issues at play within the UN, particularly in the Security Council. In many ways, *Safe Area Goražde* provides readers with an interesting case study of the multiple roles played by the UN in world politics and the complicated dynamics at play within the international organization.

Regional Organizations (e.g., NATO)

In addition to the increased relevance of the UN in the post-Cold War era, we have also seen the rise of regional organizations. Most notable for students of world politics are the European Union (EU), North Atlantic Free Trade Association (NAFTA), Arab League (AL), African Union (AU), and the myriad other regional and sub-regional organizations across the globe. One particularly interesting case is the North Atlantic Treaty Organization (NATO), which was formed during the early years of the Cold War to be a "collective defense organization" for Western allied states. Central to a collective defense organization is the tenet that "an attack on one is an attack on all." NATO's primary purpose was to provide security assurances to American allies in Western Europe and deter any possible aggression by the Soviet Union and its allies in the region. But once the Cold War ended, what purpose could NATO possibly have? Its whole reason for being had disappeared with the fall of the Berlin Wall and the collapse of the Soviet Union.

As my students learn later in the semester, the war in eastern Bosnia marked an important case study in the evolution of NATO, as it transitioned from a collective defense organization into a regional interventionist force. The opportunities, problems, and challenges associated with that transition also shed greater light on the multiple functions regional organizations can play within world politics. Sacco's work provides plenty of opportunities to engage in a discussion of both the relevance of regional organizations and the evolution of NATO.

State Sovereignty

The foundational tenet of the modern state system is the notion of sovereignty as applied to territorial states. By the 1600s, the northern European societies were organizing themselves according to the notion that political power was associated—and contained—in autonomous and territorially discrete entities known as states. The ruler of that state was the ultimate arbiter of law within that domain. There was no one above him (or her—but it was almost always him). This concept of the sovereign state is the ideal of much of contemporary Western political thought and has become the central way in which the international community is organized. When one looks at a map, it reflects the centrality of the sovereign state logic. When one thinks of the term "international community" it is almost always in terms of the collection of sovereign states. Intimately tied to the concept of sovereignty is the precept of non-interference in another state's affairs. These two beliefs—sovereignty and non-interference—are at the core of the UN's Charter.

The problem, of course, is that sovereignty is an abstract concept that is regularly ignored by powerful states. One astute observer of world politics famously quipped that sovereignty is merely "organized hypocrisy."[13] Other observers have noted how the concept is socially constructed, always in flux, and always contested.[14] Thus, the foundational tenet upon which International Relations is supposed to rest is, in fact, less than solid. The malleability of sovereignty comes into stark relief in cases of external interventions into a state's domestic affairs. The breakup of Yugoslavia was, after all, an internal development. The subsequent wars can be regarded as civil wars. States facing civil wars are usually adamant that external actors not get involved in their affairs. Such was the case during the American Civil War and is more recently the case in Syria in 2013. But is sovereignty merely a legalistic shield used by a ruling group to allow horrific uses of violence? These issues are constant themes throughout Sacco's *Safe Area Goražde*, some times explicit but often implicit. In fact, I plan to introduce a future exercise that asks students to reread the work with an eye for every time an issue relating to state sovereignty arises. I am assuming that the quantity and diversity of the issues that come to the surface will be illuminating and pedagogically useful.

Post-Conflict Reconstruction and Peacekeeping

How can societies heal after a lengthy war between neighbors? How can a post-conflict peace be achieved? Is there a role of justice, accountability, and/or retribution in the wake of sustained violence? These are but a few questions central to the field of Peace Studies in particular, and International Relations more broadly. These are questions that linger immediately after finishing Sacco's *Safe Area Goražde*. At the end of the book, the media's cameras have left, the war is declared over, and even Sacco is packing up for what appears to be his last departure from Goražde and Bosnia. Yet, as Sacco so powerfully illustrates, lives are still torn asunder, animosities run high, and former combatants are within a stone's throw of each other. Sacco notes that some of his interview subjects want to put the past behind them and move on, while others carry a seething bitterness within them, simmering below the surface.[15] Most are unable to erase their memories of the conflict, regardless of whether they want to or not.[16] It is to Sacco's credit that he ends his work with the discomforting uncertainty of the post-conflict context, for it forces the attentive reader to grapple with these monumental quandaries well after the final page is turned and we reach the supposed "end." Indeed, for many of my students, questions about post-conflict justice and constructing a lasting peace proved to be the most difficult to address of all the questions raised by *Safe Area Goražde*. I try to make the students explicitly engage in these questions—sometimes by having them propose possible peace treaty terms or by imagining what became of specific individuals in the narrative. This latter exercise is particularly fruitful, for it requires the students to engage in a level of empathy for a range of different people on both sides of the conflict.

Student Responses

When I first used *Safe Area Goražde* in the classroom, I gave the students an evaluation of the book at the end of the semester. This evaluation was specifically related to the book, because I wanted their feedback on its usefulness. The evaluation asked several questions, the last being, "Would you recommend assigning *Safe Area Goražde* to future Introduction to International Relations courses? Why/why not?" Students were unanimous in their recommendation for its continued use, though there was some variation regarding why and a few suggestions about the timing of the book in the course.

The first question asked, "What was the *most* useful element of Sacco's *Safe Area Goražde*?" Answers typically grouped into three categories. The most often cited strength of the book was its visual component. A representative quote from the evaluation was: "It was a lot easier to look at an image and understand what was going on than to read about it and try to picture or create a mental image of the status of Bosnia at the time." A few noted that it required the reader to be actively engaged, as expressed in this response: "The depictions made us pay attention to the topic, and forced us to visualize what happened. It didn't allow the reader to not be actively engaged in the reading." Another response pointed out that the graphic narrative created a stronger feeling of empathy: "Since it is a *graphic* novel, the pictures helped me understand the story and stay connected to the characters" (emphasis in original). Relatedly, many responses noted that the visual images made the horror of the war more tangible. As one student wrote: "The pictures gave a more detailed image of the horrific actions taking place in Goražde. They gave you a real life effect." These responses affirmed my primary motivation for employing Sacco's work, namely to shift away from sanitized and abstract discussions of world politics towards an appreciation of the blood, pain, and messiness of its everyday manifestations.

Several responses argued that the most useful element of the book was actually how well it related to the course's central themes. One student pointed out that it "acted as a good introduction to many of the course's core concepts, without being a dense textbook." Another response captured a number of ideas that other students expressed in various ways: "The best part was the fact that we could relate much of the other course material back to *Safe Area Goražde*. Since it was a graphic novel, it was easy to engage with and easy to recall throughout the semester." As I noted above, some students suggested that it might be more useful to assign the book towards the end of the semester, once they have a firmer understanding of a number of the book's themes, especially regarding the complex debates around humanitarian interventions.

Yet the majority of responses seemed to indicate that they found its placement at the beginning of the semester a useful introduction to the course and helpful in framing some of the themes and concepts that we encountered later.

Another theme that emerged from the responses was an appreciation of Sacco's use of multiple points of view within the narrative. This seemed to be appreciated by a number of students, one of whom wrote that "the many different perspectives it tried to achieve made the conflict more accessible by attacking its causes and consequences from multiple angles." At the same time, other students found Sacco's decision to make himself an explicit "character" in his narrative an effective device. Rather than assuming a detached authoritative voice, Sacco owns his own subject position. Some students noted that doing so increased Sacco's credibility as a journalist in their eyes. One student noted that this also increased the effectiveness of Sacco's multiple points of view approach: "I think especially with first-person accounts it really helps to see what the other people were seeing. It reaches another level of understanding about what went on."

The second question on the evaluation asked: "What was the *least* useful element of Sacco's *Safe Area Goražde*?" It is worth noting that the majority of students either provided no answer or indicated that they did not think there were any negative elements in the use of the book for the course. However, there were a handful of responses that are worth noting, and they tend to fall into two categories. The first category of responses indicated that Sacco's use of multiple points of view was "difficult to follow." Relatedly, others found the "fragmented" narrative a challenge to read and comprehend. I often use such comments to engage in a conversation about the impossibility of intellectual objectivity and how Sacco might be grappling with that by letting an array of subjectivities crowd his pages. I often ask how he might have achieved that through a more uniform narrative. Usually not seeing a viable alternative, students inevitably gain a greater appreciation of what might be at stake in the process of storytelling, especially when narrating other people's stories.

Another criticism that came up in the evaluations, but even more in our classroom discussions about the book, concerned the nature of the graphic narrative itself. In our in-class conversations, a number of students stated that they were having trouble taking the reading seriously because of its "comic book style." Many of these readers expressed that they were socialized to regard visual representations of this nature as an inferior form of communication and predominantly associated it with humor. A few students at the time were quite vocal in their concern that Sacco was denigrating the horrors of the war and people's suffering by presenting them in a "comic book." While the number of these concerns decreased by the end-of-semester evaluations, a few students continued to express concern about Sacco's use of visual imagery. As one wrote: "For me, the cartooning was almost too 'comical' in nature. It seemed to add a level of humor, which is understandable for some relief from the horrors of the topic, but I feel certain topics should be left as they are." A few other students echoed this sentiment, with one capturing the mood of several when she wrote: "I had never read a book like that before and I wasn't sure how to read it." Often, I try to address these concerns by asking about the range of ways in which humans express themselves and why certain societies privilege some forms over others. I try to frame the conversation by drawing parallels between cultural products and cultures in general, noting that differences do not necessitate value judgments (a fundamental tenet for the entire course), but that understanding might require work.

General Pedagogical Challenges

A number of scholars have recognized that graphic narratives such as *Safe Area Goražde* can be useful in introducing a range of concepts in various social scientific disciplines. Yet graphic narratives and comics in general are still considered by many to be a marginal and "slightly disreputable form of outsider art."[17] This generated a few challenges when I used *Safe Area Goražde* in the classroom. Thus, because *Safe Area Goražde* was a graphic narrative, a handful of students found it easy to discount. This reflected a previously held bias against the genre as being an inferior mode of expression rather than any substantial criticism of Sacco's work specifically. These complaints, voiced early in the class, led to productive conversations about how we characterize and value different forms of cultural production, often because of latent assumptions about social class. I usually direct this conversation towards a more focused discussion about how one "reads" a graphic narrative, taking care to pay attention to formal elements of the page—looking at panels in sequence, distinguishing between the narrative prose and word balloons, noting any tensions between text and images, and considering the deployment of gutters. I have considered assigning formal readings analyzing the comics medium, but have decided that these early objections are actually pedagogically useful. Having this conversation at the beginning of the first day helps students understand explicitly how they should "read" the text and think about where Sacco's ideological work is taking place.

Worcester notes several positive aspects of using graphic narratives in the classroom. On the simplest level, graphic narratives can excite student interest.[18] Certainly in some cases this has to do with students being drawn to visual images rather than prose-heavy texts. The same motivation may lead instructors to use films in the classroom. But, as Worcester notes, "unlike with movies and field trips, a graphic narrative has a physical form that allows for the same kind of sustained interactions that motivated readers enjoy vis-à-vis traditional texts."[19] In the classroom, we can linger on a page of Sacco's graphic narrative—such as the depiction of the international community's confused responses to ethnic cleansing in Bosnia[20]—in the way we can sustain a focus on, say, a passage from Machiavelli. In the case of Sacco's work, the prose is so rich and the visual imagery so detailed, a close reading is often required.

To that extent, assigning a graphic narrative such as *Safe Area Goražde* required extra work for both my students and me. My assumption is that most social scientists have not been trained how to make sense of aesthetic and formal issues that come to play when teaching a graphic narrative. Employing a graphic narrative does not necessarily require formal training, but I believe it does require sensitivity to a range of issues that most social scientists don't usually employ in their typical scholarly pursuits. Likewise, students should also be aware of how dense with meanings a graphic narrative can be, especially when contrasted to a typical textbook. For example, *Safe Area Goražde* portrays the discovery of mutilated bodies by the residents of Goražde and their reburial. These pages are packed with important images and ideas that might not be apparent from a cursory read. For example, why did the Serb Chetniks remove all the penises from the male bodies? Why were the stomachs of the female victims sliced open? Why did they bury a dog on top of the bodies in the mass grave? Why was the act of reburial so important to the residents? These questions opened up discussions on such topics as gender, gender-based violence, and religious traditions. Such issues are deeply important to understanding the violence during the Bosnian war (as well as other conflicts), but Sacco's engagement with them is often implicit, conveyed through rich but dense imagery.

In conclusion, Sacco's *Safe Area Goražde* proved to be extremely useful pedagogically. It opened up discussions on a wide range of topics within the course on world politics. While Sacco's narrative voice is quite strong, his reporting style presents a variety of perspectives from his interview subjects, resulting in a collection of ideas, interpretations and experiences. For the students, this meant that *Safe Area Goražde* introduced more questions than it answered, which is important within the classroom. There are no easy answers in the field of International Relations, and Sacco captures and conveys that quite nicely. Simultaneously, Sacco's detailed drawing style constructed a number of disturbing scenes that produced a visceral response from the students. Juxtaposed with the usual sanitized and abstract nature of most IR textbooks, the discomfort generated by Sacco's work was very useful pedagogically. The biggest challenge with using *Safe Area Goražde* was helping the students understanding how to "read" a graphic narrative as an academic exercise. While some were quick to discount it as "just a comic book" or assumed that Sacco was not taking the subject matter "seriously" because he was using drawings, those concerns were worked through in classroom discussions, often in very productive ways. Even those students who were initially critical or dubious of the graphic narrative concluded that *Safe Area Goražde* provided useful contributions to their understandings of world politics.

NOTES

1. Steven Smith, John Baylis, and Patricia Owens, eds., *The Globalization of World Politics: An Introduction to International Relations*, 5th ed. (New York: Oxford University Press, 2011).

2. Sven Lindqvist, *"Exterminate All the Brutes": One Man's Odyssey into the Heart of Darkness and the Origins of European Genocide* (New York: New Press, 1996).

3. Shahrbanou Tadjbakhsh and Anuradha Chenoy, *Human Security: Concepts and Implications* (New York: Routledge, 2007). See also Roland Paris, "Human Security: Paradigm Shift or Hot Air?" *International Security* 26.2 (2001): 87–102.

4. Benedict Anderson, *Imagined Communities: Reflections on the Origin and Spread of Nationalism* (New York: Verso, 1991).

5. Joe Sacco, *Safe Area Goražde: The War in Eastern Bosnia, 1992–1995* (Seattle: Fantagraphics, 2000), 18–23, 36–40.

6. Mahmood Mamdani, *When Victims Become Killers: Colonialism, Nativism and Genocide in Rwanda* (Princeton: Princeton University Press, 2002).

7. Sacco, *Safe Area Goražde*, 36–38.

8. Ibid., 21.

9. Ibid., 196–208.

10. Ibid., 117–19.

11. Ibid., 180–87.

12. Ibid., 57–67, 196–208.

13. Stephen Krasner, *Sovereignty: Organized Hypocrisy* (Princeton: Princeton University Press, 1999).

14. Thomas J. Biersteker and Cynthia Weber, eds., *State Sovereignty as Social Construct* (Cambridge: Cambridge University Press, 1996).

15. Sacco, *Safe Area Goražde*, 160–61.

16. Ibid., 212–27.

17. Kent Worcester, "Graphic Novels in the Social Science Classroom," in *Teaching Beyond the Book: Film, Texts, and New Media in the Classroom*, eds. Robert W. Glover and Daniel Tagliarina (New York: Bloomsbury, 2013), 89.

18. Ibid., 91.

19. Ibid.

20. Sacco, *Safe Area Goražde*, 184–85.

APPENDIX: JOE SACCO'S PRIMARY WORKS

Joe Sacco's work has appeared in many periodicals, anthologies, and books, ranging from work in issues of comics anthologies like *Drawn & Quarterly* #8 and *Weirdo* #23 to magazines and newspapers like *Rolling Stone* and the *Guardian*. Fortunately, Sacco's work has been collected in a number of books, making his primary works readily available. The following bibliography lists Sacco's major publications, noting when material originally published serially or separately has been collected (as in *Notes from a Defeatist*, which collects Sacco's series *Yahoo* and other comics, or *The Fixer and Other Stories*, which collects material published in two separate volumes, *The Fixer* and *War's End*). But *I Like It* and *Notes from a Defeatist* collect Sacco's early works, and *Journalism* collects stories originally published in a variety of magazines and newspapers. Since these stories are readily available in book form, I have not listed original periodical publications for short works. The final two sections of the bibliography list Sacco's collaborative books and editorial projects.

Book Publications:
Safe Area Goražde: The War in Eastern Bosnia, 1992–1995 (Seattle: Fantagraphics, 2000).
Palestine (Seattle: Fantagraphics, 2001).
Notes From a Defeatist (Seattle: Fantagraphics, 2003).
But I Like It (Seattle: Fantagraphics, 2006).
The Fixer and Other Stories (Montreal: Drawn & Quarterly, 2009)
Footnotes in Gaza (New York: Metropolitan, 2009).
Journalism (New York: Metropolitan, 2012).
The Great War: July 1, 1916, The First Day of the Battle of the Somme, An Illustrated Panorama (New York: Norton, 2013).

Earlier and Special Editions of Book Publications:
War Junkie (Seattle: Fantagraphics, 1995).
   Collected in *Notes from a Defeatist*.
Palestine: A Nation Occupied, Vol. 1 (Seattle: Fantagraphics, 1996).
   Collected in *Palestine*.
Palestine: In the Gaza Strip, Vol. 2 (Seattle: Fantagraphics, 1996).
   Collected in *Palestine*.
The Fixer: A Story from Sarajevo (Montreal: Drawn & Quarterly, 2003).
   Collected in *The Fixer and Other Stories*.
War's End: Profiles from Bosnia, 1995–1996 (Montreal: Drawn & Quarterly, 2005).
   Collected in *The Fixer and Other Stories*.
Palestine, Special Edition (Seattle: Fantagraphics, 2007).

The special edition features a preface by Joe Sacco as well as excerpts from his notebooks and photographs.

Safe Area Goražde: The War in Eastern Bosnia, 1992–1995, Special Edition (Seattle: Fantagraphics, 2011).

The special edition features a preface by Joe Sacco, excerpts from his notebooks and photographs, and an interview with Gary Groth originally published in the *Comics Journal*.

Serial Publications:

Yahoo 1–6 (Fantagraphics, October 1988–August 1992).
  Collected in *Notes from a Defeatist*.
Palestine 1–9 (Fantagraphics, February 1993–October 1995).
  Collected in *Palestine*.
Spotlight on the Genius That Is Joe Sacco (Fantagraphics, February 1994).
  Collected in *Notes from a Defeatist*.
Stories from Bosnia 1: Šoba (Drawn & Quarterly, 1998).
  Collected in *The Fixer and Other Stories*.
BUMF, Volume 1: *I Buggered the Kaiser* (Fantagraphics, November 2014).

Collaborative Work:

From the Folks Who Brought You the Weekend: A Short, Illustrated History of Labor in the United States, with Priscilla Murolo and A. B. Chitty (New York: New Press, 2001).
Best of American Splendor, with Harvey Pekar and others (New York: Ballantine, 2005).

  Joe Sacco was one of many artists to collaborate with writer Harvey Pekar on *American Splendor*. This collection contains some of Sacco's work on the series, along with that of other artists.

Days of Destruction, Days of Revolt, with Chris Hedges (New York: Nation, 2012).

Editorial Work:

Portland Permanent Press, with Tom Richards (May 1985-July 1986).
Honk! 4–5 (Fantagraphics, May 1987–July 1987).
Centrifugal Bumble-Puppy 1–8 (Fantagraphics, September 1987–June 1988).

CONTRIBUTORS

Georgiana Banita is assistant professor of US literature and media at the University of Bamberg and honorary research fellow at the United States Studies Center, University of Sydney. She is the author of *Plotting Justice: Narrative Ethics and Literary Culture after 9/11*.

Ann D'Orazio is a PhD student at the University of New Mexico.

Lan Dong is associate professor of English at the University of Illinois Springfield. She is the author of *Mulan's Legend and Legacy in China and the United States* and *Reading Amy Tan* and the editor of *Transnationalism and the Asian American Heroine* and *Teaching Comics and Graphic Narratives*.

Kevin C. Dunn is professor of political science at Hobart and William Smith Colleges. He is the author of *Politics of Origin in Africa* and *Inside African Politics*.

Alexander Dunst is assistant professor of American studies at the University of Paderborn. He is the coeditor of *The World According to Philip K. Dick*.

Jared Gardner is professor of English and director of popular culture studies at the Ohio State University. He is the author of *Projections: Comics and the History of 21st-Century Storytelling*, *The Rise and Fall of American Magazine Culture*, and *Master Plots: Race and the Founding of American Literature*.

Edward C. Holland is a postdoctoral fellow at the Havighurst Center for Russian and Post-Soviet Studies and visiting assistant professor in international studies at Miami University.

Isabel Macdonald is a doctoral candidate in communication studies at Concordia University in Montreal and the former communications director of the media watch group FAIR (Fairness & Accuracy In Reporting).

Brigid Maher is lecturer in Italian studies at La Trobe University in Melbourne, Australia. She is the author of *Recreation and Style: Translating Humorous Literature in Italian and English* and coeditor of *Words, Images and Performances in Translation* and *Perspectives on Literature and Translation: Creation, Circulation, Reception*.

Contributors

Ben Owen is a PhD candidate in the Department of English at the Ohio State University.

Rebecca Scherr is associate professor of American literature in the Department of Literature, Area Studies, and European Languages at the University of Oslo.

Maureen Shay is lecturer in the Department of English at the University of California, Los Angeles.

Marc Singer is associate professor of English at Howard University. He is the author of *Grant Morrison: Combining the Worlds of Contemporary Comics* and the coeditor of *Detective Fiction in a Postcolonial and Transnational World*.

Richard Todd Stafford is a graduate student in the Cultural Studies Department at George Mason University.

Øyvind Vågnes is a postdoctoral fellow at the University of Copenhagen. He is the author of *Zaprudered: The Kennedy Assassination Film in Visual Culture*.

Daniel Worden is associate professor of English at the University of New Mexico. He is the author of *Masculine Style: The American West and Literary Modernism* and the coeditor of *Oil Culture*.

INDEX

Page numbers in **bold** refer to illustrations.

Adam, G. Stuart, 70
Adams, Jeff, 13
Adorno, Theodor, 130
aesthetics: extraction, 104, 130; graphic narrative as medium, 97; intervention of, 134, 136; political, 168, 169; readerly identification, 132; realist, 128; traditional use of, 105, 270; visual, 101, 116, 168
African Union (AU), 264
Against the Day, 112
Agamben, Giorgio, 13, 14, 160, 161, 164
Aimes, Josey, 112
Al-Jazeera, 210
Alpheus Preparation Plant, 114, **116**, 129, 130
American Splendor, 5
Anderson, Benedict, 261
Ansar III, 146–47, 177
Arab League (AL), 264
Are You My Mother?, 188, 219
"Around Goražde, Part I," 44
Arrival, The, 228
Aspden, Peter, 67
auto-graphics, 186, 188
Azoulay, Ariella, 132, 136, 159

Badiou, Alain: ethics, 174; film, 171–72; influence, 141; isolation, 179; political philosophy, 168–69, 170; sequential comics, 173; truth procedure, 177–78
Badiou and Film, 170
Bagge, Peter, 5

Baker, Catherine, 225
Baker, Mona, 227
Bakhtin, Mikhail, 11–12, 213
Bandia, Paul, 231
Banita, Georgiana, 14, 101
Barbakh, Faris, 212
bare life, 13, 14, 160, 161, 162
Bartley, Aryn, 47, 173
Basewood, 21
Bass, Rick, 103, 114
Battle of the Somme, 6, 15
Baylis, John, 258
Beaty, Bart, 205
Bechdel, Alison, 186, 188, 214, 219, 232
Beckett & Badiou, 170
Believer, 13
Benjamin, Walter, 70, 208, 209
Bennett, Jane, 14, 142, 143, 147
"Beyond Human Rights," 160
Bill, Tony, 112
"Black Coffee," 145
Blackton, J. Stuart, 185, 188
Bonnici, Carmelo Mifsud, 162, 253
"Born in the U.S.A.," 12
Bosnia: diversity in, 50; ethnic cleansing, 270; history, 42, 45, 49; humanitarian intervention, 263; influence on Sacco work, 6, 39, 88, 91, 133; lack of reporting, 29, 46; maps/mapping of, 90–91, 93–94, 97; political conflict, 48, 175; war crimes, 262
Bosnian War: history, 48, 175; influence on Sacco's work, 3, 4, 39, 52; lack of reporting of, 26; maps/mappings of, 14, 90–91, 92, 94; presence in Sacco work, 50, 85;

278　Index

religious conflict, 261–62; safe areas, 257; study of, 13; United Nations involvement, 264–65
Boulevard of Broken Dreams, The, 185, 186
"Boys, Part One, The," 177
"Brief History of Hortisculpture, A," 215
Brister, Rose, 13
"Brother for a Day," 145
"Brotherhood and Unity," 50
Brown, Bill, 14, 141, 142, 143, 150
Broz, Josip "Tito," 49
"Bucket, The," 145
Buell, Lawrence, 251
Bugri, Ahmed, 242, 243
BUMF, Volume I: I Buggered the Kaiser, 6, 15
Burtynsky, Edward, 114
But I Like It, 5
Butler, Judith: performativity, 195; readerly identification, 132, 133, 134, 197; representation, 161; use of framing, 191

capitalist sublime, 129, 131
Caro, Niki, 112
cartography, 14, 85, 89–90, 95, 97
"Cartoon Genius," 3
Caudill, Harry, 104
Céline, Louis-Ferdinand, 40–41
Centrifugal Bumble-Puppy, 5, 8
"Chechen War, Chechen Women," 87
Chechnya, 4, 87, 158
Chitty, A. B., 6
"Christmas with Karadzic": cartography, 85, 90, 92; maps-in-text, 94–95; narrative, 91, 96
Chua, Amy, 104
Chute, Hillary, 40, 42, 173, 204

Clowes, Daniel, 5, 215
Coal: A Human History, 108
coda, 217, 218
Code of Ethics, 57
Cohn, Neil, 172
Cold War, 26, 87, 265
Colorado National Guard, 112
Colstrip, Montana, 114
Comic Books as History, 204
comic realism, 136
Comics Journal, 5, 13, 31
comics theory, 103
comix, 171
contestation, 68
conventional journalism, 13, 141, 153
Cooper, Chris, 113
Crampton, Jeremy, 89
Croatia, 175
Crumb, R., 4, 5, 8, 208, 209

"Danger Happens at the Border," 250
Darda, Joseph, 161
Days of Destruction, Days of Revolt: aesthetic intervention, 133–34, 136; collaboration, 14, 101, 123; graphic entropy, 104–5; inspiration, 6; mining, 101–2, 124; photographic aesthetic, **115, 116**; sacrifice zones, **126**, 131; truth procedure, 177
"Days of Devastation," 103, 109, 111, 112, 131
Dayton Accords, 90
de Certeau, Michel, 128, 129
Debono, Francis, 159, 162, 242, 243
Deepwater Horizon, 106
Deitch, Kim, 185, 186, 215
Derrida, Jacques, 159
Details, 6
dialogue, 193, 194, 196

Disaster and Resistance: Comics and Landscapes for the Twenty First Century, 106
discontinuity, 215, 218
Dispatches, 4, 10
Dittmer, Jason, 86
Dodge, Martin, 89, 90
Dong, Lan, 13, 39
D'Orazio, Ann, 14
drawing desire, 193, 196
Dreiser, Theodore, 108
Drexler, Clyde, 49
Duin, Steve, 105
Dunn, Kevin C., 15, 256
Dunst, Alexander, 14–15, 168

Edin, 25, 30, 49–50, 94–95
Egyptian Women's Mosque Movement, 149
Eisner, Will, 45
El Refaie, Elisabeth, 107
Elements of Journalism: What Newspeople Should Know and the Public Should Expect, The, 57–58
Enchanted Drawing, The, 185
entropy, 103, 104, 105, 107, 117
Eros Comix, 69
Ethics, 169, 174
ethnic cleansing, 39, 42, 169, 270
"Eurobeat," 33, 36
European Commission, 164
European Union (EU), 253, 264
Exterminate All the Brutes, 258, 259

"Failure," 198
Falk, Francesca, 160, 162, 165
Fantagraphics, 3, 5, 8, 69
"Feast," 204, 210, 211, 213
fidelity, 12, 168, 178, 181
"15 Minutes," 43, 71

First Intifada, 177, 178, 181
Fixer and Other Stories, The, 15, 27, 28, 29, 222, 223, 230; awards, 6; impartiality, 224; narration, **28, 29**; production of, 27; Sacco's position in, 11; subjectivity, 79; translation, 15, 222
Footnotes in Gaza: awards, 6; characters, 209; coda, 214, **216**, 217; composition, **211**; detail in work, 7, 30–31; fidelity, 181; graphic journalism, 173, 177; narration, 203–4, 205, **206**, 218; performativity, 190, 194, 196; political aesthetic, 14–15, 168, 169; reader perspective, 79, 197; Sacco's role in, 67, 187, 213; symbolism, 212; theme, 205–6; visual layout, 178–79, **180**, 190, **207**
Freese, Barbara, 108
French Revolution, 161
From the Folks Who Brought You the Weekend: A Short, Illustrated History of Labor in the United States, 6
Fun Home: A Family Tragicomic, 186, 219, 232

Gabilliet, Jean-Paul, 171
Gadassik, Alla, 50
Gardner, Jared: performance, 185, 186, 192; story-telling, 216; time manipulation, 13; voice print, 184, 193
geopolitics, 86–87
Ghassan, 32–33
Gibson, Andrew, 176
Gibson, Larry: illustration, 108, 125, **126**, 127; juxtaposition, 126; sacrifice zone, 135

Globalization of World Politics, The, 258
"Go Away," 39
Goodman, Peter, 77
Google Earth, 90, 97
Goražde: absence of reporting, 27; conflict zone, 92, 257; ethnic cleansing, 39; humanization, 45; illustration, **40**, 41, 43, 267; maps/mapping of, 50, 94; presence in Sacco's work, 12; representation in media, 46–47, **47**; resident testimony, 42; Sacco's travels to, 26, 44, 48, 51; safe area, 222–23; time movement, 25, 30, 39
Goražde. See *Safe Area Goražde: The War in Eastern Bosnia*
Gowin, Emmet, 114
Great War, The, 6, 11, 15, 116
Green, Justin, 8
Groening, Matt, 5
Groensteen, Thierry, 161, 171
Groth, Gary, 4, 11, 13, 88, 91, 95
Guardian, The, 6
Gulf of Mexico, 106
Gulf War, 5, 9, 10, 12
Guthrie, Woody, 112

Haddad, Emma, 250, 252
Hamed, Abu, 212
Handbook of Inaesthetics, 170
Haney, Bill, 110, **110**
Hannerz, Ulf, 232
Hanson, David T., 114
Harlan County War, 112
Harley, J. Brian, 89
Harper's, 6
Hatfield, Charles, 188
Hedges, Chris: collaboration with Sacco, 6, 14, 101–2; comic narrative, 135; graphic entropy, 103, 104, 105, 107, 110; illustration, **115, 116, 126**; juxtaposition, 129; mining, 112, 116, 118, 125; mountaintop removal, 117, 127–28; pillage, 109; sacrifice zones, 123, 124, 126, 136
Heizer, Neil, 111
Henstra, Sarah, 50
Herr, Michael, 4, 10
Hesford, Wendy, 198
hijab, 149, 150, 152
"Hijab," 150, 152
Hirsch, Marianne, 49, 164
Holland, Edward C., 14
Homo Sacer: Sovereign Power and Bare Life, 161, 164
Honk!, 5
"Hotel California," 12, 25, 26
"How I Loved the War," 5, 8, **9,** 12
Huffington Post, 77
hybrid medium, 169, 215

impartiality, 67, 68, 69, 71
Imperium Europa, 159
"In the Company of Long Hair," 5
inaesthetics, 170
interpreters, 224, 227, 231
Iraq War, 4, 12
Irving, Washington, 21

Jameson, Fredric, 10–11
Jenkins, Henry, 205
Jensen, Jakob Linaa, 90
Jimmy Corrigan, 21
"John the Eritrean," 246, 249–50
Jones, Francis, 231
Jones, James Earl, 113
Jones, John Paul, III, 90
Journal of Graphic Novels and Comics, 13

Journalism: collection, 158; detail, 163, **189**; empathy, 253; irony, **246**; juxtaposition, **241**; preface, 54, 61; Sacco's position in, 239; subjectivity, **244**; theory, 65
journalistic performance, 184, 187, 188, 189
journalistic text, 225
Juhish, Abu, 218

Kaloob, Ra'esa Salim Hassan, 196, 197
Karadžić, Radovan, 91, 92, 93
Katchor, Ben, 215
keffiyeh, 148–49
Kelly, Rudy, 132, 134, 135
Kenehan, Joe, 113
Khaled, 145, 209–10
"Khan Younis," 211
Kincaid, Ruby, 112
Kingsbury, Paul, 90
Kitchin, Rob, 89, 90
Klinghoffer, Leon, 31, 72
Kosofsky, Eve, 193
Kovach, Bill, 57, 58, 62
Kozol, Wendy, 13

Last Mountain, The, 109, **110,** 111, 112, 118
"Law," 74, 77
Lawrence, Jacob, 106
Lefebvre, Henri, 128, 129
Levinas, Emmanuel, 134, 161, 196
Lindqvist, Sven, 258, 259
Linfield, Susie, 132
Lippmann, Walter, 68
Logics of Worlds, 177
Lois E. Jenson v. Eveleth Taconite Co., 112
Longstreth, Alec, 21

Lowell, Norman, 243
Lowell, William, 159
Ludlow Massacre of 1914, 112
Luhman, Niklas, 23
Lunsford, Andrea A., 13, 42, 69, 79

Macdonald, Isabel, 54
Maher, Brigid, 13, 15, 222
Mahmood, Saba, 149
Malkki, Liisa, 243, 245
Mallarmè, Stèphane, 179
Manchin, Joe, 14, 22, 85–86, 118
mapping, 88–89, 90, 91, 95
mappings-in-text, 95, 97
maps-in-text, 86, 89, 94, 97
Marvel Comics, 3, 30
Massey Energy, 111
Matewan, 112, 113, 114
Matt, Joe, 215
Maus, 4, 8, 186, 188, 214, 256
Mayrhofer, Petra, 164
McCay, Winsor, 185, 188
McCloud, Scott, 45, 86, 108, 132–33, 134
McDonald, Isabel, 13
McGovern, George, 112
Memento, 24
Merz, Charles, 68
migration, 158, 162
militant art, 171, 178, 181
Milosevic, Slobodan, 49, 92
Milton, John, 231
Miracle Workers, The, 5
Mitchell, W. J. T., 162, 164–65, 192–93, 197
Mladic, Ratko, 94
"Moderate Pressure," 32, 72, 73, 145, 164
Mohammed, Abu, 213

"More Women, More Children, More Quickly," 5
Mother Jones, 7
mountaintop removal (MTR): illustration, 117, 125, 126, 128; in other works, 109; presence in Sacco's work, 14, 101, 103, 107; purpose, 104, 131; representation, 105, 127, 129
Muecke, D. C., 232
Mulholland Dr., 24
Murolo, Priscilla, 6
Muscat, Joseph, 254

Nafez, Omm, 212
Nagel, Thomas, 67
narrative techniques, 87, 88, 125, 222, 234
National Notary Association, 4
Neven, 28, 29, 223, 230, 231
Nevins, Mark, 72
New Journalism, 4, 7, 12, 31, 46, 70, 176
New York Times, 27, 77
New York Times Magazine, 6, 13, 59, 61, 62
Newton, Windsor, 185
Night Comes to the Cumberlands: A Biography of a Depressed Area, 104
North Atlantic Free Trade Association (NAFTA), 264
North Atlantic Treaty Organization (NATO), 265
North Country, 112
Notes from a Defeatist, 5, **9**, 12
Nur, Hajja, 149
Nyberg, Amy Kiste, 13, 59, 70, 71

objectivity: critique of, 13, 54, 67, 79; definitions of, 68–69; doctrine of, 57–58; intellectual, 256, 268; invention of, 55–56; in journalism, 70; in reporting, 54, 55, 56, 63; Sacco's abandonment of, 31, 59, 65, 67–68, 142; traditional use of, 71, 72, 78; visual juxtaposition, 222
Oil and Water, 105
ontology: inconsistency, 179; mapping, 86, 89–90; narratives, 227; political, 134, 169; subtractive, 172; visual, 168
"Other America," 102
Owen, Ben, 15, 203
Owens, Patricia, 258

Palestine: classification of, 70–71; coda, 214; drawing style, 79; episodic structure, 5, 23, 91; ethical criticism, 173; graphic visual, **75, 76**; illustration, 11, **34**; impartiality, 72; juxtaposition, 3; narration, 6, **73**, 155; objectivity, 14, 67–68, 143, **151**, 169; performativity, 194; publishing, 69; reader response, 102; Sacco's position in, 67, 187, 233; symbolism, 148; thing theory use, 142; translation, 15, 222, 226; use of tea in, 143, **144**, 145, 147; use of tomatoes in, 152; visual features, 33, 164, 176–77; word balloon, **227**
Palestine: conflict zone, 30, 231; patriarchal oppression, 148; political struggles, 178; Sacco visits, 5, 31–32, 223; symbolism, 147; use of visuals, 33, 133, 134; violence in, 35, 145
Palestinian Liberation Front, 31
Peace Now, 71

Pekar, Harvey, 5
performativity: emancipatory discourse, 195; framing, 192; perception, 193; presence in Sacco's work, 184–85, 198; use of, 184, 194
Persepolis, 161, 186
perspectivalism, 95
"Pilgrimage," 74, 145, 146
Pine Ridge Reservation, 3, 6, 103
Playboy, 69
Politics of Piety: The Islamic Revival and the Feminist Subject, 149
Portland Permanent Press, 4–5
Powder River Basin, 124
Precarious Life, 132, 134, 161
Priego, Ernesto, 43
Pulp Fiction, 24–25, 26, 35, 49
Pynchon, Thomas, 112

"Rafah," 211
Ramallah, 32, 33
Rancière, Jacques, 128
Rasim, 44, 45
readerly identification, 132, 135
Reagan, Ronald, 12
realism, 11, 68, 79, 128–29, 131, 135, 136
Reality Hunger, 7
"Refugeeland," 33
Rembges, Almut, 165
retheorization, 89
"Rewind," 35
Richards, Tom, 4
Riki, 12, 25, 26, 29
Rimbaud, Arthur, 179
Rip Van Winkle, 21, 22
Robinson, Arthur H., 89
"Rooms," 72, 77, 145
Rosello, Mireille, 158, 165
Rosen, Jay, 67

Rosenblatt, Adam, 13, 69, 79
Rosenstiel, Tom, 57, 58, 62
Rubenfeld, Jed, 104

sacrifice zone, 123, 124, 125, 127, 128, 130, 136
Safe Area Goražde: The War in Eastern Bosnia: awards, 6; cartography, 85, 90, **93,** 95; character recurrence, 12; conflict zone, 30, 48, 260–61; educational tool, 256–58, 267–68, 271; ethical criticism, 173; ethnic cleansing, 39; graphic narrative, 269–70; history, 45–46, 49; international law, 262, 266; juxtaposition, 3, 51; maps-in-text, 93, 94; movement of time, 24, 35–36; narration, 48; political aesthetic, 259–60, 264; publishing, 5; realism, 11; representation, 97; Sacco position in, 41, 67; splash page, **40,** 41, **47**; structure, 91; testimony, 42, 47, 92; translation, 15, 222
Said, Edward, 30, 51
Saint Paul, 170
Sameh, 35, 146, 149, 226–27, 228, 233
Satrapi, Marjane, 161, 186
Sayles, John, 112, 113
Scherr, Rebecca, 13, 15, 184
Schudson, Michael, 68, 70
Security Council, 264
Serbia, 93, 175
Shay, Maureen, 15, 239
Shields, David, 7
"Short History of America, A," 209
Sinclair, Upton, 112
Singer, Marc, 13, 67
Smith, Steven, 258

Society for Professional Journalists, 57
Sontag, Susan, 46, 192
"Spectacle," 198
Spiegelman, Art: autobiographical work, 186, 187; drawing style, 256; graphic novel, 214, 215; influence, 4, 8; narration, 217
splash page, 32, 39, 176, 209
Srebrenica, 94, 257, 262
Stafford, Richard Todd, 14, 123
"Stanton K. Pragmatron, Part of a New Breed," 3
Stewart, Kathleen, 102, 113, 118
subjectivity, 69, 178, 244, 246, 248, 259
Surface Mining Control and Reclamation Act of 1977, 129

Tagg, John, 128
Tan, Shaun, 228
Tarantino, Quentin, 24, 49
"10 Things Journalists Should Know About Fixers," 231
"Theses on the Concept of History," 208
thing theory, 14, 141–42
Thompson, Hunter S., 4
Time, 6, 25, 26, 27
Tobocman, Seth, 106
"Tomatoes," 145, 152, 154
Tomine, Adrian, 5, 215
traditional journalism model, 55, 62, 71, 225
transformation, 68
translation: as process, 15, 224; distrust of, 229; non-recognition of, 223, 225, 234; presence in Sacco's work, 222, 232; visual, 226–27
"Trauma on Loan," 188, **188**

Triple Package, The, 104
truth procedure, 175, 177, 178
Tuathail, Gearóid Ó., 87
12 Monkeys, 26
Tyler, Carol, 214

"Underground War in Gaza, The": narration, **60**; objectivity, 54, 59, 62, 65; political aesthetic, 61, 64; reporter's role, 61
Understanding Comics, 86, 132
United Mine Workers of America (UMWA), 112
United Nations (UN), 94, 160, 264
United Nations High Commissioner for Refugees (UNHCR), 239
United Nations Relief and Works Agency (UNRWA), 59, 61, 208
Universal Declaration of Human Rights, 160
"Unwanted, The": autobiographical features, 15; bare life, 162; character stories, 245, 246; detention, **163**, 164; hospitality, 159, 249; iconic solidarity, 161; irony, **246**, 252; juxtaposition, **240**; migration, 162–63, 165, 242, 247; perspective, 243; plot, 158; publishing, 239; subjectivity, **244**, 253
Usual Suspects, The, 26

Vågnes, Oyvind, 13, 14, 158, 184
verification, 68, 69
Versaci, Rocco, 42, 46, 69
Vibrant Matter: A Political Ecology of Things, 142
voice-print, 184, 186, 191, 192, 193

Walker, Tristram, 13, 44
Walzer, Belinda, 13

Wanzo, Rebecca, 205
Ward, Stephen A., 54, 55
Ware, Chris: book-length work, 214, 215; mediation, 205; music in work, 5; reading time, 21, 22; visual communication, 105–6
Weirdo, 5, 8
Weizman, Eyal, 165
Wheeler, Shannon, 105
"When Good Bombs Happen to Bad People," 5, 12
Whitlock, Gillian, 186
Whitson, Roger, 108
Williams, Kristian, 69
Wilson, 215
Witek, Joseph, 204
Wolfe, Tom, 7
Woo, Benjamin, 69–70, 71
word balloons, 226, 234, 269
World War I, 68
World War II, 3, 5, 87, 261

Yahoo, 3, 5, 11, 217
Yang, Gene Luen, 214
Yugoslavia, 88, 257, 262, 264, 266

Zelizer, Barbie, 223

www.ingramcontent.com/pod-product-compliance
Lightning Source LLC
Chambersburg PA
CBHW030611230426
43661CB00053B/1931